D0648613

MILTON AND THE HERMENEUTIC JOURNEY

MILTON

AND THE

HERMENEUTIC

JOURNEY

Gale H. Carrithers, Jr., & James D. Hardy, Jr.

Louisiana State University Press

BATON ROUGE AND LONDON

Copyright © 1994 by Louisiana State University Press
All rights reserved
Manufactured in the United States of America
First printing
03 02 01 00 99 98 97 96 95 94   5 4 3 2 1

Designer: Amanda McDonald Key
Typeface: Garamond #3
Typesetter: G & S Typesetters, Inc.
Printer and binder: Thomson-Shore, Inc.

LIBRARY OF CONGRESS CATALOGING-IN-PUBLICATION DATA

Carrithers, Gale H., date.
    Milton and the hermeneutic journey / Gale H. Carrithers, Jr., and James D.
Hardy, Jr.
        p.   cm.
    Includes bibliographical references and index.
    ISBN 0-8071-1876-1 (alk. paper)
        1. Milton, John, 1608–1674—Criticism and interpretation.
    2. Christianity and literature—History—17th century.   3. Christian
    poetry, English—History and criticism.   4. Hermeneutics—Religious
    aspects—Christianity.   I. Hardy, James D. (James Daniel), date.
    II. Title.
    PR3588.C37   1994
    821'.4—dc20   94-6781
                                                                      CIP

Portions of this book appeared previously in slightly different form as "Miltonic Dialogue and Metadialogue in *Paradise Lost,*" by Gale H. Carrithers, Jr., and James D. Hardy, Jr., in *Compendious Conversations: The Method of Dialogue in the Early Enlightenment,* edited by Kevin Cope (Verlag Peter Lang, 1992); and as "Milton's Ludlow *Mask:* From Chaos to Community," by Gale H. Carrithers, Jr., in *English Literary History,* XXXIII (1966), and in *Critical Essays on Milton from "ELH"* (Johns Hopkins University Press, 1971). Another portion appeared in slightly different form as "*Poems* (1645): On Growing Up," by Gale H. Carrithers, Jr., in *Milton Studies* XV, by James D. Simmonds, Editor. Published in 1981 by the University of Pittsburgh Press. Used by permission of the publisher.

The frontispiece is François de Nomé's *Fantastic Ruins with Saint Augustine and the Child.* Reproduced by courtesy of the Trustees, The National Gallery, London.

The paper in this book meets the guidelines for permanence and durability of the Committee on Production Guidelines for Book Longevity of the Council on Library Resources. ∞

To our wives,
Joan Carrithers and Claudia Hardy

Tri'd in sharp tribulation, and refin'd
By Faith and faithful works, to second Life
—*Paradise Lost*

CONTENTS

Preface

This book is an attempt to understand Milton's major poetry as a whole and to suggest a general interpretive matrix that can include most of the poetic corpus in a coherent although not exhaustive vision. We are convinced that Milton, in his poetry, returned constantly under various guises and in various genres to certain themes and ideas. These, predominantly religious and epistemological in nature, form a consistent pattern in his poetry and can be seen in a substantial and copious way in *Paradise Lost* and in a more restricted but not greatly different manner in Milton's other poetic works. Thus, a general synthetic interpretation of Milton's poetry insistently suggested itself to us, and in this book we attempt to develop it.

Our book represents the merging of different training regimens and concordant intellectual interests—one interest largely literary and Renaissance, the other largely historical. We found ourselves jointly responsible for a cross-disciplinary undergraduate honors course, and in our discussions and joint work we acquired a deeper understanding of G. Evelyn Hutchinson's dictum that there may be a distinction between teaching and research but there need be none between teaching and learning. We have discussed continually and revised jointly the first drafts composed in part by one, in part by the other. We regard the present text as altogether joint and as attaining a view of Milton neither of us could have come to separately. Jointly we applaud Barry Blose, the volume's editor at Louisiana State University Press.

Thomas D'Evelyn and Joan S. Bennett each read the manuscript at an intermediate stage, and we are grateful to both—to the former especially for suggestions about organization, to the latter especially for alerting us to some unintended ambiguities. We owe a great deal to the anonymous readers for LSU Press, whose readings were exemplary in their care for matters reaching from the generally philosophical to the locally syntactic. We hasten to confess what must become apparent, that we have resisted some of the wisdom offered us.

There remains the pleasure of acknowledging those at Louisiana State University who have helped in ways not apparent from the notes: Professor Billy M. Seay, dean of the Honors College, for released time; Professor John R. May, chairman of the Department of English, along with the LSU Research Council, for a Summer Research Fellowship; Polly Stevens Fields for bibliographical help; and Rebecca Powell, and earlier, Cheri Drez, Lauré Dupré, Brian Eberhardt, Deborah Jacobs, John R. LeBlanc, Deborah Liehe, Claudia Scott, and Patricia B. Stevenson. Additionally, there is in some quarters of our university a lingering presence of Eric Voegelin, and we hope we have drawn help from that. The dedication page acknowledges debts of which we are certain.

François de Nomé painted the story shown in our frontispiece. Milton probably knew of the dream of Saint Augustine's that is depicted. A boy who is pouring the ocean into a hole responds to skeptical questioning by saying that he will finish his task before Augustine can explain the Trinity. Yet Augustine launched *De trinitate*. Milton too, beside crumbling towers of the same fallen world, his own boat journey-battered, ventured on, asserting and justifying, and we attempt his readers' task.

MILTON AND THE HERMENEUTIC JOURNEY

ONE

Hermeneusis, Love, and Power

ilton in all his poetry sings a sacred song, which, as such, exceeds the merely ordinary, is ambiguous rather than univocal, asserts mystery as fundamental to human experience, and ties the human to the divine and ineffable in an antiphon loving rather than closed or debt-paying or book-balancing. In singing his own sacred song, he dealt with other sacred texts, from the Bible to Augustine to classical pagan literature, implicating the mystery and assertion of divine providence found elsewhere in his own creations. Milton reports, meditates upon, enacts, and invites a sacred journey from alienation to love and redemption, and he reflects upon the consequences of the failure to make that journey. We have found, accordingly, in hermeneutic reflection on Milton's poetry our most satisfactory engagement with it. We have found that the beginning and the end of Milton's sacred song are necessarily known in terms of each other, that the detail and the overview are mutually illuminating when seen together.

We can in a broad way identify quite simply the hermeneutic analysis that we see in Milton's poetry and that we attempt in our account of it. It is akin to, if more focused than, the normal life experience of getting to know another person, from initial introduction to intimate understanding: new information and new events modify one's sense of that person, and the deepening sense one has of the person begins to enrich one's sense of the events, and indeed of oneself. It is the procedure altogether normal to historians, as when a historian, already having a context (or Gadamerian "prejudice"), is able to recognize an archival document as significant and is moved by that to reconsider and reinforce the context, sharpening the significance of the document, so that the significance recasts more of the context, and probably the historian's initial aim. That current historical convention flattens this process resolutely to an altogether secular plane does not negate the model's suggestiveness. Milton's poetry, in contrast, touches all levels of the Great Chain of Being, from God to Satan;

both the early and the late poetry exhibit hermeneutic progression. On a more workaday plane, our text reflects and attempts to preserve and present something of Milton's multiple ontological levels while employing the techniques of hermeneutic analysis.

Moreover, since persons are significantly free, the indefinitely successive process just sketched cannot end while secular life lasts. Because of free will, because of the mind's virtually infinite trickiness, because of the radical imponderabilities of freedom, *exhaustive* definition of the hermeneutic process is certainly impossible, a bit like long-range weather forecasting. But procedures, profounder than conventions but short of absolute rules, can be recognized, and need to be observed, a bit as in short-range weather prediction. Furthermore, we are working from the conviction that language is a part of, even in some respects a generator of, being but that being is no mere artifact of language. Similarly, we take textuality to be a part of and in some respects a powerful agent of history but do not take history to be a mere artifact of textuality. Correlatively, we believe, with Heraclitus and Aristotle (though not the Sophists), in referentiality, in a world out there as well as a world in here where the mental signifieds are. Both worlds, we hold, are sufficiently shareable for the purposes of life, primarily by the agency of language when it is mobilized with energy and goodwill. Of course, neither reference nor representation is ever—save in the most limited, quasi-arithmetical cases—rigorously exact or closed, nor is the correspondence of signifieds in different minds perfect. Milton understood this as a consequence for the individual of the fall in the garden, as a consequence for corporate humanity seen in the late unpleasantness at Babel.

The imperfect determinacy of hermeneutic theory is obviously the more marked insofar as the mutually and successively defining but not exhaustively or neatly bipolar elements of the hermeneutic progression are implicated in transcendence. We would deface Milton if we were to neglect his insistence that beginnings and ends not only reciprocally and successively define each other but are inevitably conceived from a moving middle of things. And beginnings and ends are necessarily understood in relation to a radical origin and to a mysterious *telos*. So, too, part and whole are successively redefined, from the moving historical middle of things—the part in terms potentially touched by transcendence, and the whole assuredly mysterious in its comprehensiveness. Likewise the nonpolar, inexhaustible complementarity of system and similitude, of temporal succession and eternity, of truth and method, is implicated in mysterious human freedom, itself understood as an enabling gift of divine grace.[1]

For Milton, as for ourselves, one both is and is not the person one was a decade or a generation ago. Even for the most secular-minded today, the end and the beginning can never be truly seen *together* or sung through *completely* by humanity, though the secularist will not share Milton's reason: that completeness and simultaneity are attributes of God, not of persons.

For a late-twentieth-century secularist, crucial truth always exceeds method. Truth as both hidden and mysterious exceeds methodologies as tools to get at it; truth as creativity both immanent and transcendent exceeds methodologies as containers; truth as structure, hidden *or* dynamic, exceeds methodologies as universal solvents, whether structuralist or deconstructive. These metaphors are deliberate, chosen for their serviceability both antique and current. Containers and tools are invaluable even if imperfectly adequate or efficacious, as solvents are invaluable even if nonuniversal. Indeed, the very limitations in each category may be essential to the utility: no one wants a coffee cup as big as the Black Sea.

Moreover, Milton is hermeneutic because *eternal* providence—in contrast to mere efficient causation—and God's way are precisely *not* objects of linear, analytic knowledge. For one thing, the *civitas terrena* is intercalated with grace and possibilities of the *civitas dei* or "paradise within . . . happier farr" (*Paradise Lost,* XII, 587). For another thing, the free person, articulated in both attitude and relationship by knowing better and believing better and loving better, can rearticulate itself and its world. Milton's hermeneusis is ongoing being and doing with regard to reality that includes but transcends all worldly categories.

1. We are affiliating ourselves here and throughout with the hermeneutics of Paul Ricoeur, especially in *The Conflict of Interpretations* (Evanston, Ill., 1974), and of Hans Georg Gadamer, especially in *Essays in Philosophical Hermeneutics,* trans. and ed. David E. Lange (Berkeley and Los Angeles, 1976); *Truth and Method* (New York, 1975); and *Dialogue and Deconstruction: The Gadamer-Derrida Encounter,* ed. Diane P. Michelfelder and Richard E. Palmer (Albany, N.Y., 1989). We also subscribe to Joel Weinsheimer's accounts in *Gadamer's Hermeneutics: A Reading of Truth and Method* (New Haven, 1985) and *Philosophical Hermeneutics and Literary Theory* (New Haven, 1991), especially Chaps. 1 and 2. See also the valuably—and fiercely—independent position of Stanley Rosen in *Hermeneutics as Politics* (New York, 1987). Our earlier alliances include José Ortega y Gasset, in *Meditations on Quixote* (New York, 1961).

But we would see a sign, say the people—*a* sign, that is, a unifying trope. That the hermeneutic journey—for wayfaring Christian, for Bard, and implicitly for reader—*is* Milton's sign, we shall argue in the following chapters. But our argument calls for rehearsing some familiar terms here. It seems that scarcely anyone in the three and a half centuries since the 1645 edition of *Poems* has failed to note the range and reach of Milton's effort to integrate the gigantic elements of what was to be signed: the beginning (not, except to humanity, originary) *Logoi* of Genesis and Saint John, as in "On the Morning of Christs Nativity," and the commissions and creations in *Paradise Lost;* the end (termination and *telos*) of life, as in "Lycidas," *Paradise Regain'd,* and *Samson Agonistes.* The primary strategy for propounding the unifying sign, so obvious and omnipresent that it may escape reflective scrutiny, is the poet composing. He meditates upon the already scripturally revealed, and he reconsiders insofar as he is inspired and as he reacts to himself composing and having composed. His animating belief and enabling protometaphor is the scale of being, with the attendant possibilities of lapse into lower being and of gifts from higher, including regeneration and the grace to soar with "no middle flight" (I, 14), in creativity metaphorically and metonymically analogous to divine creativity.

Accordingly, in our hermeneutic reflections we have tried to reinforce recent efforts to reassert essentials, essentials procedural as well as thematic. We revise the image of a hermeneutic "circle" in order to insist on the importance of reciprocal relationships that may be incremental but need not be linear—as, for example, the relationship of beginnings to ends, of the whole to parts, of time to eternity (radical simultaneity), of God to humanity, of being to becoming. "Suppose you were devout," a celebrated Miltonist adjured his nervous seminar long ago. We have tried to deal in appropriately serious—albeit not always Miltonic—terms with Milton's sense of the divine and of divine mysteries. The truth, so elementary to Milton, that logic cannot fully explain the nature either of God or of man, nor of the concourse between them, we have tried to keep in focus. A crucial element of the Miltonic focus and of our own is the scale of being. If that metaphor no longer seems so certainly inevitable or so clearly the most valid accessible to human understanding (though perhaps it is), it remains for us an indispensable reminder of the logical discontinuities that Miltonic consideration of the divine involves and that our own hermeneutic analysis seeks to illuminate. To neglect the scale of being is riskier than navigating by Mercator projection, as a long line of critical wreckage from William Blake to A. J. A. Waldock and William Empson attests.

This rather basic and simple hermeneutic, with beginnings in Heraclitus, nonetheless has implications we have found to be far from simple. For one, the language of modern hermeneutics has seemed to some readers needlessly technical or equivocal, and its syntax is surmised to have turned copy editors to stone. The *gad* has unsolemnly but seriously been proposed as a unit of Gadamerian or other hermeneutic obscurity.[2] Such linguistic complexity, perhaps the result of excessive nominalism, is for our purposes unnecessary. The books are never completely balanced nor closed on language; full meaning is never completely communicated nor understood. Therefore some things are simply mysterious; that is how Milton saw them, and that is how we have left them. Some things simply *are* (the heavens, for example), and explanations about why they are may be interesting but do not pertain to the salvific journey; we have respected Milton's opinion about that. As a result, we have attempted to demystify the language of hermeneutics by a modest leavening of Milton's Augustinian Neoplatonism. Grace may be hard to explain, but it is easy to recognize, overwhelming to experience, and can be adverted to with some simplicity and directness—"like the sun," as Donne had remarked of mysteries.

Simplicity and directness of language, insofar as we achieve them, foster our concentrating on grace, one presenting face of that divine providence which was Milton's announced, and sustained, central concern. Once mystery is accepted as such, a hermeneutic analysis can turn to identifying the nature of the mystery and its context rather than parsing or proving it. Mystery—and grace is the great mystery of divine love—asserts truth psychologically and analogically and symbolically and metaphorically and existentially rather than consistently and logically, that is, exhaustively. Indeed, with mystery and a hermeneutic reflection upon it, exhaustiveness is the enemy of accuracy, and of course, of understanding also. So we have chosen the untidy path of a traditional and simple hermeneutic examination of grace and love, not because asserting divine providence is our task—it certainly is not—but because Milton saw it as his.

This is not, at least not intentionally, to gainsay the omnipresent ques-

2. Weinsheimer, *Gadamer's Hermeneutics*, x.

tion of the nature of belief. Again we assert a truth so familiar it may be neglected: as distinct from belief *that* (for example, that a chemical equation is balanced), belief *in* depends on (in some sense) metaphor, and (in some sense) love. Belief in a person or a poem is always a hermeneutic issue, and a problem in the special case of betrayal. No one else has ever been John Milton. No one of us is a Catholic-minded Puritan, or anything else, of the seventeenth century. Many non-seventeenth-century non-Christians have, evidently, cherished the poems for a multitude of reasons having to do, we suppose, with metaphoric recognitions of the personally meaningful. Others have felt something like betrayal in, say, Milton's presentation of Eve, God, Dalila, fallen history, or the like—particular matters about which later chapters will comment.

Part of Milton's serviceability is to push virtually every serious question in the Western tradition—including questions of interpretation, belief, and relationship—to the point at which a serious reader can recognize her or his ultimate trust interrogated and affections tested. And those are the points at which contemporary theory's vaunted pluralism, with its pretension to inclusiveness, breaks down.[3] Milton, as is increasingly said of Shakespeare, anticipates and even enacts theoretical issues that are current and may seem new.[4] So a more or less sporting taste for that kind of testing might be a reason for rereading Milton and reading reflections on his poetry such as these. Other reasons would include friendliness to the idea that containers, tools, solvents, including this one, cannot totalize, and to the related idea, of J. B. S. Haldane and Loren Eiseley, that "the world is not only queerer than we suppose, but queerer than we can suppose."[5] One in addition needs to be accessible to serious mistrust of the humanist notion that all so-called evil is *merely* error, and accessible to

3. Although this is not Ellen Rooney's language, it represents emphatic agreement with the general argument, and many particulars, of her *Seductive Reasonings: Pluralism as the Problematic of Contemporary Literary Theory* (Ithaca, N.Y., 1989).

4. See, for example, Joel Fineman, *The Subjectivity Effect in Western Literary Tradition: Essays Toward the Release of Shakespeare's Will* (Cambridge, Mass., 1991); Peter Erickson, *Rewriting Shakespeare, Rewriting Ourselves* (Berkeley and Los Angeles, 1991); Barbara Freedman, *Staging the Gaze: Postmodernism, Psychoanalysis, and Shakespearean Comedy* (Ithaca, N.Y., 1991); and Stephen Bretzius, *Shakespeare in Theory* (Forthcoming); Maureen Quilligan, *Milton's Spenser: The Politics of Reading* (Ithaca, N.Y., 1983), Introduction.

5. We take Haldane's comment from the epigraph to Loren Eiseley's *The Unexpected Universe* (New York, 1969).

love for the Miltonic gift for mighty sign and sacred song. These are not unreasonable requirements.

We argue that the common thread in all of Milton's poetry is a deep and pervasive Protestant and Augustinian Christianity rooted in the Bible, which Milton regarded as simultaneously literally and metaphorically the true and revealed "pure Word of God," in the Lutheran phrase. It is beyond argument that Milton believed profoundly and centrally in the reality of the Fall.[6] Milton conceived of the Fall as the beginning of human time and of more and less flawed conceptions of time, as the beginning of the "wandring steps" toward redemption, and as the beginning of human mischoice and misorientation in favor of power over love—love being the reflection of grace. It is also beyond argument that Milton believed profoundly and centrally in the redemption, an act of divine grace unmerited by sinful humanity and accomplished by the full, perfect, and sufficient sacrifice of the Son. Milton thus saw life as mere "wandring" that is open to being redeemed for the Augustinian journey detailed in the *Confessions,* a journey led by grace from *nox* and *aversio* to *lux* and *conversio,* a journey conducted within a context of sin but salvific in nature.

Although Milton's Christian faith and theology were basically Augustinian, the poet differed substantially from the Latin father in doctrinal emphasis and general soteriological expectations. The deep pessimism and sense of guilt, sin, and unworthiness that psychologically informed much of Augustine's writing are much less in evidence in Milton's poetry. Milton placed his personal emphasis, and his hope, on God's grace and love rather than on the fallenness and depravity and punishment of mankind. For Milton, God was a deity of more immanent love and hope; for Augustine the sins of humanity were dark and overwhelming. It is a difference in tone between Milton and Augustine, a difference manifest in poetry asserting divine providence on the one hand and polemical theology explicating the true faith and denouncing heresies on the other.[7] It is not

6. The course of our own considerations entails highlighting the Fall, of course—but intermittently, in order intermittently to occlude it and highlight other matters. For sustained and rewarding consideration of the poem in the light (so to speak) of the Fall, see Kathleen M. Swaim, *Before and After the Fall: Contrasting Modes in "Paradise Lost"* (Amherst, Mass., 1986).

7. Partly because we give greater attention to the *Confessions, Enchiridion on Faith, Hope, and Love,* and *On Christian Teaching* than to somewhat less cited works, our Augus-

a difference in general Christian theology or views of human history or the road to salvation but rather one in psychological orientation within the common faith. It is, in short, the difference between Milton's expectations of love and grace and Augustine's intolerably burdened consciousness of sin and fault and alienation.

We further argue that the exact locus of the human choice of sin over redemptive grace, so important in the theology of both Milton and Augustine, is in the dichotomy between power and love; this includes the distinction between powerful analytic polemic and loving or narrative similitude. The mode, the key, the very pace of the flight and song to provide the master sign, is love. Not only when the Bard famously proclaims "Hail wedded Love" (IV, 750) but throughout the poetic corpus, Milton presents and enacts a more than Augustinian, more than Ovidian Book of Love. Love is the gracious human metaphor of eternity, and space without love the graceless defining contrast. This statement of the nature of the polar opposites is seen in *Paradise Lost* repeatedly: in the comparison between the Son and Satan, in the comparison of the sexual relationship between Adam and Eve before and after the Fall, and again in the leap from heaven by the existentially falling angels. The selfishness of power in contrast with the selflessness and giving of love forms as well the central core of *Paradise Regain'd* and *Samson Agonistes,* and is seen also in *A Mask* and fitfully in earlier poems. The opposition between what is gracious and what is fallen—between love and loveless power—and the ultimate triumph of love form the basic component of Milton's interpretation of the Augustinian *aversio* and *conversio.*

Where do these emphases and our tactics place our book in the current dialogue—not to say heteroglossia—about Milton? Anyone likely to write about Milton, indeed anyone who has read the scholarly apparatus of modern editions, must be emphatically appreciative of a continuity of discourse. But what Edward W. Said has called the "almost Renaissance brilliance" of recent discourse in literary theory has had so many coruscations in Renaissance scholarship and Milton studies as to invite perplexity. We take it that the dominant impulse in those studies has been toward

---

tine is himself more a voice of love than the Augustine of Elaine Pagels in her valuable *Adam, Eve, and the Serpent* (New York, 1989). For generally supportive analysis and exposition of matters less crucial to our argument, see also Peter Fiore, *Milton and Augustine: Patterns of Augustinian Thought in "Paradise Lost"* (University Park, Pa., 1981).

determinacy and the dominant figure is accordingly contiguity—explicit or implicit metonymies of part to part, whole to part, part to whole, cause to effect. There are the ostensibly univocal part-to-part juxtapositions of a Miltonic element with a lexicon that may be the OED or a Renaissance rhetoric (actual, conflated, or projected), the Bible, Vergil, Calvin, Milton's own *De Doctrina Christiana,* the conventional landscape or life in the world (with its optic glass, Norwegian pine, air that "felt unusual weight" [I, 227]), or what not.[8]

Such part-to-part or part-to-quasi-part relationships grade into part-to-whole relationships. Critical Miltonic elements rewardingly analyzed and illuminated in something of this fashion have included freedom, grace, genre, sex.[9] Such containers may be implicitly synecdochic, world-signifying congeries of historically local macro and micro power relationships, variously economic, political-institutional (including gender and class), and personal—or even a golden mean or a familiar combination with regard to which divergences approach as a limit being evadable or unthinkable.[10] Reviewers explicitly use the language of contiguity when

8. Edward W. Said, "Reflections on Recent American 'Left' Literary Criticism," *Boundary 2,* VIII (1979–80), 24 (somewhat revised in *The World, the Text, and the Critic* [Cambridge, Mass., 1983], 172). For the most celebrated recension of the Viconian master tropes, see Hayden White, *Tropics of Discourse* (Baltimore, 1978). See also Roman Jakobson, "Two Aspects of Language and Two Types of Aphasic Disturbances," in *Fundamentals of Language,* ed. Roman Jakobson and Morris Halle (The Hague, 1956), 69–96, which is decisively supplemented by the analysis of the nonpolarity of metaphor and metonymy by Maria Ruegg in "Metaphor and Metonymy: The Logic of Structuralist Rhetoric," *Glyph,* VI (1979), 141–57.

9. See Joan S. Bennett, *Reviving Liberty: Radical Christian Humanism in Milton's Great Poems* (Cambridge, Mass., 1989); William H. Halewood, *The Poetry of Grace: Reformation Themes and Structures in English Seventeenth-Century Poetry* (New Haven, 1970); Barbara K. Lewalski, *"Paradise Lost" and the Rhetoric of Literary Forms* (Princeton, 1985); and James Turner, *One Flesh: Paradisal Marriage and Sexual Relations in the Age of Milton* (New York, 1987). In connection with Lewalski's article, see *Milton Studies,* XVII (1983), in its entirety.

10. For variously rhetoricized humanistic traditions—theological, political, psychosexual, and scientific—that are deployed fruitfully as containers and definers of the Miltonic achievement, see, for example, Stevie Davies, *Milton* (New York, 1991); Boyd M. Berry, *Process of Speech: Puritan Religious Writing and "Paradise Lost"* (Baltimore, 1976); John Leonard, *Naming in Paradise: Milton and the Language of Adam and Eve* (New York, 1990); Christopher Grose, *Milton's Epic Process: "Paradise Lost" and Its Miltonic Background* (New Haven, 1973); Christopher Grose, *Milton and the Sense of Tradition* (New Haven, 1988);

they speak of filling a gap. Obviously Milton's poetry would be less accessible without the triumphs such scholarly acuity has secured against wayward subjectivity and abstraction. And our footnotes attest to our efforts to learn what we needed from the available riches. So brilliant, knowledgeable, and appreciative a reader of Milton as Alexander Pope suffered in his understanding, suffered for an epistemological and ontological sophistication occluded by his culture but rehabilitated by the scholarship of ours.

Wherefore these ostensible one-to-one linkages, these containers stickbuilt on site or prefabricated and applied like templates or purse seines? When we as analysts are in a certain fury of analyzing, our animating volition is the pursuit of power. We want to get *control* of the word, the trope, the poem, whatever. Yet we reflect uneasily on the difference between loving an activity, or person, or university class (one going really well), and wanting to control an activity, or person, or class (one going not so well). Of course a good poem regularly casts a sort of control on some of the flux of—not, to be sure, experience but—understanding. Of course juxtaposing the less familiar or determinate or present to the more familiar or determinate or present is basic to all learning, is it not? Yet Lycidas is "Genius of the shoar" ("Lycidas," 183), encouraging the move that is to Milton so evidently crucial to life: the move from safe, determinate shore to tempestuous, oceanic unknown, that is, the realm of dark and even ironic similitude.

As long ago and as recently as 1941, wanting no doubt to take charge of and reform some damned nonsense about Milton abroad in the quad-

---

Stephen M. Fallon, *Milton Among the Philosophers: Poetry and Materialism in Seventeenth-Century England* (Baltimore, 1991); and Mary Ann Radzinowicz, "The Politics of *Paradise Lost*," in *Politics of Discourse: The Literature and History of Seventeenth-Century England,* ed. Kevin Sharpe and Steven N. Zwicker (Berkeley and Los Angeles, 1987), 204–29. Grose's *Milton and the Sense of Tradition* focuses on *Samson Agonistes* and *Paradise Regain'd.* For necessarily rhetoricized but more emphatically dialectical treatments, see, notably, Sanford Budick, *The Dividing Muse: Images of Sacred Disjunction in Milton's Poetry* (New Haven, 1985); R. A. Shoaf, *Milton, Poet of Duality: A Study of Semiosis in the Poetry and the Prose* (New Haven, 1985); and Regina Schwartz, *Remembering and Repeating: Biblical Creation in "Paradise Lost"* (New York, 1988). Without necessarily referring to Milton but relevant in concern, and with a differing sort of dialectic from that between ordering and chaos, a line that featured, for an earlier generation of critics, Albert Cook's *The Dark Voyage and the Golden Mean* (Cambridge, Mass., 1952) runs now to Susan Wells's *The Dialectics of Representation* (Baltimore, 1985), which addresses typicality and indeterminacy.

rangles of English universities, C. S. Lewis wrote *A Preface to "Paradise Lost."* But clearly he also wanted to celebrate Milton's magnum opus. Lewis' classical education, intelligence, and strenuous Anglicanism (which has its harmonies with Milton's Catholic-minded Puritanism), animated by his passion and articulateness, combined to catch so much of Milton's achievement that the book is still cited. Part of so brief a book's enduring power would seem to lie in its witness that Milton has caught so much of Lewis.

In 1955, apparently with the encouragement of Allen Tate, Cleanth Brooks, and perhaps Robert Penn Warren, Louisiana State University Press published W. B. C. Watkins' *An Anatomy of Milton's Verse.* It fairly represents New Criticism at its best and serves as a complementary counterpart to Lewis' book: Watkins' focus was roughly as intrinsic to the Miltonic text as Lewis' had been extrinsic. The explicative rhetorical and tropological discipline—evocative of Brooks and Warren trying to overpower the bafflements and wayward subjectivities of their LSU undergraduates—is enriched by imaginative and affectionate sensitivity beyond anything in the Renaissance rhetorics, but akin to Tate's reflections on Longinus, Dante, and Dostoyevsky.

Watkins is still cited, despite New Criticism's real or supposed abuses: the dryness of its most myopic close readings, the presumptive idiosyncrasy of multiple readings, its occasional historical or ideological parochialism, which some take to be intrinsic. Whether the last state of our discipline is better than the first admits as yet of no simple answer. In any case, in Milton studies as elsewhere, one response to New Criticism has been what an Arnoldian—and Geoffrey Hartman assures us there are many—might bemusedly call an epoch of simultaneous concentration and expansion. The concentration is toward greater determinacy, or presumed determinacy. The expansion, as we have seen, is toward a presumptively less parochial container, at least for some elements of Milton's poetic-thematic behavior. One element appropriately prominent in the latest generation of Milton scholarship—and addressed in later chapters—is of course gender. Some of the discourse about that has been countered by John Guillory in a fairly representative article that seems to us a perversely brilliant Foucauldian display of the reification and reductivity attendant on rejecting—not explaining away, but ruling out of court—theological discourse. Guillory seems to us wrong about what historians *do* with what they scrutinize, wrong about historical and discursive determinism, about ethos and psyche, about Milton and womanhood, about Adam, about astronomy. But he is right in concluding, as indeed his article manifests, that Milton is profoundly concerned with the "giant forms of discourse in conflict." [11]

That conveniently focused essay is an example of the widespread repression of theology, which we would counter partly by rearticulating crucial Miltonic terms and implications and partly by giving reminders of Paul Tillich's point that one's god is that in which one puts one's ultimate trust. But Guillory's essay also, and very positively, exemplifies the rousing motion in the assimilation of Milton's poetry by a new generation, a motion we would second. Call it acceptance of the invitation of Lycidas. The sense of generously risk-taking *disponibilité* with regard to the tempestuous energies, the potentially whelming or hurling tides actuated by Milton's inexhaustibly coursing song—that appears in Guillory and in others. [12]

Perhaps the flagship of the past decade's task force in the flotilla of Milton commentary is Louis Martz's *Poet of Exile: A Study of Milton's Poetry.* If the shore is typically the determinate world of contiguity and metonymy, then the unknown or imponderable or mysterious is characteristically—like the sea—the less predictable world of metaphor, synecdoche, and dark conceit. The Martzian vessel is powerfully constructed to explore the whole poetic map of metonymic, metaphoric, and synecdochic exile. So massively strong is it, so many the bearings taken on relatively determinate shore points, and on the sun and stars, with sensitive and sophisticated instruments, that we can scarcely fear inner vortices or cultural maelstroms. Yet the vessel is yarely responsive to the crosscurrents of Miltonic affection, anguish, and anger. [13] With Herman Rapaport's *Milton and the Postmodern,* on the other hand, we are as if on the *Glomar Challenger,* if not the *Red October.* Here be monsters, and we are down among them, clinging to Freudian and Marxian manuals as *tabulae nau-*

11. See Geoffrey Hartman, *Criticism in the Wilderness: The Study of Literature Today* (New Haven, 1980), and John Guillory, "Reading Gender into *Paradise Lost,*" in *Soliciting Interpretation: Literary Theory and Seventeenth-Century English Poetry,* ed. Elizabeth D. Harvey and Katharine Eisaman Maus (Chicago, 1990), 68–88.

12. Paul Tillich, *The Courage to Be* (New Haven, 1952); Paul Tillich, *Theology of Culture,* ed. Robert C. Kimball (New York, 1959); Gabriel Marcel, *Creative Fidelity,* trans. and intro. Robert Rosthal (New York, 1964).

13. Louis Martz, *Poet of Exile: A Study of Milton's Poetry* (New Haven, 1980).

fragiae. Even if we can match Professor Rapaport's spirit, we cannot promise so wonderfully defamiliarizing a trip.[14]

The late and magisterial New Critical analyst of the history of poetry and criticism, William K. Wimsatt, once told his friend Walter J. Ong, "I am a space man, you are a time man." The lust for determinacy conspicuous in recent Renaissance and Milton studies, including occasionally this one, may spring from an urge to control. But its sense of the medium of control is spatial, and with that, visual. Seeing is believing, from Locke's clear and distinct ideas to poststructuralist indeterminacies. Conversely, from Renaissance precursors of Locke to New Historicist plotters of power vectors and to Freud, Yeats, and some feminist critics, indeterminacy has been associated with the fuzzily or darkly unvisualizable, with the temporal and the correspondingly dynamic, and often with the feminine. It is thanks in part to the emphasis on the temporal and dynamic in current scholarship that we all have less and less excuse for being surprised that neither Freud nor anyone else would *see* in purely taxonomic terms "what women want," or men either.[15]

Ong seems to us with regard to Renaissance studies the insufficiently heeded and acknowledged master in "orality and literacy" (to draw our phrase from a title of his) and in the phenomenology and cultural dynamics of both. The very determinacy of the printed text, fixed on the page and replicable, fosters—as purely oral cultural cannot conceive or afford to do—the slow-motion replay of subtle discontinuities and centrifugalities. It is as if the printed form provided a playing field that besides permitting only certain games shaped the games it permitted, whether they were ordained by monarchs or classes or genders or national languages or modes of discourse. The determinate text may be answered by the indefinite contiguities of successive texts and may answer itself metaphorically by

14. Herman Rapaport, *Milton and the Postmodern* (Lincoln, Nebr., 1983).

15. William K. Wimsatt's remark appears in the dedication of Walter J. Ong's signally valuable *Interfaces of the Word: Studies in the Evolution of Consciousness and Culture* (Ithaca, N.Y., 1977). For identification of critical nostalgias for Renaissance "forms," and projects to reappropriate Renaissance "energies," see the Introduction and the elaborate critical-bibliographic notes to Jonathan Crewe's *Trials of Authorship: Anterior Forms and Poetic Reconstruction from Wyatt to Shakespeare* (Berkeley and Los Angeles, 1990). See, too, the wonderfully ambitious and lamentably unfinished effort to rearticulate cultures, selves, forms, and energies in Joel Fineman's *The Subjectivity Effect* and his *Shakespeare's Perjured Eye: The Invention of Poetic Subjectivity in the Sonnets* (Berkeley and Los Angeles, 1985).

disjunctions and antiphonies or respond to itself by enactment in the text or production and reproduction in the theater of our minds. Milton of course does all these things, although we shall deny that he was of the devil's party without knowing it. Wimsatt and Ong have written very little about Milton, and Mikhail Bakhtin and Paul Ricoeur, as theorists of the dialogic, or (in one of Ricoeur's titles) "time and narrative," have written virtually nothing, so far as we know.[16]

But Marshall Grossman's recent *Authors to Themselves: Milton and the Revelation of History* can serve as a signally useful representative of the open-ended temporalizing in Milton studies with which we would ally ourselves. Regarding the Bard's own phrase quoted in the book's title, and throughout the sensitively observant and cogently argued book, Grossman explores the resolution of the seeming contradiction between talking and text in the action of predicative writing. There is a dialectic of composing the self, putting verbs to subjects and objects, effecting "self-authorship . . . the temporal recuperation of the tension between self-fashioning and self-cancellation." The deliberate focus on how meaning emerges, in preference to what meaning, contributes to, among other results, Grossman thinks, the "psychogenesis of John Milton in the text

16. See Walter J. Ong, S.J., *Orality and Literacy: The Technologizing of the Word* (New York, 1982); Walter J. Ong, *Fighting for Life: Contest, Sexuality, and Consciousness* (Ithaca, N.Y., 1981); Walter J. Ong, *Rhetoric, Romance, and Technology: Studies in the Interaction of Expression and Culture* (Ithaca, N.Y., 1971); Walter J. Ong, *The Presence of the Word: Some Prolegomena for Cultural and Religious History* (New York, 1970); and Walter J. Ong, *Ramus, Method, and the Decay of Dialogue: From the Art of Discourse to the Art of Reason* (Cambridge, Mass., 1958). See, for exemplary particular application, M. T. Clanchy, *From Memory to Written Record, England, 1066–1307* (Cambridge, Mass., 1979); David Cressy, *Literacy and the Social Order: Reading and Writing in Tudor and Stuart England* (New York, 1980); and Brian Stock, *The Implications of Literacy: Written Language and the Models of Interpretation in the Eleventh and Twelfth Centuries* (Princeton, 1983). For a magisterial general survey, see Elizabeth Eisenstein, *The Printing Press as an Agent of Change: Communications and Cultural Transformations in Early Modern Europe* (2 vols.; New York, 1979), and Elizabeth Eisenstein, *The Printing Revolution in Early Modern Europe* (New York, 1983). For quite different particularized applications, more tangential to our concerns here, see Stanley Fish, "Authors-Readers: Jonson's Community of the Same," in *Representing the English Renaissance,* ed. Stephen Greenblatt (Berkeley and Los Angeles, 1988), 231–63 (reprinted from *Representations,* No. 7 [1984]); and Joseph Loewenstein, "The Script in the Marketplace," in *Representing the English Renaissance,* ed. Greenblatt, 265–78 (reprinted from *Representations,* No. 12 [1985]). The reflections of Ortega (see 3*n*1 above) can stand in this context as altogether remarkable anticipations.

of *Paradise Lost*," in explicit complementarity to William Kerrigan's well-known psychogenesis of *Paradise Lost* "in the personal history of John Milton." [17] However that may be, particular meaning, whipped to kennel, yet emerges to howl by the fire, as Grossman's own text rewardingly illustrates. Not least, his own *joie d'étudie* makes the play of predication and hope upon the field of textuality a non-zero-sum game. But we would not so disavow as he the ontology of Ricoeur—for him the Ricoeur of *The Rule of Metaphor*—and accordingly would not regard the language of Adam, Eve, or even the Bard in quite so atomistic, nominalistic, and closed a way. [18]

Our lesser resistance to the ontology of the scale of being permits us throughout the poetry a sense of a different Milton from the one to which Grossman is attuned, and of different protagonists in the three major poems. In the Miltonic universe that we find access to (not altogether a matter of seeing), even God does not create ex nihilo. Something of self-authorship occurs, but in a dialectic of love and power, and that in a metadialectic of *acceptance*—acceptance either of bad authorship that is stereotypic and decreative but never, except prospectively for Satan, Manichaeanly self-canceling, or else of creative authorship by accepted grace and responsive love.

In the necessary solitude of writing, as in the dialogue of projecting and revising together, we think of our readers as those who wonder how substantially Milton asserted eternal providence and justified the ways of God to man, or who wonder at his poetic performance in a variety of genres—and who wonder with sufficient care to pursue the matter into critical discourse. At the center of this audience, perhaps, are Renaissance scholars and Milton specialists, some of them colleagues of the mind irrespective of distances. For them we have tried, in the notes, to situate our argument within the prodigious landscape of relevant scholarship—where our argument stands both in debt and in opposition. But we write not to quarrel; we aspire to the scholarly equivalent of Rilke's poet who would write to praise. And there is another audience we wish to reach: those interested in the transmission and transmutation of ideas. So we

17. Marshall Grossman, *Authors to Themselves: Milton and the Revelation of History* (New York, 1987), viii.

18. To see Derrida arguing against the fixity of text, not quite the Derrida Grossman mobilizes, see Jacques Derrida, "Living On: Border Lines," in *Deconstruction and Criticism*, ed. Harold Bloom *et al.* (New York, 1979), 75–176.

have emphasized Milton's Augustinian heritage, mainly because it shaped the Christian matter Milton composed for his "fit audience" (*Paradise Lost*, VII, 31), but partly because it illuminates the way the inherited cultural conglomerate is passed on, preserved, and renewed with changing emphases and attitudes, in a kind of cultural hermeneutic. With Milton the theological past, reinforcing and giving substantial intentionality to—call it—a temperamental preoccupation with love, shaped his response to his circumstances most profoundly. We hope that philosophers and even, perhaps, a few historians will be interested in this phenomenon. Thus, we have attempted to produce a cross-disciplinary work, and hope that scholars from the humanities in general will find some reward in reconsidering Milton from a different perspective, thus mayhap to be renewed by a "new acquist" (*Samson Agonistes,* 1755) of experience. That is, after all, the Miltonic alternative to attempting to short-circuit, fragment, taxonomize, or otherwise overpower experience.

Finally, mingled with those two audiences and with concerns underlying but differently focused from theirs, are potential readers we have tried not to slight: the more extended, penumbral audience who feel in their minds and bones that there is something deeply wrong with the modern world, for all the local life enhancements it may proffer. Members of that audience are likely to be aware of one or another great twentieth-century portrait artist of the myth of power—Ernst Cassirer, Eric Voegelin, Lewis Mumford, Allen Tate, or Loren Eiseley, for example—and to be willing to consider that at the dawn of the new age of power, its greatest critic could offer both reflections still enhancing to life and strategies for critically reading any text that would make extreme claims to us. The bard who authors himself as the Bard, partly—early and late—by dramatizing the fallen world and partly by accepting Uranic or otherwise graceful authorship, poses a hermeneutic question. He asks, "Can I be the poet who asserts and justifies?" The answer, we judge, is not so much "Yes and no" as "May and might—still being determined by rereaders."

We return to our original two premises: a hermeneutic examination of divine grace and love. And we repeat that it is absolutely necessary to take seriously Milton's animating Christian faith and Augustinian theology. That seems not to mean that the critic must believe it but rather that the critic must entertain it—seriously, not casually. To repeat further, we agree with the argument that purely humanist scholarship must—illegitimately—pretend to discursive inclusiveness (see pp. 6–12 above).

Whatever our own illegitimate doings, we disavow that pretense of inclusiveness. We undertake not to unveil but rather to participate in a Miltonic method that disqualifies closure or pretended monopoly of truth. Therefore, this book is an attempt to suggest a general interpretive matrix that can include most of the poetic corpus in a coherent rather than exhaustive vision.

Two

The Fallen Understanding

aradise Lost, and most of Milton's poetry, is about love. Milton described and examined love in all its forms but paid particular attention to the grace of God and the proper human response, *agape.* A book about love also includes knowing and naming, since love, an overpowering condition, determines what is to be known and how it is to be named. The whole question of love is given its peculiar power and intensity in this poetry by Milton's emphasis on grace, so that love is moved beyond eroticism, or even *bienfaisance,* and ascends to the level of the meaning and purpose of life. Too little attention has been paid to love in discussing *Paradise Lost,* and indeed Milton's other major poetry. Love in Milton's poetic universe may be self-evident, and love is a Renaissance commonplace, but we have not found it commonly in the scholarship, and rarely as more than a commonplace. We agree with Rebecca West that "men resist learning truths which are too complicated and forget truths which are too simple." Declaring something self-evident is one way of doing either thing.[1]

---

1. Louis L. Martz's *Poet of Exile* is an exception, and indeed his arguments vocally and long in print—for example, in *The Paradise Within: Studies in Vaughan, Traherne, and Milton* (New Haven, 1961)—fostered our thinking on this issue. After the lines of our argument were formulated, we were delighted to find Sara Thorne-Thomsen's confirmatory *multum in parvo:* "'Hail Wedded Love': Milton's Lyric Epithalamium," *Milton Studies,* XXIV (1988), 155–85. For a more secular emphasis, see also John Kevin Newman, *The Classical Epic Tradition* (Madison, Wis., 1986), Chap. 8; and William Kerrigan and Gordon Braden, *The Idea of the Renaissance* (Baltimore, 1989), Chap. 10. For a rigorous sorites showing that God's name is Love and for the "argument of Milton's poem," see Michael Fixler, "All-Interpreting Love: God's Name in Scripture and in *Paradise Lost,*" in *Milton and Scriptural Tradition: The Bible into Poetry,* ed. James H. Sims and Leland Ryken (Columbia, Mo., 1984), 117–41. For love as glory, see, with difference of hierarchy and emphasis, John Peter Rumrich, *Matter of Glory: A New Preface to "Paradise Lost"* (Pittsburgh, 1987), and Douglas Anderson, "Unfallen Marriage and the Fallen Imagination in *Paradise Lost,*" *Studies in English Literature,* XXVI (1986), 125–44. See the Epilogue of Rebecca West's *The Meaning of Treason* (New York, 1945).

Second, it seems to us that *Paradise Lost,* with much of Milton's poetry, is a book of theology, and primarily of an Augustinian and biblically based theology. Analysis of the epic needs to begin with Protestant Christianity. Classical philosophy, accordingly, is less useful than Augustine for understanding it. Scholastic rational theology and dialectic, though important, must yield to the Bible. We would argue that Milton subscribed to the Augustinian notion that, "understanding is the reward of faith. Therefore seek not to understand that you may believe, but believe that you may understand." We argue further that Milton, like Saint Paul, saw faith as a gracious gift from God, not flowing from any merit on our part, though it is our responsibility to seek understanding and true knowledge: "Faith, therefore, works to the knowledge and love of God . . . to the end that He may be known more clearly and loved more steadfastly."[2] Since both points have been self-evident to some readers but arguable or opaque to others, we shall from time to time elaborate upon them.

Our analysis, thus rooted in Miltonic Christianity, is hermeneutic in method, as indicated in Chapter One: it involves a questioning of Milton's questions as to how understanding may come and what it may entail, and a search for and successive approximations to a general set of principles to explain the paradoxical or analogical or ambiguous relationships within Miltonic faith, love, and knowledge. Our analysis—to recapitulate further—is hermeneutic for at least five reasons: (1) it attends to the need to believe in order to understand, and to understand in order to believe; (2) it accepts the need to understand the whole in order to understand the part, and to understand the part in order to understand the whole; (3) it acknowledges the need to understand the past in order to understand the present, and to understand the present in order to understand the past; (4) it is sensitive to the need to understand the timeless in order to understand time, and to understand time to understand eternity; (5) it is aware that Milton, on good historical grounds, himself believed some-

2. "Intellectus enim merces est fidei. Ergo noli quaerere intelligere ut credas, sed crede ut intelligas" (Augustine, *In Joannis evangelium,* XXIX, 6, in *Patrologiae Cursus Completus . . . Series Latina,* ed. J. P. Migne [221 vols.; Paris, 1844–1903], XXXV, 1630). The full sentence about faith's working to the knowledge and love of God is "Valet ergo fides ad cognitionem et ad dilectionem Dei, non tanquam omnino incogniti, aut omnino non dilecti; sed quo cognoscatur manifestius, et quo firmius diligatur" (Augustine, *De trinitate,* VIII, ix, 13, in *Patrologiae . . . Latina,* ed. Migne, XLII, 960). See also Fiore, *Milton and Augustine.*

thing of this sort.[3] We in addition subscribe to the dictum of Paul Ricoeur concerning the universality of hermeneutic analysis, its spanning of the entirety of relationships between author and reader, between text and context: "Hermeneutics . . . is concerned with reconstructing the entire arc of operations by which practical experience provides itself with works,

3. We stand with Mili N. Clark against Edward W. Said, who, seemingly astigmatized by the spectacles of Foucault, begins "Abecedarian Culturae" (*Beginnings: Intention and Method* [Baltimore, 1975], 279–343) by disbarding Milton. It does not follow from Milton's epic situation that the truth is at "five removes from the reader" (p. 280), or if it were, that distance necessarily equals loss or nothingness. Clark's important, powerfully structuralist "The Mechanics of Creation: Non-Contradiction and Natural Necessity in *Paradise Lost*" (*English Literary Renaissance,* VII [1977], 207–42) argues for noncontradiction as a third term mediating sufficiency and falling, thus guaranteeing the "asymmetry of space-time" and explicating the whole poem as tragedy—and implying, *we* think, the need for a hermeneutic reading. We are less satisfied with Harold Bloom's recent assertion that "between Milton and God no mediation was necessary" (*Ruin the Sacred Truths: Poetry and Belief from the Bible to the Present* [Cambridge, Mass., 1989], 98) and that pathos held "priority over logos" (p. 101) throughout Milton's poetry. So narcissistic a Milton would scarcely bother to write and publish devotional epic. On Miltonic human time as a medium of learning (with reference to *Discursive* at *Paradise Lost,* V, 488), see Elizabeth Jane Wood, "'Improved by Tract of Time': Metaphysics and Measurement in *Paradise Lost,*" *Milton Studies,* XV (1981), 43–58. For the ultimately anti-epic grounding of such hermeneutics in rising literacy, see Walter J. Ong, "Milton's Logical Epic and Evolving Consciousness," *Proceedings of the American Philosophical Society,* CXX (1976), 295–305. See also Sanford Budick, "Milton and the Scene of Interpretation: From Typology Toward Midrash," in *Midrash and Literature,* ed. Geoffrey Hartman and Sanford Budick (New Haven, 1986), 195–212. Budick even more emphatically reads implications of interminable interpretation. Recent work illuminating as dialectic and its rhetorical features what we would include in a more variegated hermeneutic recirculation includes Marshall Grossman's "Milton's Dialectical Visions," *Modern Philology,* LXXXII (1984), 23–39 (also in his *Authors to Themselves*); and Michael McCanles' "*Paradise Lost* and the Dialectic of Providence," in *Dialectical Criticism and Renaissance Literature* (Berkeley and Los Angeles, 1975). Works tending in our view toward hermeneutic analysis or a sense of hermeneutic text include Balachandra Rajan's "*Paradise Lost:* The Uncertain Epic," *Milton Studies,* XVII (1983), 105–19 (reprinted in his *The Form of the Unfinished: English Poetics from Spenser to Pound* [Princeton, 1985]); and E. W. Tayler's *Milton's Poetry: Its Development in Time* (Pittsburgh, 1979). We have, however, many disagreements of identification and emphasis with both works. Hermeneutic recirculation can yield by degrees to ascription of rupture in Miltonic continuity or to taxonomy in the criticism. See Geoffrey Hartman on "hermeneutic structure," in "Adam on the Grass with Balsamum," in *Beyond Formalism: Literary Essays, 1958–1970* (New Haven, 1970), 124–50. For transumption as superformalism, see John Hollander, in *The Figure of Echo: A Mode of Allusion in Milton and After* (Berkeley

authors, and readers."[4] Hermeneutic analysis seeks to reduce criticism's inevitable *abstractive* understanding of poetic expression, and criticism's tendency to taxonomize relationships of form and doctrine, and its tendency toward premature closure.

On these two assumptions—that what is appropriate is a hermeneutic analysis of a hermeneutic text and that what are central are the various and contradictory forms of love—hangs all our subsequent analysis.

HERMENEUTIC MIDDLENESS

"Begin at the beginning," the White King told Alice with imperious command. Milton, a great poet, ignored such Aristotelian dicta and began *in medias res*. We, being merely commentators, will obey a royal requirement. And the beginning for us is the insight that although our essay can have a beginning, neither *Paradise Lost* itself nor a hermeneutic analysis of it can. Thus, the *point d'entrée* into either epic or analysis must be always arbitrary and disconcerting. It is disconcerting in the manner of a late entrance to a party; there is always an interruption and the feeling that much of importance has been missed. The arbitrary feel of a hermeneutic analysis of *Paradise Lost* is heightened by the sense that, already late for the party, we enter at random. This does not mean that one arbitrary entry is as good as another, for some things are central and others

---

and Los Angeles, 1981), and Harold Bloom, *A Map of Misreading* (New York, 1975), 125–43. For the imputation of mimetic and discursive discontinuities, see Mary Nyquist, "Reading the Fall: Discourse and Drama in *Paradise Lost*," *English Literary Renaissance,* XIV (1984), 199–229. See also John Guillory, "Ithuriel's Spear: History and the Language of Accommodation," in *Poetic Authority: Spenser, Milton, and Literary History* (New York, 1983; reprinted in *Critical Interpretations,* ed. Harold Bloom [New York, 1987]). Guillory offers a reading apparently irreconcilable with ours. For Milton's poetry we are using *The Complete Poetry of John Milton,* ed. John T. Shawcross (Rev. ed.; Garden City, N.Y., 1971).

4. Paul Ricoeur, *Time and Narrative,* trans. K. McLaughlin and D. Pellauer (3 vols.; Chicago, 1984), I, 53. For a somewhat analogous argument with regard to Milton's strategies in his prose, see David Loewenstein, "Introduction: 'Labouring the Word,'" in *Politics, Poetics, and Hermeneutics in Milton's Prose,* ed. David Loewenstein and James Grantham Turner (New York, 1990). Loewenstein argues that Milton practiced an "all-embracing activism" (p. 6). See also the essays in the volume. For a brief and carefully fair, albeit somewhat resistant, account, see Paul Connerton, "Gadamer's Hermeneutics," *Comparative Criticism,* V (1983), 107–28.

peripheral and it makes better sense to enter thinking about grace and love than to count the possible hours of unfallen time. Still, the middle is the middle, no matter how important the topic under consideration. Entering at a point that is of moment does nothing to change the disconcerting sense of arbitrariness and suspension, and does not alter the theological requirement that neither the epic nor the hermeneutic analysis of it can be linear or taxonomic except incidentally, nor can either be without irony, paradox, or ambiguity.

The reason for this tentativeness is the familiar one: a profoundly Christian world view and a hermeneutic analysis depend by their nature on mankind's position in the ambiguous middle of the Great Chain of Being. Situated in the middle, able to see and to comprehend the existence and something of the meaning of both higher and lower positions on the chain, mankind is always in a state of becoming, never of being. Like Saint Paul, we see here as in a glass, darkly, only hereafter face-to-face. Unable ever to be content, humanity never dwells in an essential state of repose, though rest may occur fleetingly and accidentally. Instead, mankind has the "power to degenerate into the lower forms of life, which are brutish. Thou shalt have the power, out of thy soul's judgement, to be reborn into higher forms, which are divine."[5] Constant movement is what distinguishes mankind from everything else in God's creation; movement makes man what Hermes Trismegistus called a "great miracle." The rest of creation is essentially static. The seraphim "burn with the fire of love," but that is all they do, and comparably the creatures of

5. Giovanni Pico della Mirandola, *Oration on the Dignity of Man,* para. 3, trans. Elizabeth L. Forbes, in *The Renaissance Philosophy of Man,* ed. Ernst Cassirer, Paul Oskar Kristeller, and John Herman Randall, Jr. (Chicago, 1948), 225. For a different view of the capacity of mankind, one more in line with Miltonic thought, see Augustine, *Enarrationes in Psalmos,* CXXI, 8, in *Patrologiae . . . Latina,* ed. Migne, XXXVII, 1624: "Quia homo in se non est: mutatur enim et vertitur, si non participet eius qui est idipsum" (Man in himself is not, for he is changed and altered if he does not participate in him who is the same). For an acute analysis of Miltonic rhetorical strategies attendant on the Chain of Being, see Leland Ryken, *The Apocalyptic Vision in "Paradise Lost"* (Ithaca, N.Y., 1970), a book that, however, does not have such matters as its chief focus. See further Walter R. Davis, "The Languages of Accommodation and the Styles of *Paradise Lost,*" *Milton Studies,* XVIII (1983), 103–27. On *descensus* as differentiation, see Thomas E. Maresca, *Three English Epics: Studies of "Troilus and Creseyde," "The Faerie Queene," and "Paradise Lost"* (Lincoln, Nebr., 1979), Pt. 2. On generic, imagistic, and liminal mediacy, see Patricia A. Parker, *Inescapable Romance: Studies in the Poetics of a Mode* (Princeton, 1979), Chap. 3.

nature are endlessly repetitive.[6] They are also finished, having achieved all that their station on the Great Chain of Being permits or accepts. There is nothing else for either a stone or a bright seraph to do.

The constant repetition of function and the finished nature that are the mark of creatures of both high and low degree mean that the world of nature and the hosts of heaven are perfect in their kind. Only the fallen can have movement; were it otherwise, the entire creation of God would be imperfect—for Milton, a manifest impossibility. But perfection is denied mankind, whom "sin hath impaired" (*Paradise Lost,* VI, 691). God made man

> just and right,
> Sufficient to have stood, though free to fall.
> Such I created all th' Ethereal Powers
> And Spirits, both them who stood and them who faild;
> Freely they stood who stood, and fell who fell.
>
> (III, 98–102)

For the hosts of hell, who "by thir own suggestion fell, / Self-tempted, self-deprav'd" (III, 129–30), there will be no turning to grace, only an endless descent; thus they too are in a sense perfect in their antiperfection, a state of fallenness in which no instant is essentially differentiated from another. Demons fall as the stone sits or the bright seraph loves, ex opere operato; since, unlike the stone, they have will, they sin and fall obsessively. Mankind alone, open to grace and therefore radically unfinished and functionally differentiated according to it, is imperfect and enjoys movement. We are assured by Scripture and Books XI and XII of *Paradise Lost* that this movement tends graciously upward, though "with wandring steps and slow" (XII, 648). For mankind, it is middling imperfection, it is becoming, it is an unfinished state and movement that is *sua in propria.*

The phenomenon of unfinished uniqueness may be seen from another perspective. Only mankind exists within both history and ontology. All other creatures exist only in being. In the realm of spiritual responsibility and journey the rest of creation shows no *motus ad formam,* since everything of it has already achieved the divinely ordained ends for which it

6. *Asclepius,* I, 6a, in *Hermetica,* ed. Walter Scott (4 vols.; London, 1924–36), I, 294. On the notion of perfective movement and the problem of representing it, see—or hear—G. F. Handel's Dettingen "Te Deum," with its repetition of *continually* from the Book of Common Prayer's canticle "To thee cherubim and seraphim continually do cry."

was created. If, for extrahuman creation, being describes perfectly all there is, for mankind it describes the merest surface. To define mankind by being ("isness") and matter ("whatness") goes little beyond pronouncing man a featherless biped. All that is important is omitted. Mankind acts in history, history at once personal and general, and history with direction, meaning, and importance.

Within history Miltonically construed, mankind acts in three ways, not the traditional two of macrocosm and microcosm. The first of these is certainly the classic microcosmic journey, from lostness to understanding through grace, a state decisively depicted by Saint Augustine as individual life in the city of God.[7] This journey, historical in that it occurs within time, transforms the meaning of having being though not its substance, and can take place only within being. The two other ways that mankind acts within history relate to the categorial distinction between the temporal and the eternal. On the one hand, as seen from the smaller end of the spyglass, history is temporality—the mundane, daily, fluctuating, and seemingly endless flow of events and changes of "vicissitude," the course of days in the *civitas terrena*. Purely human history, considered on its own terms, piddles along, endlessly revisiting every possible human action and reaction now as a tragedy, now as a farce, often as both, but without larger significance and with ineluctable circularity. On its own, human history goes nowhere. This is the history of meaningless changes, often misconstrued by gnostic theory, such as Marxism or Millenarianism, and almost unbearably tedious and limited.[8] How could it be otherwise? This history is merely human. But history is also more, Milton tells us, notably in Books XI and XII of *Paradise Lost*. There is eternity in God's regard of humanity and of humanity's destiny. Here the utterance of Generaloberst von Blumentritt is correct; it is absolutely true that we live in

7. For an example of one life considered as a salvific journey made possible by grace, see *The Confessions of Saint Augustine,* trans. Rex Warner (New York, 1963). A more general view of the salvific journey appears in Augustine, *The City of God,* trans. Marcus Dods, ed. Thomas Merton (New York, 1950), esp. Bks. XV–XVIII, XXII.

8. On the general topic of Millenarianism, see Norman Cohn's important study *The Pursuit of the Millennium* (New York, 1961). Milton scholars will be particularly interested in the appendix on the "ranters" during the English Revolution (pp. 321–81). For Milton's engagement in prose as well as poetry with the problem of rendering line, cycle, and end, see Achsah Guibbory, "John Milton: Providential Progress or Cyclical Decay," in *The Map of Time: Seventeenth-Century English Literature and Ideas of Pattern in History* (Urbana, Ill., 1986), Chap. 6.

a *geschichtliche Augenblick,* "in a moment" (God, VII, 154). Eternity and God's sight give meaning to the history that each person actually lives, and therefore to the history that *alone* gives meaning to mere being. For Milton, of course, the coexistence of being and history is indispensable; there is no purgatory. Ontology and history, being and becoming, stand at the core of the biblical view of mankind.[9]

And so one returns to the middle. History demands a past and a future. So wherever the poem or analysis begins, there is always something that has happened earlier. The creation of Adam is only the beginning of a specific microcosmic journey. What took place before Adam is more important to the story of Adam than Adam's own small part. Unlike nature, humanity can never escape the sins of those who have gone before, and there are always those who have gone before—or who *are* before, that is, God. To start at the beginning of temporal history is obviously not the same as starting at the beginning of eternal history, which has no beginning, or if one wishes, the beginning of which is always. When the human is connected to the divine, when history is considered in all three forms, then the shapeless and inconclusive—that is, the meaningless, graceless welter of activity—is translated into the dimension of meaning's fullness. Thus Milton employs as if typologically the epic convention of *in medias res.* His practice with other epic conventions likewise responds to the conditions of historical meaning, as we shall show. Indeed, his practice with the very epic form ontologically enlarges the political and familial, the cultural, root of previous epic. What is more, from an appreciation of Miltonic middleness analogous apprehensions concerning the poet's verse sequence, his (comic) masque, and his tragic drama depend subordinately.

The relationship of the linear to the circular, at the heart of the multidimensionality of humanity in the way the relationship bears on the contrast between being and becoming, and between the historical and the ontological, among other contrasts, figures critically in a hermeneutic understanding of *Paradise Lost.* Thus, it is back to the middle not only for history but also for an understanding and analysis of the poem. It is impossible to know about the beginning of *Paradise Lost* until the end is understood—and the reverse is true as well. The reader cannot know the

9. On this point, see Walter Clyde Curry, *Milton's Ontology, Cosmogony, and Physics* (Lexington, Ky., 1957).

parts without knowing the whole—and again the reverse is true. The fall of Lucifer is meaningless unless the redemption of humanity is clear. If humanity is not redeemed, then God is defeated, which is theologically Manichaean and biblically unsupportable. But the redemption of humanity gives the fall of Satan its full meaning, both as a metaphor for sin and as the path unredeemed by grace. It also makes the fall of the hosts of hell the nearest thing to a *felix culpa,* the prototype of God's ultimately turning all sin into an occasion for good. After all, the fall of Satan gives the full and comprehensible definition of God by means of contrast. The stature of Satan in *Paradise Lost* stands as the final measure of divine power, in that God can permit that, employ that, transmute even that.

Equally interdependent are the understanding of part and the understanding of whole. The incident of the prelapsarian naming of nature illustrates this:

> I nam'd them, as they pass'd, and understood
> Thir Nature, with such knowledge God endu'd
> My sudden apprehension
>
> (VIII, 352—54)

Such a scene, in which true name for true nature is unfailingly given, makes sense only in a context of unfallen grace *and* ultimate redemption. Certainly, we are all aware that as fallen we do not know either the true nature or the true names of God's creation. Details fit only into the context of the whole. Insofar as we are *merely* fallen, we scarcely live in God's creation but, rather, inhabit a Robert Gravesian net of mere language, itself a mere system of differences, "wandring mazes" (II, 561), as the Bard observes in hell. But even *unfallen* Adam and Eve needed names, because creation was not present to them as to God and they therefore had to create a liberating mediation.[10]

A receptivity to the interconnectedness of beginning and end and of part and whole involves one in the endless hermeneutic circle of movement from the personal through the historically temporal to the eternal. It may be superfluous to add that this clearly means that both the reader and the analyst of *Paradise Lost,* like the poet himself, are always *in medias*

---

10. See Robert Graves's poem "The Cool Web." See also Roy Harris, *Reading Saussure: A Critical Commentary on the "Cours de linguistique général"* (London, 1987). To our student Tamara Kimball we owe the suggestion about why unfallen Adam and Eve required names.

res, always being driven up the Great Chain of Being for understanding.[11] In this respect the medium is the message. In this respect, also, the hermeneutic recirculation of question and answer describes a journey and a "progress" through *Paradise Lost* itself, through Scripture, through the *Confessions* of Saint Augustine, perhaps, and through life. But the spiral that is also a journey and a "progress" has an end—salvation—even if, just as paradoxically, it does not have a beginning. Logic may find this unintelligible, but logic, though a resource for the philosopher, is of limited value to the Christian epic poet and the hermeneutic analyst. Both the poet and the analyst deal instead with the Christian promise of grace and providence:

> Mightie Father, thou thy foes
> Justly hast in derision, and secure
> Laugh'st at thir vain designes and tumults vain
>
> (V, 735–37)

The derision stands fully justified, both by grace given freely to persons and by the sacralizing of temporal history that occurs in understanding it in relation to the eternal, that is, to the wonderful work of providence.

A hermeneutic analysis of *Paradise Lost* does not operate at the level of logic or taxonomy or quantified human experience. It implicates itself instead in paradox and radical ambiguity. Human history both is and is not—at the same time and with the same act—part of the sacred and the eternal. Mankind is free, and providence is fixed: both. The human journey is both linear and circular, both toward the light and mired in original sin. Grace both saves the sinner and leaves the sin untouched, for history must be fulfilled but not repealed. Divine foreknowledge both knew of and did not affect the Fall, either of Satan or of mankind. None of these affirmations is logically compelling, and some are not even logically passable, of course, but that is because logic operates *only* at the level of humanity in the Great Chain of Being. In *Paradise Lost,* there is more to it than that. Our understanding may be fallen, impaired by sin, and thus defective, but it has not been obliterated. And for it, however one explains it, experience is not the sum total of experience.

11. From the long roster of now-canonical scholarship, we would single out Arthur O. Lovejoy's *The Great Chain of Being: A Study in the History of Ideas* (Cambridge, Mass., 1936); and Alexandre Kojève, *From the Closed Mind to the Infinite Universe* (Baltimore, 1965).

A hermeneutic analysis of *Paradise Lost* must acknowledge all the levels of the Great Chain of Being and must always begin in the middle of an endless story that also has no beginning except that which can be explained by the end. The Bible itself falls into the same category of story. It too begins in the middle, after the creation, and is, therefore, in God's terms, a commentary on the last days. [12] So the hermeneutic method must be to glory in the dialectic tension of paradox, radical ambiguity, and successive approximations, not attempt to explain these away by trivializing them through restriction to the merely human, still less to static tabulation.

So we say. But is it so? Must this be the method for a fruitful understanding of *Paradise Lost?* We can test the promise of the hermeneutic approach by examining the whole of the poem without it. If hermeneutic analysis is abandoned, the poem seems either myth or trivia. It becomes myth not only insofar as it relates a story with no referent, one too outlandish to be useful even as a metaphor and one utterly inexplicable in experiential terms, but also insofar as it relates that story arbitrarily: who, after all, is this Bard? That is the way Voltaire saw it, and so must the mythographer, who will surely ask, Who was this Adam? Is there any evidence for him? Where are these angels? Satan does not sound like anything seen around these parts recently. How can divine foreknowledge be absolute and unbinding? Worst of all, if the poem is myth, it is myth without meaning, for it tells about what cannot be so, as an explanation for what must be so. [13] The other risk of eschewing a hermeneutic analysis is encountered when the decision is made to ignore questions about the meaning of the entire poem and to concentrate exclusively on aspects or passages. Unlike the mythographic approach, this has value, but below the horizon of general explication. If that satisfies, a hermeneutic approach is not needed; indeed, no general theory is. But easy satisfaction is no argument against seeking the more robust understanding that only hermeneutics can enable.

Milton himself had hard words for the content and results of mythic or otherwise fractionalizing analysis, which leads into the limbo of vanity:

12. On this point, too important to be omitted though it is obvious, see Augustine, *The City of God,* Bk. XV.

13. On myth in this connection, see Joseph Campbell, *The Hero with a Thousand Faces* (Princeton, 1949), esp. Prologue. For more germane and helpful work, see Isabel Mac-Caffrey, *"Paradise Lost" as "Myth"* (Cambridge, Mass., 1959).

So on this windie Sea of Land, the Fiend
Walk'd up and down alone bent on his prey,
Alone, for other Creature in this place
Living or liveless to be found was none,
None yet, but store hereafter from the earth
Up hither like Aereal vapours flew
Of all things transitorie and vain . . .
New *Babels,* had they wherewithall, would build
. . . .
Here Pilgrims roam, that stray'd so farr to seek
In *Golgotha* him dead, who lives in Heav'n;
. . . Reliques, Beads,
Indulgences, Dispenses, Pardons, Bulls
      (III, 440–46, 468, 476–77, 491–92)

The various results are stigmatized as vain or flimsy because, as mere shuffles of fallen power, they are disconnected from the more solid regenerative and integrative ontology of love. A hermeneutic analysis may be disconcerting and awkward, it may lack purely human logical consistency, it may risk equivocation by dancing from level to level in the Great Chain of Being, it may be unable to unravel the dialectic of ontology and history—all this may be true. But a hermeneutic analysis does treat of humanity in the larger setting of providence and eternity, as Milton did, it consults the works of grace, as Milton did, it examines fallenness, as Milton did, it examines the whole and the parts in relation, as Milton did, and it remembers God's promise of redemption and love. Hence we attempt such an analysis, necessarily partial.

LOVING DIRECTEDNESS

As a book of love, as apotheosis of *ars amatoria* as much as of *in medias res, Paradise Lost* describes three distinct kinds of love. That is theologically appropriate for a poem dealing thematically with multiple levels of the Great Chain of Being. The love and grace of God can hardly be equated with any counterpart capacities in Satan and must also differ in kind, not degree, from the qualities in man. God's love is both creative and regenerative, and is described in terms of justice, light, life, and above all, grace and growth. Species grow, witness humanity; even divinity grows, as the Son does (III, VI). Satan's love is an antilove, marked by an endless selfishness and deterioration, as in Pandaemonium, the bridge through Chaos, and—worst eminence—the incestuous trinity of hell. Humanity's love is more complex, participating in both the demonic and the divine. At the human level of the Great Chain of Being, Milton describes love in terms of work, learning, and growth, as well as eroticism (*eros*), goodwill (*phile* or *bienfaisance*), and worship and prayer (*agape*). But he also describes it in terms of narcissism, idolatry, dispute, and the Fall. The two faces of postlapsarian human love may have been a commonplace in Milton's England, but they were not less true or important for that.

A book about love is also, of necessity, a book about knowing and naming. What is not loved but merely apprehended, it says, cannot be known but can only be recognized. Similarly, only what is well loved can be well named. This rule holds for the real names of grace as well as their approximate postlapsarian counterparts. Moreover, love impels, requires, insistently commands both naming and knowing: to name is in some sense to appropriate the named to the self and the self to the named. Satan compulsively misnames things. God receives political attributes—he is a king or the Omnipotent—whereas Eve is a goddess. Adam is called by love both to knowing and to naming, as all nature is brought "to receave / From thee thir Names, and pay thee fealtie" (VIII, 343–44). In *Paradise Lost,* knowing and naming are fundamental signs of love and are the terms in which love is generally described, whether that love is gracious or disgraceful. By knowing or naming and representing the moments of love, Milton talks of love—not perhaps in its essence but certainly in its dynamic operations and appearances—in ways that let us recognize it, poetically, theologically, and psychologically.

Milton begins the journey into the nature of love with Satan, whose kind of love is frightening, powerful, and instantly—and guiltily—recognizable. Satan's capacity for love, which is an antilove, reflects his fall, which Milton sees as strikingly similar to ours. In both, love is turned inward as the *libido dominandi,* away from God and into selfishness and self-concern, which are themselves disobedience and thus the Fall. Satan asks himself,

> Hadst thou the same free Will and Power to stand?
> Thou hadst: whom hast thou then or what t' accuse,
> But Heav'ns free Love dealt equally to all?
> Be then his Love accurst, since love or hate,
> To me alike, it deals eternal woe.

> Nay curs'd be thou; since against his thy will
> Chose freely . . .
>
> (IV, 66–72)[14]

He can only oppose that omnipotently gracious and just *equally* and *alike* by making himself less deserving of the "Love dealt" and more harmoniously woeful in hate—by turning himself into a narcissistically reduced set of similarities and differences, in contrast to the divine plenitude.[15] Thus fallen and falling, ever inward, Satan cannot love except as a ghastly and hideous parody of grace. And the object of his antilove is also the opposite of grace; it is only Satan himself. Indeed, what can fraud love if not its author? What can such love be except an antigrace, the most imposing manifestation of that power which since William Blake has moved some readers to take Satan with Manichaean seriousness: "And in the lowest deep a lower deep / Still threatning to devour me opens wide" (IV, 76–77).

Satan's antilove is described by Milton theologically in terms of evil and sin and the freely chosen embrace thereof, secondarily and psychologically in terms of the infantile fear of the devouring mother such as we have just seen:

> So farwell Hope, and with Hope farwell Fear,
> Farwell Remorse: all Good to me is lost;
> Evil be thou my Good . . .
>
> (IV, 108–10)

A counterpart to chosen sin, Satan's antilove is totally uncreative and ungenerative and can produce only loss, "distempers" (IV, 118), and degeneration. This is the more emphatically true because of Milton's constant and recurrently insistent anti-Manichaeanism. Evil is a heading or a doing; evil is not a *thing*. We gratefully invoke Ricoeur's fine essay on the dependence and insubstantiality of sin, in *Conflict of Interpretations,* which supports conclusions that can independently be inferred from Milton's usage of words like *perverse, seduce, transgress,* and the like.[16] The Bard is explicit early; Satan never

---

14. Note the pyrrhic and the spondee in the third and fourth feet of line 71, Satan *contra naturam.*

15. See Augustine, *The City of God,* Bk. XI, Secs. 13–15, Bk. XIV, Sec. 27.

16. Paul Ricoeur, "The Symbolism of Evil Interpreted," in *The Conflict of Interpretations,* 269–377.

Had ris'n or heav'd his head, but that the will
And high permission of all-ruling Heav'n
Left him at large to his own dark designs
(I, 211–13)

Milton describes this process in two distinct but related ways, referring
to physical appearance and the seven deadly sins. Appearance and sin are
mutually reflexive, almost Platonically reciprocal in the fallen world; the
outward and visible sign betokens inward and spiral disgrace. Satan's
physical ruin begins as soon as he is cast down by love, which is the sole
and essential nature of the Son, into

the wastful Deep; the monstrous sight
Strook them with horror backward, but far worse
Urg'd them behind; headlong themselvs they
    threw
Down from the verge of Heav'n
(VI, 862–65)

Satan and the fallen angels, having expelled *themselves* from paradise as the
inevitable result of the pride, fear, and anger characteristic of narcissistic
love, feel themselves "Under amazement of thir hideous change" (I, 313).
Satan *observes* Beelzebub, "how fall'n! how chang'd" (I, 84), *feels* himself
and the fallen angels to have been "astounded and amaz'd" (I, 281), and
exhibits in Bardic representation "Deep scars of Thunder . . . intrencht"
on his face, "care . . . on his faded cheek" (I, 601–602)— although he
seems imperfectly aware of the change. This theme was repeated often.
Although Satan is the "false dissembler unperceiv'd" (III, 681), he is also
the "fraudulent Impostor foul" (III, 692), with face "disfigur'd, more then
could befall / Spirit of happie sort . . . gestures fierce . . . mad demean-
our" (IV, 127–29). Ithuriel and Zephon instruct him, later in Book IV,
of his visible deterioration. But Satan's disfigurement, though evidently
unsettling, was not the end of his physical descent:

O foul descent! that I . . .
. . . am now constraind
Into a Beast, and mixt with bestial slime,
This essence to incarnate and imbrute
(IX, 163–66)

Satan hates his epic, incarnational descent to the underworld; the Son
loves his—yielding a dually ultimate version of another epic convention.

In the end, Satan is "enclos'd / In [a] Serpent" (IX, 494–95) for the purpose of deceiving Eve, and upon his ironically triumphant return to hell that form becomes confirmed, even perhaps recurrent, "some say" (X, 575): "supplanted down he fell / A monstrous Serpent on his Belly prone" (X, 513–14). The same befalls all the hellish host with hellish sympathy, like the degenerate familialism of the incestuous trinity of Satan-Sin-Death. Satan's knowing and naming have drawn them to him and him to them, centripetally, in the ultimate pathetic fallacy.

Physical decay thus matches moral decay, both happening gradually, with time and repose enough for repentance, reconsideration, and repair. There is, of course, no repentance and, accordingly, no repair; there is only further and further descent, greater and greater sin, until the epitome of antilove shall be achieved, as proclaimed *in medias:* "fardest from him is best" (I, 247).

NEGATIVE REFERENTIALITY AND REPRESENTATION

Disgrace and antilove are expressed in three general ways: intellectually by an anticreed, dramatically by the seven deadly sins repeated and refined, and imagistically by such ultimate and compound complexes as the incestuous trinity of Satan-Sin-Death. Satan pronounces his anticreed early, and it acts as a general statement of demonic ambition:

> Fall'n Cherub, to be weak is miserable
> Doing or Suffering: but of this be sure,
> To do aught good never will be our task,
> But ever to do ill our sole delight,
> As being the contrary to his high will
> Whom we resist. If then his Providence
> Out of our evil seek to bring forth good,
> Our labour must be to pervert that end,
> And out of good still to find means of evil
> (I, 157–65)

It is an ambitious program, impossible of fulfillment, theology would have us suppose, but still one that will be amply informed by the seven deadly sins. Milton manifestly designs that Satan excels at these, and in particular, at the primal, eldest curse of pride. Pride is not only the consequence but also the cause of Satan's fall. The demonic pride has many forms, all adding to Satan's loss and sense of loss: "Pride and worse Ambition threw me down / Warring in Heav'n" (IV, 40–41). Pride is also toxic shame, preventing repentance:

> is there no place
> Left for Repentance, none for Pardon left?
> None left but by submission; and that word
> *Disdain* forbids me, and my dread of shame
> Among the Spirits beneath, whom I seduc'd
> With other promises and other vaunts
>   (IV, 79–84)

The one who has rejected his generic categorical status subordinate to God is the prisoner of anxiety lest his superordination over his cohorts become subordination. Here is the powermonger's pride and concern over losing face, of being seen as the fraud and seducer that every politician in the fallen world must, for Milton, inevitably be. But there is more. Pride is always already injured and accordingly tends to the form of rage, as when Satan is caught spitting the foul dream in Eve's ear. Satan was

> overcome with rage;
> But like a proud Steed reind, went hautie on,
> Chaumping his iron curb
>   (IV, 857–59)

He is also "fill'd with scorn" (IV, 827) and with "ambitious aim" (I, 41), both of which are fulfilled, in a catastrophically ironic way, through the episode of Pandaemonium. Here Satan sits "High on a Throne of Royal State . . . by merit rais'd / To that bad eminence" (II, 1, 5–6). This ironic hummock in hell is the high point in the poem for Satan.[17] Ahead lies further physical and moral degradation. The sins of pride, ambition, and lust for power, which drove him to disobedience in the first place, are here caught in a characteristically complex metaphor of discounted "*Barbaric*" power, glory, wealth (II, 4), and effulgence "Outshon" (II, 2). But the power is illusory, the wealth worthless, the glory and effulgence fraudulent. Moreover, once having sat in that bad seat, Satan can no longer repent. Having achieved all he revolted for, having been raised in his own perception to the "eminence" he so ardently loved, he

---

17. MacCaffrey sensitively explicates Milton's metaphoricity of up and down in *"Paradise Lost" as "Myth,"* esp. Chap. 3. For further epistemological and thematic development, see Kathleen M. Swaim, "The Mimesis of Accommodation in Book 3 of *Paradise Lost,*" *Philological Quarterly,* LXIII (1984), 461–75 (reprinted in her *Before and After the Fall*).

can now love nothing else, nor know nor name anything beyond the narrow strictures of his irremediably fallen state. The quoted passage is psychologically acute, as well. We are instantly and irresistibly reminded of any politician—whether of station or of profit—whose love is fixed on "ambitious aim," whose heart "Distends with pride, and hardning in his strength / Glories" (I, 572–73), and for whom everything comes down to power. In such a world there is no room for the contrite heart.

Satan's capacity for knowing and for naming is restricted by his inability to love. Demonic knowing turns constantly inward, in a continuing downward spiral that perhaps has no end—although we shall later offer a conjecture about Milton's implication. In such a state, Satan can know and name only himself, that is, he—and by reflection, we ourselves—can give names only to various aspects of the fallenness to which we have attached our idolatrous antilove. Fallen Satan can conceive of his relationship to God only in terms of defiance and submission and of beloved fragments of himself. Having been utterly routed, he projects and declaims:

> All is not lost; th' unconquerable Will,
> And study of revenge, immortal hate,
> And courage never to submit or yield:
> And what is else not to be overcome?
> That Glory never shall his wrath or might
> Extort from me. To bow and sue for grace
> With suppliant knee, and deifie his power
> . . . that were low indeed,
> That were an ignominy and shame beneath
> This downfall
>
> (I, 106–12, 114–16)

Knowing in such political terms of force and power obliterates knowing in any other way, as Satan admits by asking "how soon / Would highth recall high thoughts, how soon unsay / What feign'd submission swore" (IV, 94–96). The theme of defective knowing and naming resonates throughout. Satan is constantly described, and describes himself, as knowing only sin and naming all things in terms such as "earthly notion can receave" (VII, 179). Upon seeing Adam and Eve together, he complains,

> Sight hateful, sight tormenting! thus these two
> Imparadis't in one anothers arms
> . . . while I to Hell am thrust,

> Where neither joy nor love, but fierce desire,
> Among our other torments not the least,
> Still unfulfill'd with pain of longing pines
>
> (IV, 505–506, 509–11)

It could be argued Milton amplifies the established subgenre of plaint much as he does the epic conventions. In keeping with that, Satan further complains,

> the more I see
> Pleasures about me, so much more I feel
> Torment within me, as from the hateful siege
> Of contraries; all good to me becomes
> Bane, and in Heav'n much worse would be my state.
>
> (IX, 119–23)

This proclaims deathly narcissism: anything differing from the self is perceived as contrarious (to use the choral word from *Samson Agonistes*) and even *hateful*. In the irremediably fallen state nothing can be known as it is, but everything must be experienced and named in terms of the fallen individual's own sin. Thus, Satan can see good only in terms of bane, conjugal love in terms of unsatisfied and burning desire. Turned totally inward, Satan is constantly besieged by the growing and finally total difference between things as they are and the sinful and loveless interpretation that he must give them. Ultimately, he loses track of everything, including himself, and becomes like the serpents who

> Chewd bitter Ashes, which th' offended taste
> With spattering noise rejected: oft they assayd,
> Hunger and thirst constraining, drug'd as oft,
> With hatefullest disrelish writh'd thir jaws
> With soot and cinders fill'd; so oft they fell
> Into the same illusion
>
> (X, 566–71)

The word *illusion* is the key to this celebrated passage, inasmuch as it describes Satan's knowing and naming. The epistemology of a total and ungracious inwardness can only encompass a perpetual and self-reflexive and self-reinforcing illusion. No nurture eventuates. No light can penetrate. The self is everything. The condition of Satan's soul matches the external landscape of hell: "No light, but rather darkness visible" (I, 63).

So Milton presents the ultimate irony. Like God, Satan has become the all in all; like God, Satan can describe himself as "I am that I am" (Exod. 3:14, KJV). But the *am* that is Satan is nothing, while the *Am* that is God is everything. The hermeneutic circle has for Satan contracted to an internality little more than a point. The parallel construction, both poetic and theological, is perfect. The constant falling of Satan reaches its logical and inevitable conclusion, the condition where antilove knows only itself and names itself endlessly. Milton has formulated a Christian ontology and—it is scarcely too much to say—a Christian phenomenology of solipsism.

The passage has a further meaning, also related to knowing and naming. The fruit, which remains fruit to Milton, and to us, and is so named by Milton, can only be ashes to Satan and the demons drawn to him, for they can know and name only inwardly. Thus the demons, who "oft . . . assayd" to eat, perform a hideous and ghastly parody of a transubstantiating Eucharist in which the accidents remain the same while the real essence is transformed. The demons take and eat in remembrance only of themselves. There is no spiritual food but only the lack thereof, and an inward and gustatory sign of that spiritual disgrace. There is neither *sacrificium* nor *beneficium* but only hunger and illusion. This view of the sacrament is reinforced by the poetic choice of fruit; in paradise fruit is nutritive even for visiting angels, whereas in hell it comes, so to speak, from the tree of unknowledge. In fallen English, the Latin root of fruit, *fruir*, "to enjoy," is muted, as at the rapist's wedding reception in the Wife of Bath's Tale, where there is no enjoyment at all. The theme of demonic sacrament is repeated with the Hell-hounds, who "lick up the draff and filth / Which mans polluting Sin with taint hath shed" (X, 630–31). Again, antilove is depicted as being unable to know or name aright, and the supreme selfishness of the fallen state is repeated. Dogs do not talk, and these dogs "nourish" only their own undoing and unbeing, as we shall argue. Moreover, the demonic anti-Eucharist may even be a periodic and thus quasi-liturgical event: "Yearly enjoynd, some say, to undergo / This annual humbling certain number'd days" (X, 575–76). The eating of ashes, in which the demons show how little they can know by knowing even less, thus becomes an anti-Easter, the high point, but also thus the low point, as the demons sink still lower. Fallenness totally inverts meaning, and so lostness is celebrated by becoming more lost, and the salvific liturgical year of Christianity is turned into an orgy of desolation and despair. [18]

The demonic sacrament and liturgical year are the culmination of Milton's comments and description of the bad that is "fardest from him" (I, 247). Unloving body and unloving temporal program are the negative coextremes in Milton's anti-Manichaean meditation on evil. The antilove that seeks decay rather than creativity, the unknowing and the incapacity to name, are carried to the ultimate level of "bad eminence" (II, 6), which is the opposite of the resurrection that redeems us all. Thereafter, Satan disappears from the epic. The ways of God to man, insofar as Satan can explain them through contrastive gracelessness, are formally explicated.

NONPOLARITY OF DIVINE REFERENCE AND REPRESENTATION

Milton began *Paradise Lost* with Satan, and there is a natural temptation to compare God with Satan, to see God as the opposite of Satan. Such a view is theologically perverse. The opposite of Satan might be described as a saint, but to apply such a concept to God is Manichaean. Can one believe Satan's boast that "Divided Empire with Heav'ns King I hold / By thee, and more then half perhaps will reigne" (IV, 111–12)? Viewing Satan as the opposite of God implies limits on God, since it means that God can somehow be known as Satan is known. But Milton insists on a God who cannot be known, not merely because of the simple conceptual distance of divinity but also because of the demands of univocation, in keeping with which knowing cannot Pelagianly promote itself up the Great Chain of Being. [19] God can only be described; indeed, we can de-

18. John E. Booty, ed., *The Book of Common Prayer, 1559: The Elizabethan Prayer Book* (Charlottesville, Va., 1976). We cite this edition because it is elegant, available, and closely approximate for our purposes to the edition of 1604 presumably most familiar to Milton. Gregory the Great was the leading organizer and redactor of Christian liturgy in general and of the Christian year in particular. See, for example, Archdale A. King, *Liturgies of the Roman Church* (Milwaukee, 1957), which is the first volume of his series Rites of Western Christendom. Regina Schwartz has argued for a markedly different Miltonic insistence on the inseparable duality of creation and chaos. See her *Remembering and Repeating*.

19. Milton, in dramatically different circumstances from Augustine, nevertheless shared in his anti-Pelagian theology. We agree on this point with Elaine Pagels in *Adam, Eve, and the Serpent*.

scribe only his shadow, that is, his works, and we can describe his works only insofar as we can understand them within the limited and fallen range of human perception. We are made to consider something like Plato's shadow of a shadow or Saint Paul's "glass darkly." But for Milton, as for Saint Paul—and more than for Plato—the image of the truth can be by grace savingly true even if not exhaustively true.

Saint Anselm understood this clearly when he stated a limited and fallen human perception of what God is: "that than which nothing greater can be conceived." [20] In this formulation, it is we, of course, who are doing the conceiving, not God. A logical and philosophical bent would produce such a description. Milton, with a Protestant and sensuous and passionate poetic inclination, saw God's shadow differently. For him, the most important of God's works, of God's shadows, was grace, which is to say that he saw God in terms of love. God's love cannot be defined nor even described directly. Like Anselm's insight, it can only be asserted.

In *Paradise Lost,* God's love is described in four general ways. It is creative generativity, of the universe, of nature, and of humanity—an enormous point for Milton, and one upon which we shall elaborate in the next chapter. God's love is also grace ever seeking repentance, contrition, and redemption, both of Satan and humanity. It is the "blessed passion, mightie resurreceyon, and gloryous ascension," as the Book of Common Prayer phrases it, which is undeserved yet freely given. And it is something to be examined through the metaphor of right order, due obedience, and men's and angels' love toward God rightly turned. Thus, although we can see Satan directly, we can understand God only through the metonymy of order or nature, or the tropes of grace, faith, and redemption.

One of the indirect ways through which Milton describes God's love is by portraying the adoration that others show toward him. When death and sin finally inhabit paradise and God describes their destined defeat,

> the heav'nly Audience loud
> Sung *Halleluia,* as the sound of Seas,
> Through multitude that sung: Just are thy ways,
> Righteous are thy Decrees on all thy Works;
> Who can extenuate thee? Next, to the Son,

20. Anselm of Canterbury, *Proslogion,* ed. F. Schmitt (Stuttgart, 1961), iii, 86.

> Destin'd restorer of Mankind, by whom
> New Heav'n and Earth shall to the Ages rise,
> Or down from Heav'n descend. Such was thir song
>
> (X, 641–48)

A similar reception awaits the Son upon his return in the triumph of having expelled Satan and his host from heaven by means of the overwhelming love—as we shall argue—that the rebellious angels could not abide:

> To meet him all his Saints, who silent stood
> Eye witnesses of his Almightie Acts,
> With Jubilie advanc'd; and as they went,
> Shaded with branching Palm, each order bright,
> Sung Triumph
>
> (VI, 882–86)

These passages, and others as well, such as the morning hymn sung by Adam and Eve while still unfallen (V, 153–208), have about them a reflection of God's love. Such reflections are, of course, limited and precise, consisting of song and hymn directed toward God at specific times and for specific reasons. These limitations of time and occasion are indications of the limits inherent in the creatures of God. The reality of God's love is clearly beyond description or imagination; what can be described and imagined is only a limited and local perception, a perception based on appropriate capacities for knowing and naming. Thus hymns are sung and greatness is praised, and these are an indication of right attitudes among the created. This Augustinian position of *conversio* is explicitly stated by a more than usually prophetic Adam:

> to obey is best,
> And love with fear the onely God, to walk
> As in his presence, ever to observe
> His providence, and on him sole depend
>
> (XII, 561–64)

A second indirect way in which God's love may be observed from our place in the Great Chain of Being is in the turning of evil to ultimate good. Thus, the Son is presented the occasion for sacrifice:

> Behold mee then, mee for him, life for life
> I offer, on mee let thine anger fall;
> Account mee man; I for his sake will leave

Thy bosom, and this glorie next to thee
Freely put off, and for him lastly die
(III, 236–40)[21]

This sacrifice, which is essentially incomprehensible, is learned by us only through revelation, which alone is capable of making known to humanity something so stupendous. The *lumen naturale rationis* is far too feeble to grasp the mystery of the incarnation, sacrifice, and resurrection. Nonetheless, for Milton what was biblically revealed was surely known, and if it could not be fully understood, it could still be poetically expressed in an approximate way, a significant and even potentially—with grace—salvific way, especially in metaphor local and extended.

Notice that Milton defines no Second Person of the Trinity who was not always such (which would be *homooisios,* the heresy of Adoptionism) but rather defines an "Onely begotten Son" (III, 80) who was always of the same substance (*homoousios*) but who grows in *love.* Doing, not substance, is Milton's emphasis. The Miltonic Son is defined by God the Father as "alone / My word, my wisdom, and effectual might" (III, 169–70), that is, as the being without whom the Trinity could scarcely relate to humanity, could have no being us-ward (in a word of Donne's). In theological terms, Milton's incarnationalism preserves his emphasis on dynamism (of which more in Chapters Four and Seven) while steering expertly between the heresies of Adoptionism and what has, less canonically, been called Christocentrism.

God's love is also seen intrinsically, that is, through the *lumen naturale rationis,* in two distinct ways—in the generative creativity of the natural world and in grace. We take Milton's sense of grace as his ultimate affirmation of God's love for humanity, and as what separates humanity from the rest of nature. We also argue that Milton viewed grace as both general and individual, as vouchsafed to all and specifically to each. Further, he understood grace within an Augustinian context, as having been made necessary by fallen will and as being, to some extent not clearly definable, prevenient. We see grace also as the poetic and theological link between God's love and human efforts at love, and its rejection as the defining mark of Satan's irrecoverable fall.

Milton's treatment of the phenomenal world in *Paradise Lost* draws

21. Note the pull of the pronouns against the metrical norm in the first, second, third and fifth of these lines.

upon the concepts of strict limits and essential perfection. Both are construed within the idea of the Great Chain of Being, with its insistence on hierarchy, plenitude, continuity, and completeness. Perfection within limits results from obedience to the divine will: plants and animals do what they are supposed to do. In the "garden of bliss" all things of nature have a right name, which can come only from the perfection given by grace. Adam "understood / Thir Nature" (VIII, 352−53), which is to say that he understood both their names and their essential perfection and limits. The sign of the perfection he grasped, and one that even fallen humanity can understand, is beauty. Paradise, and the rest of the earth as well, has

> goodliest Trees
> Planted, with Walks, and Bowers, that what I saw
> Of Earth before scarse pleasant seemd. Each Tree
> Load'n with fairest Fruit
>
> (VIII, 304−307)

Nature is perfect as the free gift of God's love. The book of nature remains today, as it did for Adam, an instruction in beauty and obedience.[22] This is part of the meaning of the recurring Miltonic images of natural beauty that quintessentialize the literary tradition of the *locus amoenus.*

Most important for humanity, God's love is seen in redemptive grace, *conversio,* which is constantly offered to all who need it. Not all accept. The Satanic hordes, "Thunder-struck, pursu'd / With terrors and with furies" (VI, 858−59), were so horrified by God's love that "themselvs they threw / Down from the verge of Heav'n" (VI, 864−65). Some men act the same way, but the love and grace of God cannot, by their rejection, be either vanquished or diminished. Much of humanity does accept God's saving grace:

> Man shall not quite be lost, but sav'd who will,
> Yet not of will in him, but grace in me
> Freely voutsaft; once more I will renew
> His lapsed powers, though forfeit and enthrall'd
> By sin to foul exorbitant desires
>
> (III, 173−77)

22. For "instruction," see Galileo, "Letter to Grand Duchess Christina," in *Discoveries and Opinions of Galileo,* trans. Stillman Drake (Garden City, N.Y., 1957). This letter, written in 1615, was not published until 1625, in Strasbourg.

This is Augustinian prevenient grace, but in a context of Miltonic love and hope more emphatic than Elaine Pagels has lately attributed to the Augustinian tradition.[23]

Grace is, therefore, for Milton the free instrument of rescue from ruin. God's love and grace enable humanity—and theoretically at least, the demons—to escape the consequences of their folly and sin. We all accept psychologically what the theology of grace teaches. We know from our own lives that such utter loving reconciliation and forgiveness are impossible except in the most fleeting and infrequent moments, and it is then, when the "offerd grace / Invites" (III, 187–88), that we all feel most keenly what Milton understood as the love of God. After all, humanity is destined to "hear me call" (III, 185), not to achieve unfallenness on its own. Milton vigorously rejects, as Augustine did, the Pelagian fantasy of self-willed perfectionism. Humanity is instructed to undertake the *imitatio Christi,* not to complete it. But that such a journey can be started, or even that it can be known whether undertaken or not, is for Milton the great sign that—as Julia Kristeva writes in one of her titles—"in the beginning was love."[24]

HUMAN MIDDLENESS AND FREEDOM

The final level of the Great Chain of Being within which Milton considers the theme of love is that of humanity, occupying the position intermediate between the angels and the beasts. "Neither a fixed abode nor a form that is thine alone nor any function that is peculiar to thyself have we given thee, Adam."[25] So says Giovanni Pico della Mirandola describing the indefinite nature of mankind. Milton would agree with humanity's place, though not with the humanistic and Pelagian implications that Pico draws from it in his famous apostrophe. Milton would also agree with Pico's emphasis on freedom. Freedom, radical free will, is one of Milton's basic assertions relating to humanity's sense of love. From the choice to offer a hymn "On the Morning of Christs Nativity" at age twenty-one until the willful rejections and inactions of the Son in *Paradise Regain'd,* dating from 1671, Milton insists upon liberty of choice even within "Bitter constraint, and sad occasion dear" ("Lycidas,"

23. Pagels, *Adam, Eve, and the Serpent,* esp. Chaps. 5, 6.
24. Julia Kristeva, *In the Beginning Was Love* (New York, 1987).
25. Pico della Mirandola, *Oration on the Dignity of Man,* para. 3.

6).[26] The other great footing of Milton's view of human love is the gigantic gap between fallen and unfallen, between the gracious and the merely human. These two elements—freedom and the distinction between grace and fallenness— give Miltonic views of human love its distinctive shape of hope, failure, and ultimate triumph through faith and grace.

Two of Milton's numerous examples economically illustrate the quality of freedom and the distinction between grace and fallenness in human love. The utter absence of grace, the state in which humanity comes closest to the continuous falling of Satan, is narcissism. In it, human love is turned totally inward, seeing and loving only the self, with God and other persons and nature completely blocked out. Narcissistic love, embraced freely when embraced at all, is consequently essentially Satanic, and in *Paradise Lost,* the clearest description of narcissism comes in the bitter and rancid monologues of Satan, in which falling becomes permanent.[27]

Although avoiding mention of the myth of Narcissus by name, Milton baptizes it into Christian service in describing Eve's first awakening in paradise. She sees herself in a pool, and admires what she sees:

> As I bent down to look, just opposite,
> A Shape within the watry gleam appeerd
> Bending to look on me, I started back,
> It started back, but pleas'd I soon returnd,
> Pleas'd it returnd as soon with answering looks
> Of sympathie and love
>
> (IV, 460–65)

But Eve does not succumb.[28] Warned away from narcissism by God, she ascends to higher forms of love in action, *eraon* and *phileon,* both of which include others in their purview, and thus incline toward God.[29]

26. See Bennett, *Reviving Liberty.*

27. For a powerful meditation on the ambiguities and contexts, historical and psychological, of narcissism, see Julia Kristeva's characteristically provocative *Tales of Love* (New York, 1987), esp. Chap. 3.

28. See Robert McMahon, *Augustine's Prayerful Ascent: An Essay on the Literary Form of the Confessions* (Athens, Ga., 1989), esp. Chap. 3, on the ascent to grace. And see Kenneth J. Knoespel, "The Limits of Allegory: Textual Expansion of Narcissus in *Paradise Lost,*" *Milton Studies,* XXII (1986), 79–99; and J. Max Patrick, "A Reconsideration of the Fall of Eve," *Etudes anglaises,* XXVIII (1975), 15–21. See also 49n1, 56n7 below.

29. For valuable elaboration on cultural traditions and contexts, see Turner, *One Flesh.* Turner defines Milton's position somewhat differently by his emphatic focus on Genesis and on *eros.*

The opposite of narcissism and dis-grace Milton describes as wedded love. Wedded love is both metonymic and metaphoric for grace and unfallen concern for others and for God. Milton refers to it in terms of divine law and "all the Charities," which is the highest praise he can bestow:

> Hail wedded Love, mysterious Law, true sourse
> Of human ofspring, sole proprietie,
> In Paradise of all things common else.
> By thee adulterous lust was driv'n from men
> Among the bestial herds to raunge, by thee
> Founded in Reason, Loyal, Just, and Pure,
> Relations dear, and all the Charities
> Of Father, Son, and Brother first were known.
>
> (IV, 750–57)

Sole and *all* are metrically accented. The marriage bed is "chast pronounc't" (IV, 761), for "Here Love his golden shafts imploies, here lights / His constant Lamp" (IV, 763–64). Wedded love embodies the closest continuing human approach to *agapaon,* which is loving God. "Pray without ceasing," wrote Saint Paul; that is, keep constantly in mind the love and obedience owed God by making life a constant prayer. Only wedded love, Milton maintains, is the path to that ideal, to that duty. Not for Milton is the monastic ideal, already condemned in the limbo of vanities with its population of "Eremits and Friers" (III, 474) who had abandoned wedded love for variations of the sterile love of Narcissus; they here become metaphorically the sport of winds because directionless and insubstantial. Milton shows the varieties of human love and their differing content of grace through the extremes, the Satanic self-destruction and hellish ungenerativity of narcissism and the *caritas* of wedded love. All else in between can be left to the imagination and experience of the readers (including the experience of *A Mask* and the 1645 edition of *Poems*), or—as it turns out—to elaboration in *Paradise Regain'd* and *Samson Agonistes.*

One further element of grace in human love must be mentioned. This involves the freedom of service to God and the forms and choices that service might take. *Agape* might be the morning hymn sung by both Adam and Eve, their "Orisons, each Morning duly paid" (V, 145), fluent and exclamatory:

These are thy glorious works, Parent of good,
Almightie, thine this universal Frame,
Thus wondrous fair; thyself how wondrous then!
(V, 153–55)

Hymns and prayer were, of course, always appropriate, but they were not necessarily expressed in the guise of song. Work, as Saint Benedict of Nursia knew, was also a form of prayer through which human love mediated by grace might be expressed.[30] And accordingly, as the bard observes, their "work . . . declares [their] Dignitie" (IV, 618–19)—not exclusively a Puritan sentiment. Adam calls, in a sacralized aubade,

Awake, the morning shines, and the fresh field
Calls us, we lose the prime, to mark how spring
Our tended Plants, how blows the Citron Grove,
What drops the Myrrh, and what the balmie Reed,
How Nature paints her colours
(V, 20–24)[31]

30. The Rule of Saint Benedict may be found in *Patrologiae . . . Latina*, ed. Migne, LXVI, 215–930. For a convenient modern translation, see *The Rule of St. Benedict,* trans. Anthony Meisel and M. L. del Mastro (Garden City, N.Y., 1975).

31. Louis L. Martz was the first we know to have identified *sacred parody,* the sacralizing (like Adam and Eve's *aubade*) of secular poetic *topoi,* as a kind of allegory of regeneration. See his *The Poetry of Meditation: A Study in English Literature* (New Haven, 1954). Thus, with *topoi,* as with conventions, modes, and genres, Milton gives his literary inheritance a hermeneutic turn or two, making it not merely new, as Ezra Pound later asked of poets, but ontologically more intense. For instances, see 44*n*28 above, as well as O. B. Hardison, Jr., "*In Medias Res* in *Paradise Lost,*" *Milton Studies,* XVII (1983), 24–41; James A. Freeman, *Milton and the Martial Muse: "Paradise Lost" and European Traditions of War* (Princeton, 1980); Stella P. Revard, *The War in Heaven: "Paradise Lost" and the Tradition of Satan's Rebellion* (Ithaca, N.Y., 1980); Barbara Everett, "The End of Big Names: Milton's Epic Catalogues," in *English Renaissance Studies Presented to Dame Helen Gardner in Honour of Her Seventieth Birthday,* ed. John Carey (New York, 1980), 254–70; Francis Blessington, "'That Undisturbed Song of Pure Concent': *Paradise Lost* and the Epic-Hymn," in *Renaissance Genres: Essays on Theory, History, and Interpretation,* ed. Barbara K. Lewalski (Cambridge, Mass., 1986), 468–95; and Leland Ryken, "*Paradise Lost* and Its Biblical Epic Models," in *Milton and Scriptural Tradition: The Bible into Poetry,* ed. James H. Sims and Leland Ryken (Columbia, Mo., 1984), 43–81. But for an argument that, ostensibly on semiotic grounds, contends that there was a Miltonic "breakdown" and failure, see Stephen A. Nimis, *Narrative Semiotics in the Epic Tradition: The Simile* (Bloomington, Ind., 1987), 161–77.

Or unfallen love might take the form of perfect marital giving, as described by Milton in the lines on the "blissful Bower" (IV, 690): "With Flowers, Garlands, and sweet-smelling Herbs / Espoused *Eve* deckt first her Nuptial Bed" (IV, 709–10). Unfallen love might also be found in service, as Eve prepares the dinner to be offered to Raphael. In all these situations, the right and appropriate choice is freely made, for unfallen love reflects nothing less than the free service to God.

Choice also appears in the dismal depths of fallen love, the carnal and hateful deterioration that selfishness always produces in *Paradise Lost*. Such choice, or at least some choices of the sort, are cataloged in Milton's description of fallen love:

> the bought smile
> Of Harlots, loveless, joyless, unindeard,
> Casual fruition, nor in Court Amours,
> Mixt Dance, or wanton Mask, or Midnight Ball,
> Or Serenate, which the starv'd Lover sings
> To his proud fair, best quitted with disdain.
>
> (IV, 765–70)

Milton's condemnation of courtly love, with its conventions of song, sonnet, and illicit pursuit could hardly have been more severe, nor less unexpected. It is a poetically and ministerially powerful salvo against the ancient enemy, both political and clerical. It also fits the Miltonic pattern of judging human love. All that is associated with the courtly love tradition, whether its elaborate and artificial conventions, its emphasis on adultery, its penchant for deception, its themes of social class, sexual power, and endless longing or sinister seizure of the day—all these are in stark and even savage contrast to Milton's hymn to *agape* inherent in wedded love.

The significance that Milton gives to fallen love as a spiritually unhealthy condition can be seen in the reappearance of the description of carnality with reference to Adam and Eve after the Fall. Adam was the first to feel the pangs of this sin:

> Carnal desire enflaming, hee on *Eve*
> Began to cast lascivious Eyes, she him
> As wantonly repaid; in Lust they burn:
> Till *Adam* thus 'gan *Eve* to dalliance move.
>
> (IX, 1013–16)

With *on*, the ostensibly beloved other is described as mere object. The same theme is repeated again, though within the larger context of all the sins unleashed by the Fall, when Adam and Eve confront God. Our "first Parents" (III, 65) are in a state of original sin, begun with them though primal in us all, and the meeting with God is not a happy occasion. They approach, reluctantly:

> discount'nanc't both, and discompos'd;
> Love was not in thir looks, either to God
> Or to each other, but apparent guilt,
> And shame, and perturbation, and despair,
> Anger, and obstinacie, and hate, and guile.
> (X, 110–14)

The Fall had brought as its recompense the failure of joy and of poise, of integrity, and of duty toward both God and themselves, thus of their joint and several identities. The pair falter in dis-grace.

We argue that this description of the consequences of the Fall, and thus the nature of it, is found not only in an exceptionally poignant description of descent from *agapaon* to narcissism but also in the Miltonic description of original sin. It seems to us that Milton conceives of original sin as consisting of three parts: idolatry (for example, "uxorious King," I, 444; "Was shee thy God," X, 145); the sins that we are, particularly the seven deadly ones (X, 110–14); and the sense of loss, a kind of nameless woe of guilt and regret (X, XII, conclusions). Original sin should be understood, accordingly, as a separation from the proper and necessary love for God and from appreciation for God's works, grace, and care—as a loss of the very ability to be in a state of *agape.* For Milton, humanity loving moves between the entropic falling dis-grace of Satan and the salvific grace God offers. Thus this epic characterizes *caritas,* which, lost by humanity, can still be glimpsed through the book of nature and the book of Scripture, through duty, worship, and the acknowledgment of sin in confession, and through married love, when that makes life a journey of prayer, faith, and grace.

THREE

The Dynamics of Nature and History

ivine creativity, for Milton, frames the movement and dynamism that humanity calls nature and culture. He examines the divinely given and the humanly made, nature and culture, both as metaphors for "Fixt Fate, free will, foreknowledge absolute" (*Paradise Lost*, II, 560) and as real examples of the movement of man and nature according to the divine plan. He emphasizes *working*, whether the working of God or the working of human intelligence and perception. Accordingly, the *infelix culpa* is subsumed in the pageant of divine creativity, and so *Paradise Lost* is, we will argue, a Christian and neo-Ovidian book of changes as well as an Augustinian journey.[1] Further, the congruence of divine creativity with the continuous making of man in the divine image is necessarily a journey in grace and favor, in both nature and culture. Thus *Paradise Lost* not merely resonates with the theology of divine love and good but presents and enacts the becoming implied in work and journey, and meant by the terms *call* and *purpose*.

PARADOXICAL TEMPORALITY

The pageant of divine creativity and temporality in Book VII unfolds at the approximate beginning of the second half of the epic. It shows com-

---

1. See Martz, *Poet of Exile*, esp. Chaps. 12, 13, 14. Of what has been written since, see Charles Martindale, "Paradise Metamorphosed: Ovid in Milton," *Comparative Literature*, XXXVII (1985), 301–303; Richard J. DuRocher, *Milton and Ovid* (Ithaca, N.Y., 1985); and John K. Hale, "Milton Playing with Ovid," *Milton Studies*, XXV (1989), 3–19. John Peter Rumrich, in "Metamorphosis in *Paradise Lost*," *Viator*, XX (1989), 311–26, is a welcome ally in his emphasis on love. Rumrich works through *eros* to urge, rightly, that Adam and Eve transcend Ovidian prototypes as Christianity does classical cultures (p. 324), but he leaves the Savior of *Paradise Regain'd* and Samson merely reflecting "fortitude and balance." See also Arthur O. Lovejoy, "Milton and the Paradox of the Fortunate Fall," *English Literary History*, IV (1937), 161–79 (reprinted in his *Essays in the History of Ideas* [Baltimore, 1948], 277–95); and for rebuttal, Mili Clark, "The Mechanics of Creation," esp. 207–11.

plexity, fertility, and rightly oriented love. Book VII also contrasts with the inconclusive disorder and uproar of war in heaven, and with heaven's abruptly conclusive reordering, but it no less consequentially and profoundly presents an alternative to the conventional metaphor of time imagined as space.[2] That metaphor so pervades modern Western culture and appears so frequently with Milton himself that we had long supposed the matter of getting the notion of eternity into the poem to be one of the most intractable problems for him. But he solved that epistemological problem. Time and the timeless are imaged, almost indexed, by a scale of understanding. Milton inherited the paradox of conceiving human time and ignorance to concur simultaneously with divine and eternal time and divine foreknowledge. Human time, as a succession of things and moments, resists poetic definition. Yet, what is lived is known, experientially. It is time as eternal, without end or beginning, radically simultaneous for God, and yet also ongoing and finite and divisible, that needs explanation. Saint Augustine addressed this paradox:

> You are before all the past in the sublimity of your ever-present eternity, and You are above all future things because they are still to come, and when they have come they will be past, but "Thou are the Same and Thy years fail not." Your years neither go nor come, but these years of ours go and come, so they may all come. Your years stand still all together . . . there is no passing from one state to another, but these years of ours will not all be until all will have ceased to be. Your years are all in one day . . . because your day is followed by no tomorrow and comes after no yesterday. Your today is eternity. . . . You

2. Wood notes the "self-referential circularity of Satanic motion" and argues that time as space is "mere fate" ("'Improved by Tract of Time': Metaphysics," 48–50). Ricardo Quinones argues that "any straight line approach to time is disrupted" for the human characters. See his *The Renaissance Discovery of Time* (Cambridge, Mass., 1972), 474. See Quinones' study, especially pp. 459–76, for a valuable discussion of comparative literary, as well as Miltonic, texts. Harold Fisch's *Jerusalem and Albion* (New York, 1968) remains a valuable work on the cultural movement toward visuality and spatiality, as does Ong's *Ramus, Method, and the Decay of Dialogue* on orality and print literacy, along with Lewis Mumford's *The Myth of the Machine* (2 vols.; New York, 1967–70), esp. Vol. I, Chaps. 9–12, Vol. II, Chaps. 1–3. For a more particular but diverse focus on Miltonic time, space, and eternity and the attendant paradoxes, see Jackson Cope, *The Metaphoric Structure of "Paradise Lost"* (Baltimore, 1962); Rosalie Colie, "Time and Eternity: Paradox and Structure in *Paradise Lost*," in *Paradoxia Epidemica: The Renaissance Tradition of Paradox* (Princeton, 1966), Chap. 8; and S. K. Heninger, "Sidney and Milton: The Poet as Maker," in *Milton and the Line of Vision*, ed. Joseph A. Wittreich (Madison, Wis., 1975), 57–95.

made all times and before all times You are, nor was there ever a time in which there was no time.[3]

As we might say, for God all is present (*praesans*); for us, all is past or future as we subsist on the "knife edge of the present," as Josiah Royce somewhere says. Time is both measured and infinite, both continuous and simultaneous, both ours and not ours, and it contains both future and absolute foreknowledge—all, so to speak, at the same time. But the tension here is more seeming than real. The paradox lies mainly in language, and one resolution appears in the realm of rational theology. There one may invoke not experience but hierarchy, and have recourse to the concept of the Great Chain of Being with its various levels separated by differences that are absolute. Because a level of being cannot adequately define or understand any level above it, even the faithful Abdiel so far fails to comprehend the nature of God that he accepts the Apostate's advice to carry tidings "to th' anointed King; / And fly, ere evil intercept thy flight" (V, 870–71). But God, who constitutes time itself, already knows, and has always known, and it is impossible that he not know. The difference in relation to temporality between God and all creation is absolute, and necessary rather than contingent.[4]

Unproblematically enough, on the human, mortal, and finite level of being, time is and was, as Milton has Raphael acknowledge, the brief succession of hours and years and the chronology of events that fill them:

> (For Time, though in Eternitie, appli'd
> To motion, measures all things durable
> By present, past, and future)
> (V, 580–82)

3. *The Confessions of Saint Augustine*, Bk. XI, Chap. 13, 267. Similarly, in Bk. XI, Chap. 11, we are told that in eternity nothing is ephemeral, all is present (*praesans*). Wood finds a Miltonic demurrer to Augustine's distinction between the temporal world and the eternal one. See her "'Improved by Tract of Time': Metaphysics," 54–56.

4. The fundamental book on this topic remains Lovejoy's *The Great Chain of Being*. In a general way, Christian meditation, proceeding as it does from lower to higher, provides an excellent way to tie hierarchy, different levels of being, and experience together. See, for example, *The Spiritual Exercises of Saint Ignatius*, ed. David S. Fleming, S.J. (St. Louis, 1978). An earlier example is Saint Bonaventura's *The Mind's Road to God*. On the integrative employment of such meditative paradigms by seventeenth-century poets, see the already classic argument by Martz in *The Poetry of Meditation* and *The Paradise Within*.

Adam's human view of time contrasts with a higher one, as when he opines that Michael has

> Measur'd this transient World, the Race of time,
> Till time stand fixt: beyond is all abyss,
> Eternitie, whose end no eye can reach.
>
> (XII, 554–56)

Adam claims to be "Greatly instructed" (XII, 557), but we may doubt that, both because we have just heard Michael speaking of "endless date" (XII, 549) and "eternal Bliss" (XII, 551) and because we have noted Adam's overspatialized and overstatic terms. We must certainly recall yet again Raphael's pronouncement:

> Immediate are the Acts of God, more swift
> Then time or motion, but to human ears
> Cannot without process of speech be told
>
> (VII, 176–78)

The process of speech, the mediation by speech, is the source of the difficulty, carrying the paradox. The reality, and even the nature, of God's time was perfectly clear. Ironically, though appropriately for the poet of the salvific journey, it was the word that failed, though not the Word.

The problem that the Great Chain of Being—again considered as the structure of being—does not solve and, indeed, invents is language. How does one describe God? Milton causes all the speakers in *Paradise Lost* to name God, and to move toward naming themselves in doing so. The names they employ almost irresistibly narrow to descriptive attributes. God is the

> Father . . . Omnipotent,
> Immutable, Immortal, Infinite,
> Eternal King; thee Author of all being,
> Fountain of Light
>
> (III, 372–75)

These are certainly good names, and they by no means exhaust the list, but unsurprisingly, they do not define God. Imagine a snail trying to name mankind or to name unique persons. Indeed, the essential differences in being and consciousness between levels of being are most apparent in language. When applied to God, perfectly useful words lose their sharp bite of definition, become slippery, vague, their meaning blunted.

When applied to God, useful human words slip inexorably into paradox, in the phenomenon known as equivocation, with a single word having two mutually incompatible meanings at two different levels of being. This problem of language, so common we often overlook it or handle it by rough and ready approximation, remains for Milton no mere puzzle but a theological mystery for poetic identification. It is a question of representing, through "accommodation" to human faculties, the hierarchical relationship between God and humanity, between Creator and created.

Thus, more or less fallen understanding limps through temporality; perfect love is a condition of eternity, eternity as instantaneity ("Immediate are the Acts of God, more swift / Then time or motion," VII, 176–77). Although the falling—because rebelliously unloving—angels persuade even the faithful Abdiel that God and his hosts do not know of the conspiracy *yet,* perfect hatred is for Milton an existential and theological impossibility. It would be a sort of nullity or black hole in the space of being. But the near-perfect hatred (so to speak) of hell is eternity as paradoxical near-static space marked by merely local tumults: "Nine times the Space that measures Day and Night" (I, 50) the angels fell, "To bottomless perdition" (I, 47). They are paradoxically *at* a place and condition that, as we are given to understand, they make yet more, ever more, lost.

SCALES OF NOTION AND STAGES OF CREATION

The Bard unfolds a series of contrasts. In Books I and II, God ambiguously either creates hell or allows falling psyches to materialize it, as a projection of the fit place for the now-fallen angels. Thus Books I and II are a pageant of decreative change or uncreative activity. Books III and IV follow with a pageant of contrasting divine creativity and change. Book V stands as an emblematic prolepsis of history, a larger version of the often-noticed local proleptic bits in the text of the first two books. The would-be disorderly change and quasi decreativity of the rebellious angels in Book VI is then posed against the divine creation of worldly nature and of new *modes* in Book VII. These appear quickly after the victory celebration, itself suggestive of the Passion, resurrection, and redemption, at the end of Book VI. The God who permits, so to speak, hell in Book I, then introduces a full divine partner in Book III, creates a vision of felicity for the reader as for Adam and Eve in Book IV, creates the world in

Book VII, creates a situation permitting tragic stature to his dual protagonists in Book IX, and creates the world of culture, real human history, and boundless potentialities of fruitful change in the fallen human world in Books XI and XII.

Milton makes unimpeachable authority speak of day (for example, at VI, 685, X, 53) in ways that suggest that temporal terms are radically *provisional*. Something Adam hears, but misunderstands, from Raphael in Book VII deserves the emphatic attention the Bard invites for it. Early in the book, God the Father is made to say,

> I can repair
> That detriment, if such it be to lose
> Self-lost, and in a moment will create
> Another World, out of one man a Race
> Of men innumerable, there to dwell
> (VII, 152–56)

Note the phrase *in a moment,* to which we will return in connection with the week of creation. A little later, after directions have been given to the Son, Raphael reports,

> So spake th' Almightie, and to what he spake
> His Word, the filial Godhead, gave effect.
> Immediate are the Acts of God, more swift
> Then time or motion, but to human ears
> Cannot without process of speech be told,
> So told as earthly notion can receave.
> (VII, 174–79)

Here Milton connects creativity and perception in a concentrated hermeneutic reflection on the creation story of Genesis that he relates in Book VII.[5] Earthly notion includes, and its limitations are suggested by, the inadequate categories of "time or motion."

---

5. Arnold Williams makes it clear that Milton was as imperiously independent with regard to the divergent biblical commentarists as he was toward other categories of writers. See his *The Common Expositor: An Account of the Commentaries on Genesis, 1527–1633* (Chapel Hill, N.C., 1948), esp. Chap. 3. See also A. S. P. Woodhouse, "Notes on Milton's Views on the Creation: The Initial Phases," *Philological Quarterly,* XXVIII (1949), 211–36. For the unargued assertion of the "allegory of maturing consciousness that it was for Milton," see Gale H. Carrithers, Jr., *Donne at Sermons: A Christian Existential World* (Albany, N.Y., 1972), 139.

What, then, are the *metaphoric* moments or days of creation in Book VII—of that divine activity to be understood as "more swift / Then time or motion"? Whether or not lay Christians in previous centuries had judged or literalized, with Moses, about the matter, there was certainly a Christian intellectual tradition that divine creation was instantaneous (as in VII, 176) and ex nihilo, a tradition embattled by Aristotelian and Stoic postulation of an external world, by Epicurean postulation of an accidental creation, and by Cartesian mechanism.[6] So what does Milton make of the Mosaic moments? They are mainly, even if not exclusively, moments or opportunities of perception, consonant with the development of human consciousness in the individual. Milton presents the divine week of creation by an analogy with the ecclesiological and liturgical notion of the Christian year—as a paradigm of *modes* and occasions for loving allegiance to God with and through that which, in the words of Psalm 19, declares his glory and "sheweth his handywork." Like the Christian year, too, the successive occasions and opportunities, though recurrent, would not be mechanically cyclical, because of the freedom intrinsic to the complexity of perception, the complexity of history, and the creativity of divine love as grace. Milton, it will be recalled, was interested in cultural develop-

6. See, for example, Augustine, *De Genesi ad litteram, imperfectus liber,* 4.33−34, 5.23, 6.3; and Honorius of Autun, *De imagine mundi,* in *Patrologiae . . . Latina,* ed. Migne, CLXXII, 121. We owe both these citations to Robert McMahon. See, indispensably, Paolo Rossi, *The Dark Abyss of Time* (Chicago, 1984), esp. Chap. 5, which is on Bishop Stilling-fleet's contending in 1662 against the various theses of noninstantaneity, and Chap. 8, on the party, represented in 1665 and earlier by Robert Boyle, and later by Newton, that held that "the laws of nature have no history," and on Moses as popularizer, a prudent accommodator. Descartes (*Principia,* 3, Sec. 45; 1644) is cited by Rossi as one who genuflected to a world created perfect at once, then slyly proposed quasi-biological growth *as if* it were a farfetched but accommodating metaphor instead of the virtual sign he intended it to be. See Rossi, *The Dark Abyss of Time,* 42−44. Milton, in contrast, took the Mosaic signifieds as *necessarily* metaphorical, and meditated upon their signification, finding it in the terrain of the mind to which the signifieds were an accommodation. Williams cites Ecclus. 18:1 ("He that liveth forever created all things together [*simul*]") and, similarly, Philo and Origen but reports that only Brocardus among his commentators took the Mosaic days as manifestations or accommodations of divine instantaneity to human sense. Compare John Donne: "In paradise, the fruits were ripe, the first minute" (Sermon on Christmas Day in the evening, 1624 in his *The Sermons,* ed. George Potter and Evelyn Simpson [10 vols.; Berkeley and London, 1951−59], VII, 172; first published in *LXXX Sermons* [1640]). See also Thomas F. Merrill, "Miltonic God-Talk: The Creation in *Paradise Lost*," *Language and Style,* XVI (1983), 296−312. See, as well, the texts listed in 59n8 below.

ment and in the development of the child's mind and the education of children, with a view to repairing the ruin of our first parents.[7]

The first day is obviously enough the dawn of perception and, we would suggest, the dawn of awareness of primary bounds, of the fact of distinction. There is a suggestion in the lines about "brooding wings" (VII, 235) and "vital vertue infus'd, and vital warmth" (VII, 236) of maternal plenitude and the infant's closeness to the maternal source of care and sustenance. The second day, of firmament and waters, seems to be an elaboration of the fact of distinction. Sameness and difference involve partition firm and sure, as against infirm continuity like "circumfluous Waters calm" (VII, 270), and involve still more a sense of exception from the "loud misrule / Of *Chaos* farr remov'd" (VII, 271–72). Is it too much to liken what must be sensed to the reassuring sort of firm support, not necessarily immovable, that is important to infants, in contrast to the shaky support and loud noises evidently distressing to them?

The third day, with its "Womb . . . Of Waters" (VII, 276–77) and "great Mother to conceave" (VII, 281), is in some sense a celebration of vegetable life and appetitive process. It suggests, also, a second birth— "Mountains huge appeer . . . broad bare backs upheave" (VII, 286–87)— with an awareness of sensory dynamism and more elaborated distinctions than on the first two days. Newly present are differing sorts of vegetable life, and dynamic trees rising "as in Dance" (VII, 324); the almost jocose

7. The phrase will be recognized from the essay "Of Education." For a similar view of human development as a gloss on an epic, see Fabius Planciades Fulgentius, *Expositio virgilianae continentiae secundum philosophos moralis,* in *Fabii Planciadis Fulgentii Virgilianae Continentiae Opera,* ed. R. Helm (2nd ed.; Stuttgart, 1970), 81–107. For a general analysis of Fulgentius and his time, and on his later currency, see M. L. W. Laistner, *The Intellectual Heritage of the Early Middle Ages* (Ithaca, N.Y., 1987), 202–15; and M. L. W. Laistner, *Christianity and Pagan Culture in the Later Roman Empire* (Ithaca, N.Y., 1951). For the connection of Fulgentius to Milton, see Douglas Bush, *Mythology and the Renaissance Tradition in English Poetry* (2nd ed.; New York, 1963), 295. On mythography in seventeenth-century England, see A. M. Cinquemani, "Henry Reynolds' 'Mythomystes' and the Continuity of Ancient Modes of Allegoresis in Seventeenth Century England," *PMLA,* LXXXV (1970), 1041–49. For Reynolds' text, see E. W. Tayler, ed., *Literary Criticism of Seventeenth-Century England* (New York, 1967), 225–58. In Chapter 6 below, we shall address variations on this theme, in the children "timely tried" in *A Mask* and the poet educating himself—with foils in "L'Allegro" and "Il Penseroso"—in the 1645 edition of the *Poems.* Alvin Snider focuses helpfully on Eve and on a kind of hermeneutics in and of her reflection, in "The Self-Mirroring Mind in Milton and Traherne," *University of Toronto Quarterly,* LV (1986), 313–27.

imagery emphasizes a new degree of independence perhaps to be understood as the *playful* degree.

The fourth day in the Bardic meditation, the day of stars in the sky, brings a more abstract envisioning of distance and more abstract distinctions of time and degree: "for Signes, / For Seasons, and for Dayes, and circling Years" (VII, 341–42). This enacts more mature signification. In addition, on the fourth day there is a perception of, and gratitude for, divinely ordained regularity, in contrast to "vicissitude" (VII, 351). Phrases such as "sowd with Starrs the Heav'n thick as a field" (VII, 358) and "as to thir Fountain other Starrs" (VII, 364) remind us of the divine fecundity of creativity and the opportunity for perception, belief, and loving praise.

The fifth day, the day of fowl, snakes, and fish, is the first on which the soul is mentioned. It is a day of complex natural order in a complex but largely preordained life world, though with increasing emphasis on consciousness and something like choice. We find birds that "more wise / In common, rang'd in figure wedge thir way, / Intelligent of seasons" (VII, 425–27), as well as the "prudent Crane" (VII, 430), and the like. It may be in recognition of the increasing perception of diversities and complexities of natural order that the Bard declares the evening and morning of the fifth day "solemniz'd" (VII, 448), not "recorded" (VII, 338) like the third day or "crownd" (VII, 386) like the fourth.

The sixth day, inevitably, in Bardic meditation as in Genesis, is the day of the creation of human life, though emphatically with Milton also of higher animal life, which famously rises as from the very clods. A new category of consciousness is introduced: ambiguity, as in the "River Horse and scalie Crocodile" (VII, 474) that are "ambiguous between Sea and Land" (VII, 473). The proleptic reference to "Summers pride" (VII, 478) is a warning. In a Renaissance commonplace, Milton accepts the conventional emphasis on man's upright stature, but he does so with unsurpassed, indeed almost phenomenological, insistence:

> not prone
> And Brute as other Creatures, but endu'd
> With Sanctitie of Reason, might erect
> His Stature, and upright with Front serene
> Govern the rest, self-knowing, and from thence
> Magnanimous to correspond with Heav'n
>
> (VII, 506–11)

The higher animals rising from the clods and man rising in upright stature from the earth seem to emblematize the capacity for spiritual freedom from mechanized time and constraining place, and self-consciousness certainly intensifies that consideration. The metaphoric sequence of stages in time opens by a trope of grammar into something beyond the temporality of the indicative mood. The magnanimity that is "to correspond with Heav'n" is affirmed in the infinitive mood, a part of the indefinite temporality of man's ongoing creation amid change, reaching potentially from sign to symbol and even, by grace, to transcendence.

Milton's seventh day is the day of the most truly dignifying and liberating order of creation: it is the day of love. The prayer and praise and society his account of the seventh day depicts are reasoned justice and love in action, the reasoned justice and love of which the account speaks. These are not abstractly cerebral, nor do they anticipate Lockean visual clarity: "incense Clouds . . . hid the Mount" (VII, 599–600), for example. The blind Bard will not idolatrize sight, but reasoned justice and love reiterate the continuing nature of divine creativity: "to create / Is greater then created to destroy" (VII, 606–607). Lines spoken by God the Son shortly thereafter are much more than anti-Manichaeanism:

> Who seeks
> To lessen thee, against his purpose serves
> To manifest the more thy might
> (VII, 613–15)

These words imply the dynamic of ongoing attempts at decreativity that divine creativity subsumes and that occur parallel with fallen humanity's efforts of loving understanding in history. This is analogous in Milton's construal to the boundlessly varied, divinely ordained, yet free historical world of culture.

HISTORY AS VICISSITUDE OR GRACE

A variant in creativity and dynamism in *Paradise Lost* is the dual meaning Milton gives to the idea of history, which he treats as both existential and teleological. Books VIII, IX, and X, counterparts to Books III and IV, are emblematically about the beginning of history, in which events are individual and unique, not mythic or replicable, though there may be analogies between them. Even when tragic, the events appear in a divine continuum of time that will be different and better at its ending than at its beginning. Miltonic history is not cyclical. Philosophically sound, the conclusion that it is not cyclical is also theologically inevitable. Christianity is a historical religion, depending on the reality of events for both ministerial effectiveness and fundamental truth. The Bible is, in large part, a description, commentary, and explication of events. Thus, emphasizing the role of history in the emergence of order from chaos seems entirely in keeping with the character of Christian revelation.[8] But human history, even if divinely directed in a teleologically coherent mission, must still be human.[9] It must present itself "as earthly notion can receave" (VII, 179). Human history is a process—not an event—that is ongoing but has been and always will be the same, at least with regard to tychastic time.[10] History has its being and focus between, on the one hand, the

8. See also Fabius Fulgentius, *De aetatibus mundi et hominis,* in *Fabii Planciadis Fulgentii Virgilianae Continentiae Opera,* ed. Helm, 127–79. For an English translation, see *Fulgentius the Mythographer,* trans. Leslie George Whitbread (Columbus, Ohio, 1971); for an examination of the meaning of history in terms of the purposive mode, see pp. 179–231. In the general area of the dialectic of the creation, uncreation, and re-creation of order in *Paradise Lost,* see Michael Lieb, *The Dialectic of Creation: Patterns of Birth and Regeneration in "Paradise Lost"* (Amherst, Mass., 1970), esp. 200–229. By 1680, Thomas Burnet could argue that Moses pastorally "consulted the public safety" in selecting the option of geocentric imagery in the creation story. See Rossi, *The Dark Abyss of Time,* 40–41. See also G. A. Wilkes's interpretive article "'Full of Doubt I Stand': The Final Implications of *Paradise Lost,*" *English Renaissance Studies Presented to Dame Helen Gardner in Honour of Her Seventieth Birthday,* ed. John Carey (New York, 1980), 271–78.

9. "This having learnt, thou hast attaind the sum / Of wisdom" (*Paradise Lost,* XII, 575–76). For the epistemological consequences of this requirement, see Robert L. Entzminger, "Epistemology and the Tutelary Word in *Paradise Lost,*" *Milton Studies,* X (1977), 93–109. See also Marcia L. Colish, *The Mirror of Language: A Study in the Medieval Theory of Knowledge* (New Haven, 1968). An opposing view, according to which history is essentially apocalyptic, can be found in Thomas Amorose's "Milton the Apocalyptic Historian: Competing Genres in *Paradise Lost,* Books XI–XII," *Milton Studies,* XVII (1983), 141–62. See also C. A. Patrides, "'Something like Prophetic Strain': Apocalyptic Configurations in Milton," *English Language Notes,* XIX (1982), 193–207.

10. See, as an example, Mary Ann Radzinowicz, "Man as a 'Probationer of Immortality': *Paradise Lost* XI–XII," in *Approaches to "Paradise Lost,"* ed. C. A. Patrides (Toronto, 1968), 31–51. We disagree, however, with Radzinowicz' assertion that Adam learns. For the attribution of a cyclical view of history to Milton, see John T. Shawcross, "Stasis, and John Milton and the Myths of Time," *Cithara,* XVIII (1978), 3–17. See also Robert L. Entzminger, "Michael's Options and Milton's Poetry: *Paradise Lost* XI and XII," *English Literary Renaissance,* VIII (1978), 197–211.

allegory of a journey essential for good health and the avoidance of hetero-
dox cyclicism and Manichaeanism, and on the other, the mundane and
chance concatenation of facts. If the journey is forgotten or remains un-
found, one will live without purpose and die unshriven; if the facts are
ignored, the journey will be lost, because the past will be lost.[11] Thus
human history in human time with human meanings is also a constituent
of divine history, the purposive journey. What is lower must reflect, imperfectly of course, the perfection from above, somehow in similitude.[12]

Books XI and XII, the last two humanly temporal books of the epic,
should be construed as an explanation of history on both a human and
divine level by a poet of amplitude and spiritual growth. This section of
Paradise Lost is often, though erroneously, called the education of Adam.[13]

11. Consider, for example, the current efforts in the former Soviet Union to recover
from the rewriting of history, which painted so false a picture of the past that the society
and the government are having enormous, perhaps insurmountable, difficulty in managing
the present and defining the future.

12. Our word is meant to recall Michel Foucault's *The Order of Things: An Archaeology
of the Human Sciences* (New York, 1970; translation of *Les Mots et les Choses* [1966]),
Chap. 2, and to open generally and appreciatively into the wealth of modern scholarship
on this Miltonic matter. Two essays are particularly useful for our purposes. Clearly reinforcing a line of explicative rhetorical scholarship back to James Whaler is Linda Gregerson's "The Limbs of Truth: Milton's Use of Simile in *Paradise Lost*," *Milton Studies*, XIV
(1980), 135–52. John Guillory's "Ithuriel's Spear" is provocative and valuable for its
differing assumptions and preoccupations and its variant representation of hermeneutic
and typological tradition from Immanuel Kant to William Kerrigan. Alongside our many
disagreements with Guillory is our agreement with his highlighting of the figure of *transumption*—the ABBA chiastic human rhythm of revisionary repetition. See also Colie,
"Time and Eternity," in *Paradoxia Epidemica*. William Madsen emphasizes Miltonic dynamism in his much-cited *From Shadowy Types to Truth: Studies in Milton's Symbolism* (New
Haven, 1968), esp. Chap. 3, and pp. 166–80. For the impact on similitude of the idea
of multiple levels of being, see, of course, Lovejoy, *The Great Chain of Being*. See, though
somewhat tangentially, Albert C. Labriola, "The Medieval View of Christian History in
Paradise Lost," in *Milton and the Middle Ages*, ed. John Mulryan (Lewisburg, Pa., 1982),
115–32. Two recent, remarkably contrastive, studies seem to us to illuminate the hermeneutic structure we try to define in yet other terms. In "Milton's Dialectical Visions,"
Grossman addresses the epistemology and semantics of Milton's strategy, finding moments
in a dialectical practice moving from metaphor to synecdoche. We emphasize the movement, and so does Budick, who, in "Milton and the Scene of Interpretation," finds Milton's
cosmos an interpretive engine with edified and engraved heart wandering and interpreting.

13. See, for example, George Williamson, "The Education of Adam," *Modern Philology*, LXI (1963), 96–109. See also Colie, "Time and Eternity," 132–33; Entzminger,
"Michael's Options and Milton's Poetry," 199–201; Lawrence A. Sasek, "The Drama of

The foretelling for Adam, which is the retelling for us, changes nothing in the cosmic journey of regeneration unless it changes us; the Bardic presentation is quite orthodox. What was earlier given in philosophical snippets now appears in extenso. The metaphor here, repeating the theme of development in Book VII, is history, on both a microcosmic and macrocosmic stage.[14]

The purely human—which is thus inconsequential except as exemplum—appears in Book XI, where Adam sees the extent of pagan history:

> His Eye might there command wherever stood
> City of old or modern Fame, the Seat
> Of mightiest Empire, from the destind Walls
> Of *Cambalu*, seat of *Cathaian Can*
> And *Samarchand* by *Oxus*, *Temirs* Throne,
> To *Paquin* of *Sinaean* Kings, and thence
> To *Agra* and *Labor* of great *Mogul*
> Down to the golden *Chersonese*, or where
> The *Persian* in *Ecbatan* sate, or since
> In *Hispahan*, or where the *Russian Ksar*
> In *Mosco*, or the Sultan in *Bizance*,
> *Turchestan*-born; nor could his eye not ken
> Th' Empire of *Negus* to his utmost Port
> *Ercoco* and the less Maritime Kings
> *Mombaza*, and *Quiloa*, and *Melind*,
> And *Sofala* thought *Ophir*, to the Realm
> Of *Congo*, and *Angola* fardest South;

Paradise Lost, Books XI and XII," in *Milton: Modern Essays in Criticism*, ed. Arthur Barker (London, 1968), 342–56; Radzinowicz, "Man as 'Probationer of Immortality'"; Balachandra Rajan, *The Lofty Rhyme* (Coral Gables, Fla., 1970), Chap. 9; and Denis Burden, *The Logical Epic: A Study of the Argument of "Paradise Lost"* (Cambridge, Mass., 1967), Chap. 9. But see Golda Werman's provocative argument that Adam and Eve's very penitence elevates them, in "Repentance in *Paradise Lost*," *Milton Studies*, XXII (1986), 121–39. We would say that it Augustinianly—and temporarily—*reorients* them.

14. See Barbara Lewalski, "Structure and the Symbolism of Vision in Michael's Prophecy, *Paradise Lost* XI–XII," *Philological Quarterly*, XLII (1963), 25–35. Lewalski points out that Milton's treatment owes something to the widespread tradition that finds similitude between the six Mosaic days of creation and the six stages of history. Our own focus is on Milton's characteristically bold reconception of this tradition. See also William Walker, "Typology and *Paradise Lost*, Book XI and XII," *Milton Studies*, XXV (1989), 245–64. For "stage," more emphatically, see John G. Demaray, *Milton's Theatrical Epic: The Invention and Design of "Paradise Lost"* (Cambridge, Mass., 1980).

> Or thence from *Niger* Flood to *Atlas* Mount
> The Kingdoms of *Almansor, Fez* and *Sus,*
> *Marocco* and *Algiers,* and *Tremisen;*
> On *Europe* thence, and where *Rome* was to sway
> The World
>
> (XI, 385–406)

The geographical, rather than chronological, focus emphasizes the post-lapsarian bias in the catalog. The whole of Old World history is laid out like a text, looking from left to right. We readers as understanders are invited to see it whole, all at once, as an angel would see it—God knowing it before it is. The humanity of human history is shown by disregarding all that man finds familiar and comfortable. What is familiar and comfortable to *fallen* man is, of course, alien to God. The inconsequentiality of the *merely* human is that it fails to join the regeneration of order that is the whole purpose of the macrocosmic journey. Ophir and Mombaza, colorful though they are, stand apart from the divinely commanded human journey.

This point is driven home by Milton's consideration of agriculture, metalworking, and war. Here what is ordinary and familiar is described in common terms and uncommon context. The ambiguous nature of the human arts, for example, appears in the passages on metalworking. The vision of Book XI reflects a description similar to that of technology in hell, where "*Mammon* led them on" (I, 678) in building Pandaemonium, there likened to "*Babel,* and the works of *Memphian* Kings" (I, 694). The Memphian kings are on a par with the Persian in Ecbatan and the kingdoms of Almansor, Fez, and Sus. Merely human activity is, at the very least, potentially demonic.[15]

The correlation of hell with the utterly secular can be seen in Milton's descriptions of war:

> Concours in Arms, fierce Faces threatning Warr,
> Giants of mightie Bone, and bould emprise;
> Part wield thir Arms, part courb the foaming Steed,
> Single or in Array of Battel rang'd
>
> . . . .

---

15. Martz has made essentially the same point from the other direction, with reference to the worldliness of hell implicit in the mundane metaphoric vehicles in Books I and II. See Martz, *The Paradise Within,* 114–16, 138. See also 51*n*4 above.

> With Carcasses and Arms th' ensanguind Field
> Deserted: Others to a Citie strong
> Lay Siege, encampt; by Batterie, Scale, and Mine,
> Assaulting; others from the wall defend
> With Dart and Jav'lin, Stones and sulfurous Fire
>   (XI, 641–44, 654–58)

Much the same terms are used to describe Moloch's address to the consult in Pandaemonium. He compulsively reiterates the failed strategy of war in heaven, which the reader will hermeneutically reconsider in Book VI:

> let us rather choose
> Arm'd with Hell flames and fury all at once
> O're Heav'ns high Towrs to force resistless way,
> Turning our Tortures into horrid Arms
> Against the Torturer
>   (II, 60–64) [16]

It seems clear that history, from the arts of war to those of peace, has more than one meaning, depending on the context. Whether the context is regenerative or fallen depends entirely on grace. Without grace there would be no journey, on either the personal or the general level; indeed, without grace the very idea of journey would be lost. There could be only raging energy, passive speculation, aimless technique, or subversion, as the successive proposals of Moloch, Belial, Mammon, and Beelzebub witness in Book II. Grace prevenient, in the Augustinian sense, is required before the rescue of fallen man can begin. [17] Even prayer is useless without the grace to pray:

> Thus they in lowliest plight repentant stood
> Praying, for from the Mercie-seat above

16. On the Satanically mechanical and uncreative, especially the sulfurous, see Lieb, *The Dialectic of Creation*, 239–43.

17. See *The Confessions of Saint Augustine*, esp. Bk. I. On the whole notion of the vision of Adam and the biblical theology underlying it, see Jason P. Rosenblatt, "Adam's Pisgah Vision: *Paradise Lost*, Books XI and XII," *English Literary History*, XXXIX (1972), 66–86. This is an important article that will repay careful reading. See also Jon S. Lawry's important book *The Shadow of Heaven: Matter and Stance in Milton's Poetry* (Ithaca, N.Y., 1978), 267–88. And see Robert A. Bryan, "Adam's Tragic Vision in *Paradise Lost*," *Studies in Philology*, LXII (1965), 197–214. These works present an overview of Milton's description of history. Donne likewise expressed dependence on prevenient grace in his Holy Sonnet "Thou hast made me" and in "A Litanie."

> Prevenient Grace descending had remov'd
> The stonie from thir hearts
>
> (XI, 1–4)

Grace not merely transforms humanity, it transforms history as well. History without grace would be merely an amassing of episodes, existential, meaningless, and without purpose, and tending inexorably to corrupt an already corrupted humanity further. Within the context of grace, however, history becomes the slow but not necessarily wandering steps toward salvation, toward order as love. It becomes the unfolding of the revealed Word of God.

This regenerate and meaningful history Milton also relates. Most of Books XI and XII are in greater part devoted to that theme. The presentation of creative and regenerate history follows two paths. The first is a recapitulation of biblical history beginning with Genesis; the second is an explanation, which owes a great deal to Anselm, of why gracious history, which is the overlapping of human and eternal time, is the fulfillment of the incarnation.

Regenerate history begins with Cain and Abel (XI, 441–49), though this story is merely a bridge from one typology to another. In *Paradise Lost,* the working of grace in history really begins with Enoch:

> To Council in the Citie Gates: anon
>
> . . . .
>
> Of middle Age one rising, eminent
> In wise deport, spake much of Right and Wrong,
> Of Justice, of Religion, Truth and Peace,
> And Judgement from above
>
> (XI, 661, 665–68)

Enoch acts as a paradigm, for both the recapitulation of Adam and the prefiguring of the Christus. He is the single one who looks to God, who exhibits God's grace.[18] Wise council cannot come unaided. God's own judgment on man is clear: "His heart I know, how variable and vain / Self-left" (XI, 92–93). So is the theme replayed, through fallen mankind, with prevenient grace working repeatedly in one person at a time. So continues the macrocosmic journey toward the order of love.

18. J. B. Broadbent noted Milton's predilection for the solitary figure, in *Some Graver Subject: An Essay on "Paradise Lost"* (London, 1960), 289. See also, more substantially, J. Douglas Canfield, *Word as Bond* (Philadelphia, 1989), esp. Afterword.

The working of grace receives fuller theological treatment in the story of Noah:

> God observ'd
> The one just Man alive; by his command
> Shall build a wondrous Ark, as thou beheldst,
> To save himself and houshold from amidst
> A World devote to universal rack.
>
> (XI, 817–21)

Again it is in the single individual that grace is found. It occurs in the *sheareth*, the remnant—in Christian terms, in the *ecclesiola*, which is the true church found in the midst of secularism, sin, and of God's commands a general disregard. For Milton, the Calvinist, such a concept was not merely familiar but true.[19]

The theme of the faithful remnant, reduced again to just one man, is repeated by Milton in the story of Abraham, from whom, both remnant and renewer, there is a "Nation from one faithful man to spring" (XII, 113). The same thought reappears with Isaac and Jacob (XII, 153, 155–65). Renewal is constantly needed and, through grace, constantly attained. With Isaac and Jacob, the idea of the regenerative journey is merely mentioned, but Moses and Aaron receive more ample treatment. The reasons for our extended education here—with Adam as our locum tenens—lie in the related realms of the law and of the church and ritual, both of which are first mentioned in the Bible. The additions of law

19. Although the concepts of the remnant and the little church work in the same way to the same end in Books XI and XII of *Paradise Lost,* it should be noted that they have some profoundly different theological implications. The remnant implies a reduction of the faithful to a handful, perhaps only one or two, who will then renew the community. The *ecclesiola* defines the true church as a hidden minority existing within the corrupted husk of the institutional church. The hidden faithful are not a remnant but have existed always, and they are not going to renew the community. The community is lost to the sin and idolatry of the world. For a modern fictional treatment of this theme, see André Schwarz-Bart, *Le Dernier des justes* (Paris, 1959). See also Julie Nall Knowles's interesting though tangential article " 'The Course of Time': A Calvinist *Paradise Lost,*" *Milton Studies,* XVIII (1983), 173–93. More on the point, see Dennis Danielson, "Milton's Arminianism and *Paradise Lost,*" *Milton Studies,* XII (1979), 47–75; Dennis Danielson, *Milton's Good God: A Study in Literary Theodicy* (New York, 1982); William J. Rewak, S.J., "Book III of Paradise Lost: Milton's Satisfaction of Redemption," *Milton Quarterly,* XI (1977), 97–102; Desmond Hamlet, *One Greater Man: Justice and Damnation in "Paradise Lost"* (Lewisburg, Pa., 1976); and Gary D. Hamilton, "Milton's Defensive God: A Reappraisal," *Studies in Philology,* LXIX (1972), 87–100.

and church to the covenant are part of the unfolding revelation of the Word, so that the remnant may better understand the journey, and the love of God may be seen through something other than nature. Merely human life thereby comes to accrue continuous divine meaning (see XII, 227–31, 249–53).

The direction of the Augustinian journey is not always easily seen in the telling of it. The kingdom is the destination, and Milton uses the Davidic kingdom to prefigure the divine one (XII, 315–71). Earthly kingdoms, unlike the remnant, do not renew, and unlike the *ecclesiola,* do not sustain. They are either symbols, like the kingdom of David, or useless, like Ophir and Mombaza. The divine gloss on human time carries the meaning.

The motif of prefiguring, so important for real, that is, divine, history, is mostly implied in Books XI and XII, but one of the few occasions when it is explicitly mentioned is particularly important:

> *Moses* in figure beares, to introduce
> One greater, of whose day he shall foretell,
> And all the Prophets in thir Age the times
> Of great *Messiah* shall sing.
>
> (XII, 241–44)

In this light must the constancy of God, the renewal of the remnant, the macrocosmic journey toward order, the dual meaning of time, and the meaning of history be understood.

DEBT THEOLOGY OUTDONE AS LOVE

Stating the ways of God for man is, as Milton well knew, not the same as explaining them. The need for redemption is obvious, but the reasons the journey toward order takes the form it does also have to be addressed. The explanation Milton offers assumes a traditional schema, though it is untraditionally expressed. He draws on the feudal debt theology of Saint Anselm of Canterbury, which began with conventional notions of original sin. According to it, man, having fallen, lies utterly in thrall to sin, unable to help himself in any way.[20] Man's state is utterly degenerative:

20. To argue otherwise is to fall into Pelagianism, the doctrine that Adam's sin injured him alone, that what we do may include good, and thus that we can earn salvation. Augustine opposed all three ideas. See *The Confessions of Saint Augustine,* esp. Bk. X. See

> But hard be hard'n'd, blind be blinded more,
> That they may stumble on, and deeper fall;
>
> . . . .
>
> Disloyal breaks his fealtie, and sinns
> Against the high Supremacie of Heav'n
>   (III, 200–201, 204–205)

So low has man fallen that grace prevenient is needed just to understand the nature of the soteriological journey, quite apart from beginning it. Man, owing everything to God, cannot repay the debt, because true repayment would have to come out of what he does not already owe. Milton puts *unredeemed* debt theology into the mouth of Satan: "The debt immense of endless gratitude, / So burthensome still paying, still to ow" (IV, 52–53). The debt owed to God only grows by the derivative repaying that human beings are capable of, as grace prevenient is added to the burden. Yet, the debt somehow must permit of being paid. Were it otherwise, God would be treating sin and grace as the same thing and in the same way, thus degrading the name of justice in a Manichaean way. For the debt to be paid, there would be needed a sacrifice so stupendous that humanity could not make it. For man, "Indebted and undon, hath none to bring" (III, 235). A worthy satisfaction of the debt can be found only in the free gift offered by the Son to sacrifice himself in man's place, "mee for him, life for life" (III, 236).[21] Because theologically the Son of God is

---

also Augustine, "On the Grace of Christ," trans. Peter Holmes, in *St. Augustin: Anti-Pelagian Writings,* ed. Philip Schaff, Select Library of Nicene and Post-Nicene Writings, V (New York, 1887), 217–36. See, in the same volume, Augustine's treatises "On Original Sin" and "On the Proceedings of Pelagius." A brief examination of the issues can be found in Paul Lehmann's "The Anti-Pelagian Writings," in *A Companion to the Study of Saint Augustine,* ed. Roy Battenhouse (New York, 1955), 203–35. For a simultaneously rigorous and generous critique of Augustine's embattled position, see Paul Ricoeur, *The Conflict of Interpretations,* Pt. IV. Ricoeur distinguishes, for example, the juridical category of debt from the biological category of inheritance. See also Pagels, *Adam, Eve, and the Serpent,* 124–32.

21. It should be noted that this freewill leap of faith by the Son, while sustaining the debt theology, has been mistakenly construed to put Milton into the posture of Arianism. The allegation has been so frequent as to have become a cliché, and thus we will not cite authorities. For an article that nonetheless affirms both the Arian nature of Milton's views on the godhead and the too casual acceptance by scholars of Miltonic Arianism, see Karl Lewis Winegarden, "No Hasty Conclusions: Milton's Anti-Nicean Pneumatology," *Milton Quarterly,* XI (1977), 102.

understood as owing nothing but paying all as a gift, that is to say, *as an act of love rather than a burden,* we have the prayer-book formula of a "full, perfect, and sufficient sacrifice, oblation, and satisfaction, for the sins of the whole world." [22] Milton, much like the compilers of the Book of Common Prayer, conceived that only in such a way could the wounded condition of man be made whole, could man be made debt-free, and could the divine plan be completed. [23] Hellish hate shall be outdone and debt calculations transcended by heavenly love more fundamentally than by heavenly light:

> So onely can high Justice rest appaid.
> The Law of God exact he shall fulfill
> Both by obedience and by love, though love
> Alone fulfill the Law
>
> (XII, 401–404) [24]

All is paid by uniquely unexampled love. The macrocosmic order is restored, and *Paradise Lost* is, in a paradox similar to that of the nature of time as it relates to the development of creation from chaos, also the story of *Paradise Regain'd.*

The philosophical and rational problems posed by Books VII, XI, and XII of *Paradise Lost* are not insoluble, though they do not yield to logic or a merely literal interpretation of the poem. The Neoplatonic concepts of multiple levels of being, and of a hierarchy of increasing reality, given a Christian application, are the appropriate tools, along with the Augustinian notion—hermeneutic, we believe—of faith, hope, and love work-

22. Booty, ed., *The Book of Common Prayer, 1559,* 263. This appears in the service of Holy Communion.

23. See *Anselm of Canterbury: Why God Became Man and the Virgin Conception and Original Sin,* trans. and ed. Joseph M. Colleran (Albany, N.Y., 1969), esp. *Why God Became Man (Cur Deus Homo),* Bk. I, Chaps. 9, 12–15, Bk. II, Chaps. 6–7, 9, 14–16, 18. Milton dissented from the strict necessitarian view of the incarnation. See pp. 80–92 below. See also Rewak, "Book III of Paradise Lost."

24. Despite what seems to us Albert R. Cirillo's misconception of the "transcendent symbol of noon" as the "basic metaphor" and as a concluding *fumet* of Manichaeanism, we acknowledge the extensive collateral material and kindred argument marshaled by him in "Noon-Midnight and the Temporal Structure of *Paradise Lost*," *English Literary History,* XXIX (1962), 372–95 (reprinted in *Critical Essays on Milton from "ELH"* [Baltimore, 1971]).

ing dynamically in the mind.[25] The relation of the higher to the lower, of creation to development, of eternity to history, stands at the core of the epic. Human development and history are real only on the microcosmic level, the human level in the Great Chain of Being. On God's level they only seem. "Nay, I know not seems," says Hamlet. Milton knew it well. Seeming is the fundamental metaphor for being, and the special seeming of human love is the metaphor for divinely eternal being. Milton obviously understood that metaphor always works partly by the tense force of simultaneous similarity and contrast.

More particularly, different *categories* (as we conventionally say) of seeming are metaphors for different *aspects* (as we might say) of being, for the heavenly "righteousness and peace and love" (XII, 550) of which Michael speaks. At the risk of making the epic and dynamic Milton sound too much like the sage and serious Spenser of *Fowre Hymns,* we can say that for him too the aspect of eternity animated by perfect love and administered in perfect righteousness is heavenly peace.[26] "Reason also is choice," says God (III, 108); accordingly, the linearity of human thought is a medium of re- or degeneration, and human time is ambiguously a metaphor of perfect heavenly freedom. For human perception, philadelphic peace is a metaphor of eternity divinely replete; war—paradoxically empty and constricting—is a somewhat spatial definition by contrast, publicly and privately. Of Adam and Eve's "fruitless hours" (IX, 1188) of "vain contest [there] appeer'd no end" (IX, 1189). Human love, in contrast, the crowning mode of perception, metaphorically suggests eternity and the social order of heavenly righteousness, and suggests it

---

25. The notion is pervasive, as we understand Augustine, but see his *De trinitate,* esp. IX, X.

26. Williams suggests that God's creation of a world "Answering his great Idea" (*Paradise Lost,* VII, 557) recuperates "A goodly Paterne" in Spenser's "Hymne in Honour of Beautee" (line 32). See Williams, *The Common Expositor,* 44. See also Marsilio Ficino, *Commentary on Plato's Symposium,* trans. Sears Jayne (2nd ed.; Dallas, 1985); and Marsilio Ficino, *Theologica platonica de immortalite animorum: XVIII libaris comprehensa* (New York, 1975). Ficino's theories were the starting point for Renaissance and Baroque commentaries on love. See as well Paul Oskar Kristeller, *Studies in Renaissance Thought and Letters* (Rome, 1956), and Paul Oskar Kristeller, *The Philosophy of Marsilio Ficino* (New York, 1943). On the specific issue of Marsilian Platonism, see M. J. B. Allen, *The Platonism of Marsilio Ficino: A Study of His Phaedrus Commentary, Its Sources and Genesis* (Berkeley and Los Angeles, 1984).

better than logic can. Thus categories of becoming cross-refer metaphorically to the aspects of being and to one another. Grosser levels or stages of perception associate with quantities differentiated, moved, mined, and manipulated, including the elemental phenomena of Adam and Eve's technologized sex after the Fall. Suggesting by metaphoric similarity, if not indeed metonymic participations, the *civitas dei* of righteousness and the end of history moves prophetic figures. Individually, such just men move in the defining metaphoric contrast of the *civitas terrena*. Starker contrasts loom when less and less saintly dispensations, though in teleological history, decline to welters of mere chronicle. Satan is a Manichaean, but Milton is not. Hence, in *Paradise Lost* the never quite perfect unrighteousness, never quite perfect strife, never quite perfect unlove of hell both stand and fall—like human becomings at their worst—as *contrastive* but meaningful metaphoric definitions of heavenly freedom, joy, and eternity.

FOUR

Movement and Dynamism

aradise Lost is often—at least implicitly—called a curiously static poem, by which is meant that calm is pervasive and nothing happens. Change is oftener apparent than real, and where change is real, it is unimportant. Criticism biased toward narrative may lean toward such a view; theologically oriented criticism does tend toward it, whether Judeo-Christian, structuralist, or poststructuralist; so do ideological readings of a Marxian or Freudian sort. For example, the fall of Satan, though colorful and real and permanent, is without consequence in the poem, some will say, since the divine plan proceeds to its loving conclusion anyway. The discursive or psychic or political economy displays itself endlessly. The fall of man is inconsequential, too, even though real, since the *culpa* is supposed *felix* and the incarnation will occur.[1] The events of human history, though capable of discommoding individual human beings, are in themselves unimportant, by reason of the incarnational good news. The very pageant of the heavenly bodies is the same always, "regular / Then most, when most irregular they seem" (*Paradise Lost*, V, 623–24). Everything, including hell, is fixed, if not in a constant state of grace, at least in a constant state of ultimate ineluctability.

This view of Miltonic dynamism is not necessarily incorrect, but it is both wildly incomplete and dependent upon blinking the ultimate un-

---

1. On this, see Arthur O. Lovejoy, "Milton and the Paradox of the Fortunate Fall," *Essays in the History of Ideas*, 277–95; and John C. Ulreich, Jr., "Milton and the Fortunate Fall," *Journal of the History of Ideas*, XXXII (1971), 351–66. Ulreich's article is rigorous and engages the issue. Earlier, the felicity had been denied by Dick Taylor in "Milton and the Paradox of the Fortunate Fall Once More," *Tulane Studies in English*, IX (1959), 35–51; it had been problematized by Earl Miner in "*Felix Culpa* in the Redemptive Order of *Paradise Lost*," *Philological Quarterly*, XLVII (1968), 43–54. Subsequently, Wilkes has differentiated the logical and experiential, somewhat as we wish to do in "'Full of Doubt I Stand': The Final Implications of *Paradise Lost*."

knowability that attaches to the divine. The conception of the universe as fixed or static is incomplete because it adverts only to the divine level of vision. To God, being and becoming are the same thing, since all time is one.[2] But Milton deems the monistic apprehension of reality, however conventional in the Renaissance, to be available only to God; it hardly describes human experience. Mankind sees change constantly, and individuals are themselves in a constant state of becoming, as matter is endlessly made into form.[3] Man's becoming may also be described in Augustinian terms, as proceeding from *aversio* to *conversio,* from "lostness" to redemption. That is a journey Milton considers of no small consequence, as he makes plain in Adam's familiar last speech, which can be abbreviated for present purposes:

> Greatly instructed I shall hence depart,
> Greatly in peace of thought . . .
> And love with fear the onely God, to walk
> As in his presence, . . .
> Acknowledge my Redeemer ever blest.
>
> (XII, 557–58, 562–63, 573)

An interpretation of *Paradise Lost* that omits humanity's sense of struggle—ironically occluded by Adam's supposition—and humanity's journey and possibility of redemption, can hardly be called complete, or even balanced.

Furthermore, the God's-eye view is presumptive rather than knowable. From a Protestant theological perspective, what is known about God is revealed in Scripture, and that knowledge is tantalizingly incomplete. Scripture famously conceals as well as reveals. Revelation is also hard to understand. Words that have valid and reliable meaning when describing

---

2. On this point see *The Confessions of Saint Augustine,* Bk. XI, Chaps. 13–28. See also 73*n*4 below.

3. Milton could both draw on and draw away from Greek conceptions, from Heraclitean flow or fire to Platonic *metaxy* to Aristotelian taxonomies in the *Physics* and elsewhere. Ann Gossman has taxonomized some of the most important movement in the poem in terms of the opposition between ring (good) and maze (bad). See her "The Ring Pattern: Image, Structure, and Theme in *Paradise Lost,*" *Studies in Philology,* LXVIII (1971), 326–39. Philip Brockbank has written sensitively of rhythms and disruptions of temporality as motion, in "'Within the Visible Diurnal Sphere': The Moving World of *Paradise Lost,*" in *Approaches to "Paradise Lost,*" ed. C. A. Patrides (Toronto, 1968), 199–221.

things, and may seem to have it when describing human activities, become hopelessly and obviously equivocal when applied to God. It is not necessary to subscribe without reservation to the line, from Ockham to Karl Barth, of radical voluntarists who assert God is *wholly* Other to accept and appreciate the awesome Otherness in God. Radical voluntarism implies that even metaphor cannot accommodate human understanding to the divine—as Milton clearly believed it could. But seventeenth-century Calvinists thoroughly appreciated the theological implications of the hidden God who has nothing really in common with man. An interpretation of *Paradise Lost* that finds in it a static universe where change is either unreal or inconsequential closes its eye to equivocation and divine Otherness, and also the psychologically and theologically important action that occupies the entire epic.

We would emphasize more forcefully than any recent critic known to us that *Paradise Lost,* far from being static, is filled with movement and dynamism. Milton presents, represents, and thematically insists upon change. *Paradise Lost* is, among other things, a book of changes. The changes are Christian, of course, including both the Fall and redemption from it through the gracious and providential journey undertaken by those "who are called according to his purpose" (Rom. 8:28). The changes are also neo-Ovidian, insofar as the exaggeration and enlargement of preexisting characteristics are the basis for them.[4] Further, the changes are important and real; the differences between our prelapsarian and postlapsarian condition could hardly be greater. The changes are psychological and physical as well as theological. Milton's epic is filled with movement, colorful, dramatic, sometimes surprising, and including all but God, whose immutability, postulated but not known, would obviate movement; human understanding can accommodate itself to divine plenitude, however, by metaphors of change or movement. As with epic conventions, so with Ovidian metamorphosis: Milton's theology gives him means—and should we say spirit?—to intensify overwhelmingly his classical precedent. Those undergoing change are not so much absorbed into benign nature as fulfilled justly and lovingly in supernature.

4. In *The Gods Made Flesh: Metamorphosis and the Pursuit of Paganism* (New Haven, 1986), Leonard Barkan explores Ovidian transformations and transformations of Ovid through the Continental Renaissance and Shakespeare. See also 71*n*1 above.

SATAN'S DETERIORATION

The most spectacular of the changes that inform *Paradise Lost* is the falling of Satan, an entropic decay that begins within the precincts of the epic but continues indefinitely, endowing the epic with a sort of open-endedness, or an ending *in medias res*. The fall of Satan is a continuing flight from *caritas,* though, ironically for Satan, the "allness" of God makes it also a fall toward grace. We maintain that for Milton the falling of Satan is real, even though human language for it entails metaphoricity; for those as aversive to Christian belief as William Empson, the more radically metaphorical view of the fall of the demons may provide comfort, but it impedes an understanding of the epic. Satan's fall is a neo-Ovidian change; Satan being proud and disobedient changes into greater and greater pride and resistance to grace. His fall is endlessly reductive, a fall ultimately into ontological nothingness. Milton thought that all creatures, including the unfallen angels, Satan, and the demons, lived and were within space-time, that only God had being independent of time and space, and that, in this fundamental sense, God alone had Being, while all of manifold creation had both being and becoming.[5]

The falling of Satan in the Miltonic epic "begins" in eternity with the anointing of the Son, at which, "All seemd well pleas'd, all seem'd, but were not all" (V, 617). Satan, consumed with envy, wrath, and pride, "thought himself impaird" (V, 665), "thence conceiving . . . resolv'd . . . to dislodge, and leave" (V, 666–69). For Satan, the thought is swiftly followed by words and other deeds, bringing him to a throne "High in the midst exalted as a God" (VI, 99). The progression to this point,

---

5. "Esse, nomen est immutabilitatis" (Being is a term for immutability; Augustine, *Sermones ad populum,* VII, 7, in *Patrologiae Cursus Completus . . . Series Latina,* ed. J. P. Migne [221 vols.; Paris, 1844–1903], XXXVIII, 66). For a comment on the relationship of man to God within an ontological framework, see Augustine, *Enarrationes in Psalmos,* CXXI, 8, in *Patrologiae . . . Latina,* ed. Migne, XXXVII, 1624. Milton was anticipated in his view of the descent of Satan into ontological nothingness by Anselm. See Anselm of Canterbury, *De casu diaboli,* trans. and ed. Jasper Hopkins and Herbert Richardson, in *Truth, Freedom, and Evil: Three Philosophical Dialogues by Anselm of Canterbury* (New York, 1967), esp. Chaps. 1, 4, 9. Milton placed more emphasis on freedom than he did on necessity. Robert Martin Adams argues that Satan's entailment of hell and its contributions to ordering structure are goods out of evil. See his "A Little Look at Chaos," in *Illustrious Evidence: Approaches to English Literature of the Early Seventeenth Century,* ed. Earl Miner (Berkeley and Los Angeles, 1975), 71–89.

spread over more than three hundred lines, includes actions (as we must call them) by others, such as the divine observation and "derision" (V, 736) and the rejection of apostasy by Abdiel. That the revolt began with thoughts in Book V—before the book of the revolt in heaven—invites questions about when Adam and Eve should be understood to begin to fall, and to die.

The Miltonic description of the disobedience and defiance of Satan has about it the ring of psychological truth. It is how mankind, now fallen, would have acted. One sees similar progressions: the envious thought, hypocritically suppressed, breaking out in envy and rancor, as if disparagement of another would enhance the self. Then rancor, no longer satisfied with abuse and jealous wrath, spills over into deeds of betrayal and assault as disappointment and dissatisfaction are fastened upon another.

The underlying theology of the oneness of sin, and its sad effects, is poetically heightened by both defamiliarization and domestication, by describing human characteristics in a nonhuman setting and hellish characteristics in terms suitable to fisher, farmer, matron, bourgeois, and burglar.[6] In less than a dozen lines, Milton drew the outlines of original sin. The monstrous idolatry of Satan, in which the archfiend is depicted worshiping himself, appears in patterns theologically precise and psychologically familiar. The false always imitates the true. Seeming or fraud is the medium of idolatry, as the lust for power or control is its animating energy. And with Satan, the idolatry of self-worship begins when "All seemd well pleas'd" (V, 617), in a seeming that went unnoticed by all but God, to whom "all hearts be open, all desires known, and from whom no secrets are hid."[7]

Specific sins, such as envy, wrath, and pride, may be understood to have been, until that instant, existent only in the mind of God, external to Satan while he was still unfallen and still whole. But with Satan, as with Adam, Eve, and ourselves, the Fall is the figure of these sins' movement inward, making them a part of us. Pride and envy and wrath and the rest are no longer merely potential properties of acts carried out in disobedience; they characterize, both for Satan and for mankind, what we are. After the Fall, Milton takes care to insist, Satan no longer commits sin; he is sin.

6. See Martz, "The Earthly City," in his *The Paradise Within,* 110–16.

7. Booty, ed., *The Book of Common Prayer, 1559,* 248. Milton is careful, always, to illuminate the difference between God and God's creation, whether that creation is falling (Satan), fallen (humanity), or perfect in its way (nature, unfallen angels).

Milton describes Satan after the Fall in terms of all but nameless woe. Satan "thought himself impaird" (V, 665), and so he was, though not as he imagined. The fallen imagination characteristically deceives. Considering repentance, the fatally impaired Satan will not, in the Book of Common Prayer's formula, "turn from his wickedness and live" but will only turn away, his woe never rightly named or understood:

> troubl'd thoughts, and from the bottom stirr
> The Hell within him, for within him Hell
> He brings, and round about him, nor from Hell
> One step no more then from himself can fly
> By change of place: Now conscience wakes despair
>
> (IV, 19–23)

The hell may be endlessly stirred, but it is never changed. It is always "Me miserable! which way shall I flie / Infinite wrauth, and infinite despair?" (IV, 73–74). His woe, real and pervasive but tenuous and shapeless, like death in Book II, resists descriptive naming. In the fallen state, knowing and naming have woeful limitations.

The Satanic fall was evidently not for Milton an *event,* so much as was the case for humanity generally. Satan falls endlessly, his idolatry, his sin, and his narcissistic inwardness and woe always growing. He can paradoxically get "to" perdition (I, 47), but perdition is "bottomless" (VI, 866). Falling and being have become merged into a single state. Were Satan to stop falling, he would cease to be Satanic, but that is an event theologically and mythically reserved for the end of ordinary time. The continuous falling is marked by Milton's emphasis on Satan's pride, the primal curse of sin. "Proud, art thou met?" (VI, 131) is the greeting given the now rebellious Satan on the eve of insane battle. As battle ends, when "Warr wearied hath perform'd what Warr can do" (VI, 695), and Satan is expelled from Heaven by love, his fall takes on a physical dimension. The demonic horde fall nine days as "confounded *Chaos* roard" (VI, 871) and the fallen angels begin their journey through common time. This is when Satan's heart starts endlessly distending "with pride" and "hardning in his strength" (I, 572), a process Milton emphasizes by referring again and again to Satan's proud refusal to accept grace and repentance.

Satan and his progeny and followers—the author of evil and the instrumentalities—warp and weft into experience the text of evil hitherto hidden as a concept in the mind of God. They are routed by love. Milton's angelic figure may compare with Paul Ricoeur's human figure possessed by "dread . . . of not being able to love any more, the danger of being a dead man in the realm of ends."[8] But Satan is a relentless enumerator and is construed as the author of all ill, of sin, of evil (II, 381, 864, VI, 262). "Author," from *auctor,* suggests the enlarger of evil, presumably at the expense of love and good (for example, I, 157–68). Satan regularly conceives existence as a zero-sum game, being as unable to conceive the paradox of a non-zero-sum game to either extreme—all winners or all losers—as he is to conceive the metaphoricity of a "bruise" to "Serpents head" (X, 1031–32; XII, 149–50). Hence, for the Satanic, will "terrour be in Love" (IX, 490), as Satan remarks of Eve; hence, earlier, is the devil "abasht" by the "youthful beautie" and "grace / Invincible" of the cherub (IV, 845–46). God promises that heavenly love shall "outdo" (III, 298) hellish hate, rather than, say, outweigh it—an idea with Pauline sanction (*pondus gloriae*)—or even outshine it. But it is noteworthy that it is heavenly *love*—which is so ideal it cannot be named by the fallen word *power*—that shall outdo hellish hate.[9] When the Son in "Chariot of Paternal Deitie" (VI, 750) sallies forth "with fresh Flowrets Hill and Valley smil'd" (VI, 784) and he announces that "Number to this dayes work is not ordain'd" (VI, 809), though "by strength / They measure all" (VI, 820–21). It is not the eyes of the Son but rather the eyes of the chariot that "shot forth pernicious fire" (VI, 849), proleptic of the "contagious Fire" (IX, 1036) of the eyes of the newly fallen Adam and Eve. With regard to the falling angels, the fire from the chariot's eyes

> Witherd all thir strength,
> And of thir wonted vigour left them draind,
> Exhausted, spiritless, afflicted, fall'n.
> (VI, 850–52)

They are castrated, one might say, intending by the word a psychospiritual disabling. Because the "Golden Scepter . . . Is now an Iron Rod"

---

8. Paul Ricoeur, *The Symbolism of Evil* (New York, 1967), 30. He writes of "consciousness of defilement" (p. 31).

9. Not dissimilarly, Adam at last exclaims that "over wrauth grace shall abound" (*Paradise Lost,* XII, 478). Milton explicitly accords to the fallen his insight that love (grace) shall outdo mere power—a not unimportant point and one solidly based on Scripture.

(V, 886–87) to the rebels, as Abdiel remarks, and the Son has into "terrour chang'd / His count'nance too severe to be beheld" (VI, 824–25), we conclude that only the love of the Son for the Father and of God for the rebel angels can account for the terror they feel. The Son's *countenance* may be imageless in severity, but the Son is the image of the divine "word, . . . wisdom, and effectual might" (III, 170), in that and other contexts an image of redemptive or creative love.

So grace, repentance, and love are available to all, Satan not excluded. Milton insists on the recognizable possibility of Satanic repentance:

> with his good
> Upbraided none; nor was his service hard.
> What could be less then to afford him praise,
> The easiest recompence, and pay him thanks,
> How due!
>
> (IV, 44–48)

Due, certainly, but not to be given, and negatively prejudged by Satan's chosen economic metaphor. Satan's response to himself was to have "sdeined subjection" (IV, 50), which was never asked, the basic Christian position being that only in God's service can perfect freedom be found. But by feeling and misconstruing unequally potent love as unequal power, Satan continues to fall, a declension marked unerringly by Satan's comment on the love of God: "Be then his Love accurst, since love or hate, / To me alike, it deals eternal woe" (IV, 69–70). No one who has not utterly rejected God's love and offer of salvation can possibly make such a statement, and only Satan can make it endlessly. Since knowing and naming are dependent on love, Satan's curse on God's love marks the ultimate and continuing descent into lostness. And Satan's intelligence is aware of this, even as the affections of his will suffer: "thy will / Chose freely what it now so justly rues" (IV, 71–72). So still he goes to a "worse relapse, / And heavier fall" (IV, 100–101). Milton has brought theological and psychological truth together. Love turned totally inward to narcissism is, as Ovid knew, hate turned out to all the world and beyond. If Blakeans have been beguiled by Satan's "bad eminence" (II, 6), here is the hideous truth, self-confessed and self-condemned, of Satan Lost. There are further and equally vivid descriptions of Satan and his works. But it is all elaboration, seeing in detail what is here seen whole. All the rest, as Rabbi Hillel once remarked, is commentary.

The fall of Satan is not merely endless, it is an ontological degradation as well. Because God is "Author of all being" (III, 374), the Fall must lead ultimately only to grace and good except in Satan's case, where it leads to nothingness. Milton's devotion to that theological and pastoral tenet can hardly be in doubt. But the Fall also leads to the destruction of the fallen. The *culpa* is *felix* only for God—a point fundamentally simple but so much abused as to deserve review in the next section. Milton portrays the fall of Satan as progressive, with each stage of the descent worse than the one before. The final extended glimpse of Satan in *Paradise Lost*, in Book X, is of progressive and endless decay: "down he fell / A monstrous Serpent on his Belly prone" (X, 513–14). All of the words are there: *down, fell, prone.* The proneness upon the lake of fire comes to mind. That was bad, but this is worse. And, a "heavier fall" (IV, 101) awaits, a fall that ends in nothingness. Satan ultimately loses being. He ceases to be since his fall into nothingness, into entropy, is complete. So we read God's apocalyptic vision (X, 635; like the Son's, at III, 259), which mentions the effects, sin and death (elsewhere the shadow of sin), but not their progenitor, Satan.

Ontological entropy is not only a theologically necessary extrapolation from Milton's description of Satan in Books IV and X, it is also required by the nature of time, within which Satan lives and changes. One may think of Satan's fall from being into nothingness in terms of Minkowskian space-time geometry, made necessary by relativity, with Satan spiraling slowly into total entropy. For Satan, of course, grace is entropy and nothingness is divine love. Whether this is described as destruction or redemption is immaterial. For Satan, it comes to the same thing. It also, incidentally, introduces the Christian reader to the theology of *Paradise Regain'd,* in which the waxing reality of the Savior is in stark contrast to the futile and fading reality of the Fall. [10]

10. This point is little altered even if one accepts William Kerrigan's psychoanalytically ingenious allegation of ambiguity at *Paradise Regain'd,* IV, 583. See his *The Sacred Complex: On the Psychogenesis of "Paradise Lost"* (Cambridge, Mass., 1988), 90–91, 102. Leonora Leet Brodwin has glossed a debt to Socinianism, in "The Dissolution of Satan in *Paradise Lost:* A Study of Milton's Heretical Eschatology," *Milton Studies,* VIII (1975), 165–207. Jules David Law convincingly argues dissolution on rhetorical and ontological grounds, maintaining that abrogation of proper boundaries entails loss of identity. See his "Eruption and Containment: The Satanic Predicament in *Paradise Lost,*" *Milton Studies,* XVI (1982), 35–60.

THE "FORTUNATE FALL"

We now turn from, as they say in chemistry, qualitative to quantitative analysis, from the plenitude of movement and the *motus ad formam* (or the phenomenology of hatred) to the structure of the Fall. The Miltonic lines are psychologically precise and express clearly the theological paradox of "Light out of darkness" (XII, 473) and "evil turn to good" (XII, 471) that is the necessary result of grace. At the human level, the paradox of fallenness as the precondition for salvation—and thus going to the greater glory of God—has been fully stated with admirable clarity by Arthur O. Lovejoy: "If [the sin and fall] had never occurred, the Incarnation and Redemption could never have occurred. These sublime mysteries would have had no occasion and no meaning; and therefore the plenitude of divine goodness and power could never have been exercised nor have become known to men."[11] Lovejoy remarks that Milton took cognizance of the fortunate fall, not omitting it, as he might easily have done, but instead using care to keep it away from his descriptions of the Fall itself, lest the magnitude of the Fall or its sad consequences seem diminished. Thus the *felix culpa* is reserved for the end of Book XII, with the entire archangelic description of human history, both biblical and profane, separating it from the description of the fallen pair who are "discount'nanc't both, and discompos'd" (X, 110).

By separating this description, certainly not redolent of fortune or happiness, from the *felix culpa,* Milton was able to draw upon the paradox of the fortunate fall, "even better than the simple belief in a future millennium or celestial bliss, to give to . . . history as a whole the character, not of tragedy, but of a divine comedy."[12] Even more, Milton was able to accept, without comment or explanation, a "paradox which has at least the look of a formal antinomy," and he was able to do that in a way that did not require him to decide whether it is really a contradiction or merely seems to be one, or even if the fall is fortunate or not.[13] We wish to suggest three things: that the paradox of the fortunate fall is an apparent and linguistic (that is to say, fallen linguistic) rather than real antinomy; that there was nothing fortunate about the Fall as Milton understood it;

11. Lovejoy, "Milton and the Paradox of the Fortunate Fall," in *Essays in the History of Ideas,* 277–78.

12. *Ibid.,* 278.

13. *Ibid.,* 279, 277.

and that Milton used the paradox, as Lovejoy caught brilliantly, to help us see how human history, a generally sorry chronicle, is a salvific and divine comedy. In supporting our suggestions, we shall look at Christian liturgy, and we shall also look at systematic theology, particularly as it pertains to the Great Chain of Being and the problems of freedom and necessity in the will of God.

Milton's introduction of the idea of the fortunate fall was less than an endorsement or analysis but more than an allusion. The lines of Adam's exclamation in Book XII show its middling place in the epic:

> O goodness infinite, goodness immense!
> That all this good of evil shall produce,
> And evil turn to good; more wonderful
> Then that which by creation first brought forth
> Light out of darkness! full of doubt I stand,
> Whether I should repent me now of sin
> By mee done and occasiond, or rejoyce
> Much more, that much more good thereof shall spring,
> To God more glory, more good will to Men
> From God, and over wrauth grace shall abound.
>
> (XII, 469–78)

Milton does not name the *felix culpa,* and he presents the paradox only in personal terms, in ruminations acknowledged to be doubtful by Adam, who is newly fallen but has already shown a readiness both for confusion and for self-serving interpretation. And Adam himself does not expand on the theme of the Fall but goes on to ask about the faithful left on earth after the Redeemer's "mighty resurrection and glorious ascension." [14] It is this question that the archangel Michael answers, and the *felix culpa* remains without Bardic, archangelic, divine, or Satanic comment. Elsewhere, the voice of God is represented as adducing a desolately *infelix culpa:*

> O Sons, like one of us Man is become
> To know both Good and Evil, since his taste
> Of that defended Fruit; but let him boast
> His knowledge of Good lost, and Evil got,
> Happier, had it suffic'd him to have known
> Good by it self, and Evil not at all.
>
> (XI, 84–89)

14. *Ibid.,* 277–78.

Here Milton's God is made to define mankind's fall as one into hermeneusis: from knowing even so critical an entity as good "by it self" to knowing all by relationship, indeed by successive reciprocal approximations.

Yet an epic that seeks to "assert Eternal Providence / and justifie the wayes of God to men" (I, 25–26) cannot avoid an at least implicit position on the *felix culpa,* and the general tenor of the entire poem opposes the notion of a *felix culpa,* in our opinion, at least as it pertains to the conduct and fate of mankind. As Diane McColley has decisively put it, "Nothing could be more repugnant to Milton's thought than the idea that disobeying God could be good for you." [15] The *culpa* is, accordingly, exactly what one would imagine: a moral, willful, and rational failure, the occasion for original sin, the origin of death, and the beginning of fallen human history. To refer to the Fall as presented in *Paradise Lost* as *felix* rather than *infelix,* without heavy qualification, fosters the perpetuation of a cardboard God, as well as other confusions. We shall examine the *infelix culpa,* therefore, as Milton saw it: as a disaster for which the repair, though adequate and sufficient, undoes only the ultimate, not the immediate, and the general, not necessarily the personal, damage. It does not at all make the damage illusory or render the *culpa,* so to say, damageless. "So Heav'nly love shall outdo Hellish hate" (III, 298), but, the hate and the sin of human disobedience allied with it remain real and damaging and *infelix.*

The term *felix culpa* itself comes from the Christian liturgy and has been traced back to the sixth-century *Liturgia Gallicana,* edited by Saint Germanus, bishop of Paris. [16] Within the chanted prayer, "exultet iam angelica turba caelorum," sung by the deacon during the Easter Even service, appear cries of exultation:

> O certe necessarium Ada'e peccatum, quod
> Christi morte deletum est! O felix culpa,
> quae talem ac tantum meruit habere
> Redemptorum: O beata nox, quae sola meruit
> scire tempus et horam, in qua Christus ab
> inferis resurrexit! [17]

15. Diane McColley, "Eve's Dream," *Milton Studies,* XII (1978), 25. For an oblique comment on the fortunate fall, see McColley's article as a whole, pp. 25–45 (reprinted in her *Milton's Eve* [Urbana, Ill., 1983]).

16. Saint Germanus, *De Liturgica Gallicana,* III, xxxii, in *Patrologiae . . . Latina,* ed. Migne, LXXII, 269.

17. *Ibid.*

These exclamations are appropriate for the liturgy of the Word, which is part of a specific language of faith.[18] The liturgy of the Word calls the believer to embrace the gift of salvation and the truth of the faith, not primarily because of explanation but because of illustration, through participation in story and song, by recognition of the force of sacred text and prayer. The experience and ambience of prayer concern the spirit, for it is the spirit that gives life. Shakespeare's Claudius perceives this, though from a negative perspective: "My words fly up, my thoughts remain below; / Words without thoughts never to heaven go."[19] What is being sent to heaven in the "Exultet" is the formal joy at Christ's mighty resurrection, and the personal joy that we ourselves may participate in it also. The liturgical action is designed to invite and foster the participants' thoughts and feeling coming on Easter Even; the "Exultet" lies at the heart of the good news, in which, though unworthy, we have been invited to share and benefit through Christ's

> Full, perfect, and sufficient sacrifice,
> oblation, and satisfaction, for the sins
> of the whole world.[20]

A sense of awe and wonder and gratitude is what informs that eucharistic prayer of consecration. The exclamations of *felix culpa* and *beata nox* enact and foster our wonder at a God who can turn rampant evil into ultimate good, and turn sin to his, not its own, account.

Understood within the context of prayer, the words of the "Exultet" take on more subtle shades of meaning than they show when decontextualized. By considering the nature of prayer, it is possible to rise from translation to interpretation. No longer are we tempted to think that the Fall, *culpa,* is either fortunate or happy. Rather, we see that we are both fortunate and happy in spite of the nature and existence of original sin, which remains as heinous as ever. In the poetry of Milton, as in the "Exultet," the substantive *culpa* is distinguished and separated from the descriptive *felix.* In *Paradise Lost* this is made clear by the description

18. On the character of the language of liturgy, see Joyce Ann Zimmerman, *Liturgy as Language of Faith: A Liturgical Methodology in the Mode of Paul Ricoeur's Textual Hermeneutics* (New York, 1988). A long-standard work on early Christian liturgy is Dom Gregory Dix's *The Shape of the Liturgy* (London, 1945).

19. *Hamlet,* III, iii.

20. Booty, ed., *The Book of Common Prayer, 1559,* 263.

of fallenness: "Let us seek Death, or he not found, supply / With our own hands his Office on our selves" (X, 1001–1002).[21] This hardly sounds like a description of felicity, though it is convincing enough as an element of the *culpa*. In turning from love to power, Adam and Eve *found* death. That is so not only in the folktale motif familiarly represented by Chaucer's three revelers in "The Pardoner's Tale" but also in the interpretation of Genesis. No one could properly be made glad by a carnality or wantonness such as Adam and Eve's lust (IX, 1013–15). Although such scenes are common on television, it is hard to imagine Milton describing anything of the sort as fortunate. And it is the same in the "Exultet" itself. It is not the *culpa* that is being celebrated; it is the *redemptorum*.

A metaphorical reading also fits the *beata nox. Nox,* which has the dual meaning in this context of "night" and "evil," is in no way blessed itself. The *nox* will, rather, be dispelled, both personally and ultimately, by the blessedness that results when "Christus ab inferis resurrexit." The *beata nox,* like the *felix culpa,* reminds the faithful that good can come out of evil, and come not in any way strange or paradoxical; in life we see it every day. The liturgy of the "Exultet" is not a precise exposition of the relationship of the Fall to the redemption. Unsurpassed in expressing the awe felt at the glory of the "mighty resurrection and glorious ascension," it has to be read in the metaphorical context of a specialized language of faith, of a "believing in order to understand." There are, of course, logical difficulties in a literal reading of *certe necessarium, felix culpa,* and *beata nox.* But it will be recalled that liturgy—etymologically, "the people's work"—by design and definition subsumes and exceeds logic, somewhat as poetry typically aspires to do.[22]

One may rise above logic in daily living and in the mysteries of faith,

21. Eve would here appropriate offices, as of the unfallen or regenerate order (the equivalent of liturgy), for fallen improvisation (the equivalent of theater). We have been helped to this recognition by Stephen Mullaney's remarks on *Measure for Measure* in *The Place of the Stage: License, Play, and Power in Renaissance England* (Chicago, 1988). For illuminating elaboration on Renaissance Ovidian and Petrarchan contexts and on Adam and Eve "mirroring images of each other" after the Fall, see William Kerrigan and Gordon Braden, *The Idea of the Renaissance* (Baltimore, 1989), Chap. 10.

22. We are led by Elaine Pagels to consider Julian of Eclanum in this connection. See her *Adam, Eve, and the Serpent,* 132–33. But Milton needed no Julian, preserved mainly in Augustine's anti-Pelagian *Opus imperfectum contra Julianum,* nor did he need the biblical

and it is essential to good mental health to do so, but logic is essential to theology. Faith is not on this side of reason but is beyond it, Donne remarked, recognizing reason to be necessary but not sufficient. Systematic theology is a specialized language, that of the interpretation of faith. As Saint Anselm of Canterbury reminds us, theology is *fidens quaerens intellectum,* faith seeking understanding. The same message comes from Saint Augustine.[23] Faith is primary, and we have given pride of place to the language of faith, but understanding is a state of comparative blessedness toward which faith leads. And it is to the logical language of theology that we turn now.

Among the theologians who produced detailed and important descriptions of the fortunate fall were Pope Gregory the Great and John Milton himself. Pope Gregory, though accepting the existence of the paradox, does not use the word *felix* to describe the *culpa.* It is, instead, *maior,* an altogether different thing: "What greater fault than that by which all die? And what greater goodness than that by which all are liberated from death? And had Adam not sinned, it would not have behooved our Redeemer to take on our flesh."[24] Milton himself had the same view, of the *culpa* as *maior.* Concerned in his *De Doctrina Christiana* that the original sin might be too lightly considered, Milton was emphatic: "For what fault is there which man did not commit in committing this sin? He was to be condemned both for trusting Satan and for not trusting God; he was faithless, ungreatful, disobedient, greedy, uxorious; she, negligent of her husband's welfare; both of them committed theft, robbery with violence, murder against their children [*i.e.,* the whole human race]; each was sacrilegious and deceitful, cunningly aspiring to divinity

---

commentarists Justin Martyr, Clement of Alexandria, or Irenaeus. Nor was it necessary for him to have known the remarkable series of five sermons by John Donne published in 1649 on Ps. 38:2–4, which develop with imaginative bravura the orthodox interpretation that sin is a kind of dying. See Donne, *The Sermons,* II, Sermons 1–5.

23. "Intellectus enim merces est fidei. Ergo noli quaerere intelligere ut credas, sed crede ut intelligas" (Augustine, *In Joannis evangelium,* XXIX, 6, in *Patrologiae . . . Latina,* ed. Migne, XXXV, 1630).

24. "Nam quae maior culpe, quam illa, que omnes morimur. Et quae maior bonitas, quam illa, per quam a morte liberamur? Et quidem, nisi Adam peccaret, Redemptorum nostram carnem suscipere nostram non oporteret" (Pope Gregory the Great, *In librum primum regum,* IV, 7, in *Patrologiae . . . Latina,* ed. Migne, LXXIX, 222).

although thoroughly unworthy of it, proud and arrogant."[25] This is not a happy list.

The list from *Paradise Lost* is no happier, and the poetry of theology bears some resemblance to the dry prose of godly instruction. Adam and Eve are described as "destitute and bare / Of all thir vertue: silent, and in face / Confounded" (IX, 1062−64). Thus Milton uses here and in Book X the same terms in describing the Fall, and whether the description is set prior to Michael's instruction and the composition of the Bible (*Paradise Lost*) or subsequent to it (*De Doctrina Christiana*). His terms denote sin, calamity, loss, and alienation of the severest magnitude.

Milton obviously did not dispute the description of the Fall as *maior;* indeed, no other understanding is possible within standard Christian theology, since the redemption, turning history from the Old to the New Covenant, is the central action in the human journey. Too, the Fall must be crucial if only on the general grounds of equivalence. Milton's theology, however, and orthodox Christianity in general, do not equate importance with felicity. Thus the Fall cannot be called fortunate, at least from the perspective of Milton's ideas on freedom, necessity, and the nature of sin.

Milton is most emphatic about freedom, particularly the freedom of the human will. He amplifies the point by enunciating it in the very voice of God in Book III. Moreover,

> Foreknowledge had no influence on their fault,
> Which had no less prov'd certain unforeknown.
> So without least impulse or shadow of Fate,
> Or aught by me immutablie foreseen,
> They trespass, Authors to themselves in all
> Both what they judge and what they choose; for so
> I formd them free, and free they must remain
>
> (III, 118−24)

Milton's insistence on human free will, in all situations including salvation, as with "those who, when they may, accept not grace" (III, 302), is repeated three times and can hardly be doubted.

Humanity's radical free will has some interesting implications. If the human will is free even unto the uttermost, then the will of God must

---

25. John Milton, *De Doctrina Christiana*, Bk. I, in *Complete Prose Work of John Milton,* ed. Don M. Wolfe *et al.* (8 vols.; New Haven, 1953−82), VI, 383−84.

also be free. Moreover, the freedom of God's will must be greater than the freedom of mankind's, because God is greater than man, and this must be so even if, as Milton does, one defines radical free will as complete. Therefore, whatever the implications of freedom are when applied to God—and the pitfalls of equivocation only permit us to guess—they are obviously greater on the divine level than on the human. The freedom of the human will can be described as able to "accept not grace," but the freedom of God's will is beyond description and definition, for it is beyond language.[26]

The validity of this line of thought can hardly be doubted. If mankind's will is free but God's will is not, then mankind is greater than God, a manifest absurdity. The biblical position, on which Milton relied—on which all Christian theologians rely—is perfectly clear: "So God created man in his own image, in the image of God created he him; male and female created he them" (Gen. 1 : 27). The Creator and the created were clearly differentiated, and no philosopher or theologian would assert that the created was greater than or anterior to the creator. Furthermore, if one wishes to maintain that mankind's will was absolutely free but God's will was bound to the "mighty resurrection and glorious ascension" by the sin of man, then mankind the created would possess an attribute that God the Creator could not give because he did not have it. Placing God in the position of giving more than he had was not an idea likely to recommend itself to either Christian theology or Christian mythology. Nor did classical philosophy countenance such a possibility. The necessary, God, is always greater than the contingent, mankind.[27]

This reasoning may be directed against a further point: the notion that God *must* use the redemption of Christ as the repair for mankind's sin, a notion that is a clear corollary to the conception of God's will as bound

26. This holds even if, as Bennett argues, Milton subscribes like Richard Hooker to a God whose governing will is "consistent with His reason," which is accessible to men. See her *Reviving Liberty,* Chap. 1. What must be accessible for human salvation, like what does not offend the human sense of noncontradiction—even like what may be asserted or justified with Urania's inspiration—need not be conceived as All. Generally, Bennett's book should stand for this generation as the definitive treatment of freedom in Milton's prose and poetry.

27. We assume Milton's awareness of, and infer his agreement with, Aquinas' cosmological proof.

while mankind's is free. Is anyone really ready to accept the position that the absolute and unimaginable freedom of God's will *must* be limited by the repair that everyone is familiar with: that of the Son's putting on humanity and becoming the "full, perfect and sufficient sacrifice" for the sins of mankind? Is this the *only* solution possible for God? We argue that this corollary and therefore subsidiary description of the limitations on God's freedom is no more valid than the primary limitation can be, that is, than it can be that God's freedom is less than mankind's. Something other than the sacrifice and redemption of Christ may be unimaginable to mankind, but mankind's deficiencies do not bind God, nor even mankind necessarily, as Milton made clear in *Paradise Regain'd*. We suggest, therefore, that the most that can be said—and this is a wholly human proposition—is that the humanity, passion, and resurrection of the Son *may* (possibly) be the only solution to human sin that God can imagine. Just to state this proposition exposes one to ridicule, however, its logical consistency notwithstanding. Therefore, it seems to us that the position of "certain necessity," *certe necessarium,* advanced in the "Exultet," must, on every logical level, fail.

But what of the position advanced by Saint Augustine and Pope Gregory the Great? Here, we suggest, the *felix culpa* is much less vulnerable to charges of logical absurdity and theological contradiction. Pope Gregory the Great, writing of the *maior culpa,* rather than the *felix culpa,* did not assert the "certain necessity" whereby the divine will was bound either by mankind's will or by the requirement of the resurrection. The pope wrote, in the excellent translation by Lovejoy, that "unless Adam had sinned, it would not have behooved (*oporteret*) Our Lord to put on (*suscipere*) our flesh."[28] The argument here is from convenience rather than necessity. This may be doubted, but not disproved.

Pope Gregory also emphasized the idea that good would arise from evil: "Out of that evil which brought death, almighty God provided a good which would overcome that evil. What faithful believer cannot see how wonderfully the greatness of good excels evil? Indeed, great are the evils which we rightly suffer through that first fault, but who among the elect would not suffer worse evils than not to have such a redeemer?"[29]

---

28. Lovejoy, "Milton and the Paradox of the Fortunate Fall," 288.

29. "Ex illo malo, quo morituri erant, bonum quod malum illum vinceret, omnipotens Deus esse facturum providerat. Cuius profecto boni magnitudo, quis fidelis non vi-

The pope described the ultimate triumph of God's plan as the "good which will overcome evil" and which "excels evil." There is no suggestion that the redemption was *caused* by man's sin; rather, it was the occasion of repair. Pope Gregory the Great was far too good a theologian to commit an overt and clumsy fallacy of *post hoc, ergo propter hoc;* he clearly understood the important difference between causality and mere posteriority.

Saint Augustine, the patristic writer to whom Milton was theologically most akin, took a similar cautious line in discussing the *felix culpa.* In his *Enchiridion,* he wrote that when mankind sins, "yet by that very will of the creature whereby it does what the Creator did not will, it fulfills what He willed—God, as supremely good, putting even evils to good use." [30] The literal yet fluid translation of Professor Lovejoy shows the emphasis on the macrocosmic turning (*conversio*) of all things to God's purpose, including, of course, the *maior culpa* of initial sin. Causality, the major theological difficulty with the "Exultet," is neither explicit nor implicit in this passage. The emphasis is on the miraculous, and hence the mysterious. Indeed the subtle yet unmistakable implication of the thought of both Latin fathers ran precisely opposite to the causality usually implied in the concept of the *felix culpa.* Both Gregory and Augustine asserted that, on the macrocosmic level, the sin of mankind caused nothing but was only another occasion, like the fall of Satan, for the triumphant grace and will of God to prevail.

Milton evidently embraces this theological position. *Paradise Lost,* taken as a whole, maintains that ultimately nothing can derogate from divine truth and grace. Grace may be rejected, individually and for the moment; freedom demands that. In the end, however, humanity is redeemed, not because humanity sinned but because God is, by virtue of being God, the Redeemer. Milton specifically states this position in the very passage where the *"felix" culpa* is described by a fallen, dazzled Adam, in the exclamation (XII, 466–78), to which we return once more:

---

deat quam mirabiliter excellat? Magne quippe sunt mala, quae per primae culpae meritum patimur, sed quis electus nollet pejora mala perpeti, quam tantum Redemptorem non habere?" (Gregory the Great, *In librum primum regnum,* IV, 7, in *Patrologiae . . . Latina,* ed. Migne, LXXIX, 222).

30. "Sed quod voluit ipsa fecisset, etiam per eamdem creaturae voluntatem, qua factum est quod Creator noluit, impleret ipse quod voluit, bene utens et malis, tanquam summe bonus" (Augustine, *Enchiridion . . . de fide, spe et caritate,* C, 26, in *Patrologiae . . . Latina,* ed. Migne, XXXV, 279).

O goodness infinite, goodness immense!
That all this good of evil shall produce,
. . . and over wrauth grace shall abound.
(XII, 469–70, 478)

Milton both described and denied the *felix culpa* in a single poetic passage. For Milton, as for Gregory and Augustine, causality and necessity vanish. Milton replaced these with the grace that "over wrauth . . . shall abound." Metaphoric transfiguration supersedes metonymic conjuncture. This serves powerfully as yet another reminder, one of a series in the poem, that *Paradise Lost* is hermeneutic commentary on sacred text and is, above all, an epic about love.

Still, we are left with the problem of how the *felix culpa* has survived as a living part of Christian liturgy and theology since the time of the Merovingians. Its vigor and vitality must resonate with Christianity or, indeed, with secular life in general. We suggest two reasons for the idea's persistence and popularity, one involving the psychology of desire, the other having to do with the power of analogy. In each case, the symbolic or even semiotic view of life has transcended the logical.

The psychology of the *felix culpa* seems both simple and profound. Certainly this is true of the world view expressed by Saint Paul: "And we know that all things work together for good to them that love God, to them who are the called according to his purpose" (Rom. 8:28). Everyone wishes for the scales to be balanced, for good to come out of evil, for even the most hideous of men or events to advance, however distantly, the cause of good. If the "mighty resurrection and glorious ascension" is understood as the result of the "hideous ruin and combustion" (I, 46) of the Fall, the world not only makes sense but also offers comfort and consolation. The questions posed by Boethius are no different from those asked by the Book of Common Prayer's "company of all faithful people," and the idea of the *felix culpa* provides answers that cover the entire spectrum of faith, hope, and *caritas*. Nothing is more plausible than that the Fall should be thought of as fortunate.

The *felix culpa* also speaks with the authority of analogy. The idea that the Fall is fortunate is something of a paradox (Lovejoy's "look of a formal antinomy"). But paradox and antinomy are exactly the modes for describing God. The description the Bible gives is instructive, particularly inasmuch as Milton clearly believed it came directly from God: "And God said unto Moses, I AM THAT I AM" (Exod. 3:14). Saint Augustine also struggled with naming and describing what is utterly beyond human logical and linguistic resources. The Latin father used paradox as a way to hint at the "allness" and "otherness" of God: "He is the one true and perfect God, who never was not, never will not be . . . than whom nothing is more hidden, nothing more present."[31] Augustine admitted that this was far from being perfectly comprehensible, but he held that all we can do is "understand God, if we can, as far as we can."[32] He made another attempt: "being good without quality, great without quantity, a creator though he lacks nothing, governing but from no position, sustaining all things without having them, in his wholeness everywhere, yet without location, eternal without time."[33] All this, and even Augustine's best effort, that God can "be called his own deity"—this whole semiotic cloud—only reaffirms the need to see God through human paradox.[34]

If God must be defined and understood by paradox, then, by analogy, all the important mysteries of the faith must be so approached. Mindful of the aphorism generally ascribed to Tertullian, "Credo, quia absurdum," Christians were hardly unprepared to substitute paradox and belief for strict logic.[35] Analogy served where syllogism failed, and it brought all the mysteries and beliefs of the faith into a whole. The *felix culpa* was like the Eucharist or the resurrection; it could be described, believed, and understood concordantly with those great mysteries. It could be taken in. And so it was, in some personal, existential, and analogical sense, true and right.

We return to the starting point, to the language of faith. That lan-

---

31. "Unum Deum verum atque perfectum, qui nunquam non fuerit, nunquam non erit, nunquam aliter fuerit, nunquam aliter erit; quo nihil sit secretus, nihil praesentius" (Augustine, *De qualitate animae,* XXXIV, 77, in *Patrologiae . . . Latina,* ed. Migne, XXXII, 1077).

32. "Ut sic intelligamus Deum, si possumus, quantum possumus" (Augustine, *De trinitate,* V, i, 2, in *Patrologiae . . . Latina,* ed. Migne, XLII, 912).

33. "Sine qualitate bonum, sine qualitate magnum, sine indigentia creatorem, sine situ presidentum, sine habitu omnia continentem, sine loco ubique totum, sine tempore sempiternum, sine ulla sui mutatione mutabilia facientum, nihilque patentem" (*Ibid.*).

34. "Unus Deus, solus, bonus, magnus, aeternus, omnipotens, *ipse sibi unitas deitas,* magnitudo, bonitos, aeternitas, omnipotentia" (Augustine, *De trinitate,* V, xi, 12, in *Patrologiae . . . Latina,* ed. Migne, XLII, 919).

35. The aphorism "credo quia absurdum," though it expresses the meaning of the passage by Tertullian, is not accurate: "Mortuus est Dei Filius; prorsus credibile est, quia ineptum est" (Tertullian [Quintus Septimius Florentius Tertullianus], *De Carne Christi,* V, in *Patrologiae . . . Latina,* ed. Migne, II, 806).

guage is not, in this case, the Christian liturgy, but is, instead, Milton's poetry. The faith that Milton expressed in *Paradise Lost* about the *felix culpa* is twofold, and thus, for believers, twice blessed. It is, in the first place, faith that out of evil, even the ultimate evil of Satan's and humanity's double fraud, there must ultimately come good and there must come ultimate good. The circle remains always unbroken that lets "evil turn to good" (XII, 471). This was described by the voice of Adam as "more wonderful" (XII, 471) than the creation of "Light out of darkness" (XII, 473), with which it is coupled in explicit analogy. What may be seen in individual life though all too rarely—a good result from an evil intention—is by faith expanded to include the whole of God's creation and human history. Thus Milton's poetry covers the entire spectrum from macrocosm to microcosm, from God's eternal plan to a single human event, in a single analogy the variant details of which are supplied by the reader.

The language of faith was also applied by Milton to Adam himself, and through Adam to us all. Adam is made to stand "full of doubt" (XII, 473) whether he should repent of his sin or rejoice that after the sin came the passion and resurrection of the Son. He should, of course, stand on his mountain pinnacle assured of his need to do both, thereby making doubt the language of faith. The doubt properly applies not to love or faith in grace, but to form of explanation and articulation, to naming and knowing. Perhaps we should understand inconstant Adam as saying through the medium of doubt no worse than that he does not at that moment have the proper name to describe the wondrous gift of the Son, nor the capacity to know completely and logically its full implication.

So Milton dealt with the fortunate fall in a way that befits the ambivalence of the idea itself. Far too good a theologian to assert the logic of the *felix culpa* as systematic theology, Milton nonetheless acknowledged its enduring appeal as an illustration of the mystery and paradox of the faith. It thus became, for him, not truth in itself but a reflection of the great and central Christian truth that "over wrauth grace shall abound" (XII, 478).

ADAM AND EVE IN TRANSIT

In Augustine's *De doctrina christiana,* there occurs a phrase we have quoted previously because it seems so central to the Augustine who enabled Milton: "interpretation [that] leads toward the reign of love" (ad regnem caritatis interpretatio perducatur).[36] Let us concentrate on the word *ad,* "toward," and the sense of movement that it conveys. Humanity lives within time, constantly moving toward something, constantly becoming, constantly defining its being by reference to dynamism instead of stasis. Real movement, in space-time and in receptivity to grace, is not incidental to humanity but is of the very essence of human existence. Milton presents human movement as progressivist in the individual or cultural scale, but only in God's scale as meliorist. We believe that Milton was here following the systematic theology of Augustine, in which humanity finds life a constant choice, each instance of choice having implications with regard to salvation. We argue, too, that the constant movement of life is independent of fallenness: obedience is required as much in paradise as afterward, the will is free in both settings, and movement is the essence of life regardless of sin.

All this is seen within *Paradise Lost,* initially in the extended conversation between Raphael and Adam, in a section of the epic that might uncritically be called the initial education of Adam—uncritically because the exchange is totally unsuccessful in educating Adam. Early on, before the relation of the war in heaven and the creation of the universe, Adam gives assurances that he understands his duty:

> Yet that we never shall forget to love
> Our maker, and obey him whose command
> Single, is yet so just, my constant thoughts
> Assur'd me, and still assure
>
> (V, 550–53)

We do not doubt his good intentions. Adam promises to love God, and should that promise be kept, should his life be a prayer without ceasing, all will be well. Yet, everyone already knows better. Adam's will, which will be irreparably damaged in the Fall, is already weaker than his reason. Augustine's acute analysis of human weakness finds its echo in Milton.

Adam's love of God, which infallibly leads *ad regnem caritatis,* weakens substantially during the short span of Raphael's instruction. Though avowing that Raphael "largely hast allayd / The thirst I had of knowledge" (VIII, 7–8), Adam does not mean it. He follows pious reassurances with

---

36. Augustine, *De doctrina christiana,* III, xv, in *Patrologiae . . . Latina,* ed. Migne, XXXIV, 157.

an itchy question that reveals he has not understood Raphael well at all. He asks, in effect, whether God really knows what he is doing:

> When I behold this goodly Frame, this World
> Of Heav'n and Earth consisting, . . .
> How Nature wise and frugal could commit
> Such disproportions, with superfluous hand
> So many nobler Bodies to create,
> Greater so manifold to this one use
>
> (VIII, 15–16, 26–29)

Raphael is not pleased at this falling away from due love for God into a search to understand God's ways—not to admire them but to know them as God does:

> To ask or search I blame thee not, for Heav'n
> Is as the Book of God before thee set,
> Wherein to read his wondrous Works, and learn
>
> (VIII, 66–68)

Nonetheless, Adam should "Rather admire" (VIII, 75) than seek to scan God's secrets (VIII, 74), scanning implying computation if not indeed control, Raphael replies, and then proceeds to explain in such a way that Adam can neither understand nor admire. Adam as schoolmaster had lectured Eve, responding to her markedly less tendentious question (IV, 657) and showing ironic appreciation of cosmological constancy. Adam's response here is to go from bad to worse. "Cleerd of doubt" (VIII, 179), he replies that he is fully satisfied. He is, of course, neither satisfied nor in possession of a doubt-removing clarity. Nor could anyone else be. Milton could have provided Raphael with a clear explanation of the heavens; the Galileic account had been out for a generation, and the Ptolemaic for much longer, and both were clear. But the Bard chose otherwise. Raphael favors Adam with a muddled and confused explanation, and concludes it with an oral injunction:

> Think onely what concerns thee and thy being;
> Dream not of other Worlds, what Creatures there
> Live, in what state, condition or degree,
> Contented that thus farr hath been reveal'd
> Not of Earth onely but of highest Heav'n.
>
> (VIII, 174–78)

Raphael's injunction to Adam to return to the praise and love of God, and to ignore those things which do not lead to that end, gives the first hint of disobedience. Adam's lust for knowledge, much like that of Oedipus, can only lead downward to self-absorption, to an increasingly narcissistic concern with human power. If Adam is primarily concerned with knowledge rather than love, he will, inevitably, no longer "all temptation to transgress repel" (VIII, 643).

The Miltonic Adam and Eve, like the Miltonic Satan, always embody the tendency to move in the direction of incompleteness. It is the result of freedom; there is, in Milton's theological universe, no compulsion to love. Both in Satan and in Adam and Eve, the movement toward incompleteness instead of *ad regnem caritatis* appears first as physical separation from God, and in the case of Adam and Eve, from each other. Eve suggests to Adam, "Let us divide our labours" (IX, 214), making each separate from the other. The pair will be rendered incomplete. Adam thinks this is a bad idea, but he is not able to explain why convincingly. He can only say that Satan is subtle, "who could seduce / Angels" (IX, 307–308). But the answer, although true in itself, misses the point: that the couple apart love less completely than while together. This is true both spatially and existentially. Adam's famous quasi concession is the nub: "Go; for thy stay, not free, absents thee more" (IX, 372). He tempts her or distracts her with the power she has just expressed anxiety at not having in "narrow circuit" (IX, 323).[37] She can say she has won a concession. He

37. Here there is a cornucopia. According to Joan S. Bennett, Adam fails. See her "'Go': Milton's Antinomianism and the Separation Scene in *Paradise Lost*, Book 9," *PMLA*, XCVIII (1983), 388–404. F. Peczenik parses a reciprocity not before the Fall hierarchical, in "Fit Help: The Egalitarian Marriage in *Paradise Lost*," *Mosaic*, XVII (1984), 29–48. See also Joan M. Webber, "The Politics of Poetry: Feminism and *Paradise Lost*," *Milton Studies*, XIV (1980), 3–24. Largely parallel to this segment of our argument is Joseph Wittreich's "'John, John, I Blush for Thee!': Mapping Gender Discourses in *Paradise Lost*," in *Out of Bounds: Male Writers and Gender(ed) Criticism*, ed. Laura Claridge and Elizabeth Langland (Amherst, Mass., 1990), 22–54. He notes that the infamous phrase "shee for God in him" (IV, 299) indicates what *Satan* supposed he saw. Too late for use here was the elegant Aristotelian analysis in Debora K. Shuger's "The Temptation of Eve," in *Traditions and Innovations: Essays on British Literature of the Middle Ages and the Renaissance,* ed. David G. Allen and Robert A. White (Newark, Del., 1990), 187–99. In *Traditions and Innovations,* see also Kathleen Kelly, "Narcissus in *Paradise Lost* and *Upon Appleton House:* Disenchanting the Renaissance Lyric," 200–213. Kelly argues that Eve is *not* narcissistic at the pool, but is at the Fall, and Adam likewise. For a view irreconcilably

has pretended to a power not his: he cannot—to use the words of the Lady in *A Mask*—touch the freedom of her mind; only she can do that. At the same time, his love has turned inward: he is very close to saying, I can't stand you scowling instead of smiling at me. Eve's replies are equally true, and beside the point. She cites free will and argues from a Renaissance notion of affections of the will:

> thus to dwell
> In narrow circuit strait'n'd by a Foe,
> Suttle or violent, we not endu'd
> Single with like defence, wherever met,
> How are we happie, still in fear of harm?
>   (IX, 322–26)

In the end, Eve, like Adam before her, gets her way. Adam was instructed in astronomy, and Eve wanders off alone. Incompleteness, though not yet fallen, triumphs.

As yet, of course, incompleteness is still proleptic, still essentially imaginative and metaphorical, still a tendency rather than a fact. The Fall, the "rash hand in evil hour" (IX, 780), will transform incompleteness radically into a condition of further travel. That Adam also ate must be understood not as demonstrating great love for Eve but as manifesting excessive trust that human power, rather than divine love, can effect the cure. Adam fell into desperation, even despair—a symptom of radical retreat into himself, radical incompleteness, and radical disregard of God.[38]

---

at odds with the position that Milton honors Eve—the position variously argued in the articles just cited and by us throughout—see Christine Froula, "When Eve Reads Milton: Undoing the Canonical Economy," *Critical Inquiry*, X (1983), 321–47.

38. Irene Samuel observed a generation ago that Adam has the choice of offering himself as a ransom for Eve, to behave on a lower level analogously to the Son. Instead, he chooses—as we would put it—to reign below like Satan. See Samuel, "The Dialogue in Heaven: A Reconsideration of *Paradise Lost* III, 1–471," *PMLA*, LXXII (1957), 609–11. In accepting that, we disagree with one point in Maureen Quilligan's valuable "The Gender of Milton's Muse and the Problem of the Fit Reader," in *John Milton's "Paradise Lost": Modern Critical Interpretations,* ed. Harold Bloom (New York, 1987). Of Adam's actually "offered sacrifice," she supposes that "one may heretically suspect" that it "derives from the divinity within him for which Eve was made" (p. 131). This is more Romantic than heretical, perhaps, but still misconstrued, we judge. See in this connection Witt reich, "'John, John, I Blush for Thee!": Mapping Gender." Variously expansive on relationships of Adam to Eve and Eve to Adam, and Bard to both and to reader are Nyquist's

The immediate consequence of the double fall is carnality. Separated from the proper love for God, Adam and Eve, though together, are radically alone. Fallen, they can know nothing rightly, especially themselves and each other. Their incompleteness means that each now regards the other as an occasion for exercising power in response to appetite, not for acting continuously with the love of God. Adam's carnal attention is fixed "on Eve" (IX, 1013) in lust; the other's identity fades in the desirer's self-absorption. Carnality is soon joined by "guilt / And shame, and perturbation, and despair / Anger" (X, 112–14), and so forth—by all the characteristics that humanity recognizes as signposts of defective love and downward movement. The next chapter will look at the communicative dysfunctionality of such attributes with regard to naming and knowing when they are called to account, in Book X. At present the subject is their dynamism, their essential nature as becoming, which renders the deadly sins more than a mere state of existence. Milton lumps all of them together in a literal and emblematic moment of discovery, hideous moments of recognition of multiple sin capable of coming to anyone. Nonetheless, in the central moment (X, 110–11), he explains becoming and movement in terms of being. He was perfectly capable of distinguishing the condition of original sin from the transient sins of the moment, and of distinguishing the continuous self-recognition of fallenness from the discountenancings of the moment. Though theologically clear, the poetry of the Fall does have epistemological subtlety.

Beyond this, fallenness neither invents nor erases the interior movements toward and away from the love owed to God. After the Fall, of course, the journey toward love of God takes place in radically different

"Reading the Fall," 199–229, and "Gynesis, Genesis, Exegesis, and Milton's Eve," in *Cannibals, Witches, and Divorce: Estranging the Renaissance,* ed. Marjorie Garber (Baltimore, 1987), 147–208; John Shawcross' *With Mortal Voice: The Creation of "Paradise Lost"* (Lexington, Ky., 1982), esp. Chaps. 8, 10, 12; and Stella P. Revard's "Eve and the Doctrine of Responsibility in *Paradise Lost,*" *PMLA,* LXXXVIII (1973), 69–78. We would respond to Nyquist that any submission of Eve's "desire to the paternal will" ("Gynesis, Genesis," 203) is rendered by Uranic Bard in the mother tongue, not in patristic Latinity. For a focus of attention alternative to ours, with detailed attention to Satan in relation to power, and to the action in *Paradise Regain'd* and *Samson Agonistes,* see John M. Steadman, *Milton and the Paradoxes of Renaissance Heroism* (Baton Rouge, 1987). This is a hermeneutic reengagement, reinforcement, and advance on themes Professor Steadman has long studied—for example, in *The Hill and the Labyrinth: Discourse and Certitude in Milton and His Near-Contemporaries* (Berkeley and Los Angeles, 1984).

circumstances of sin and disobedience, though not of debt. Always it is the same: "of thine own have we given thee," as the Book of Common Prayer has it. But before the Fall, the interior movements toward and away also occur. For both Adam and Eve, knowledge obscures *agape*. Eve, psychologically driven by her evil dream to know and understand the nature of sin and Satan, seeks to know herself through single trial. She will obtain knowledge as a result of contact with Satan. The knowledge Adam seeks is about astronomy, less threatening than what awaits Eve—but he has had a less vivid initiation to the imagining of sin. The seductiveness of knowledge in *Paradise Lost* not only is biblically based, it seems also a personal Miltonic touch, a self-deprecatory tribute to Milton's own passion, a tribute that has in it a certain wry charm, like Donne speaking of his own "hydroptic thirst" for knowledge. It illustrates again Milton's basic view that all human activity ought to be conducted within an attitude of life as a prayer without ceasing.

The interior movements toward and away from loving God before all else appear first in the postlapsarian conduct of Adam and Eve when it seems that they will repeat the experience of Satan and the hosts of hell, whose motion, in Platonic terms rectilinear, was straight from heaven to hell in a nine-day fall.[39] Their first movement does not conform with Satan's proposal in Eve's dream of ascending "in the Air . . . to Heav'n" (V, 79–80). After the Fall, the interior motion is manifestly and inconclusively reciprocal between Adam and Eve:

> Thus they in mutual accusation spent
> The fruitless hours, but neither self-condemning,
> And of thir vain contest appeer'd no end.
> (IX, 1187–89)

Their fall—a journey to a false end or to no end—continues to the point that they consider suicide, with Eve proposing "Destruction with destruction to destroy" (X, 1006). But her suggestion is too much. Adam is prepared to wrangle with her endlessly and is intermittently willing to die with her but is not willing to die right then. He argues that death would provoke the Highest to worse punishment (X, 1020–28) and that, moreover, death only "cuts us off from hope" (X, 1043). Adam proposes to use the tools God has given, the capacity to work and bear children, as

---

39. See Thomas Ramey Watson, "God's Geometry: Motion in the English Poetry of George Herbert," *George Herbert Journal*, IX (1985), 17–25.

well as reason for the creation of knowledge. He argues that God will "instruct us praying, and of Grace" (X, 1081). Unlike Moloch, Belial, Mammon, or Beelzebub in Book Two, he proposes repentance:

> Thus they in lowliest plight repentant stood
> Praying, for from the Mercie-seat above
> Prevenient Grace descending had remov'd
> The stonie from thir hearts
>
> (XI, 1–4)

And so the flight away from God ends and the return to origins begins.[40] In Platonic terms, the motion of the human soul has turned from rectilinear to spiral. In Augustinian terms, the human soul, though severely damaged in will, memory, and reason, still has the possibility of ultimate salvation, of turning. But Milton renders *conversio* with intermittances, returns, and reinforced reconsiderations that both invite and enact the spiral of hermeneutic advance. The Miltonic *psychomachia* ends in victory, that is, in the triumph of faith, hope, and love (*caritas*) over multimeasured sin (X, 112–14), and so again whenever resung by the Bard—as at the end of *Paradise Regain'd*—or Bardically replayed in the mind of the audience. Whether the dialogue between Adam and Eve, a dialogue assisted by grace prevenient, is seen as history (contiguous events, metonymy) or metaphor, the result is the same. The human steps may be "wandring" and they may be "slow," but they are steps just the same.

40. See McMahon, *Augustine's Prayerful Ascent,* 118.

FIVE

Knowing and Naming: Adam, Eve, and Bard

In *Paradise Lost,* characters are defined primarily if not completely by their capacities—which, in the best Heraclitean mode, are their destiny. God is defined by his infinite capacity for love and generation. Satan, "Artificer of fraud" (*Paradise Lost,* IV, 121), who himself is hell, exhibits malice, cunning, hypocrisy, flattery, and deceit at all times and in all places. Adam and Eve are defined by their capacities—which means by their ways of naming and knowing. Both, of course, know partially through the body, and the poet makes little differentiation between them on that point, taken narrowly but generally. Separately, Adam knows within the epic primarily by discourse of reason (V, 487–88), largely from Raphael and Michael, but he is also the privileged recipient of an epiphany from God. Eve learns also by "process of speech" (VII, 178), but she understands even more by dream vision. She does not need to be told at great length; she understands even when she does not know. She sees less in detail but more in the whole. Thus differentiated, "our Grand Parents" (I, 29) cohere as "unfeign'd / Union of Mind, or . . . both one Soul" (VIII, 603–604), probably a Miltonic subsumption of the familiar story in Plato's *Symposium.* In any case, each is incomplete without the other.

Knowing and naming are not only major definitions of humanity, both before and after the Fall, they are also a central manifestation of grace. Grace, the outpouring of God's love, is experienced by humanity in several ways, faith being one of them, knowing and naming another. It is worth recalling that Milton's God describes himself as "I AM THAT I AM." The view of divinity associated with that was reinforced philosophically by the concept of the Great Chain of Being, and mythically by the story of Semele.[1] The otherness of God means that even the love of God must

1. The fundamental book on this topic remains Lovejoy's *The Great Chain of Being.* See also DuRocher, *Milton and Ovid,* esp. Chap. 2. See, conveniently, Ovid, *The Metamorphoses,* trans. Horace Gregory (New York, 1958), iii, 92–94; and Euripides, *The Bacchae,*

be experienced indirectly and in a manner suitable for humanity. That manner was, for Milton, divine grace.

The grace of God and the human capacity for knowing and naming operate, for Milton, within a context of radical free will. Humanity is totally free to disobey, refuse grace, know wrongly, and name badly.[2] Knowing and naming, of course, imply choice; there is more than one name for any object or event, more than one way of knowing and under-standing what life means. Knowing and naming as free choice are made explicit by Milton in his use of numerous names for God. The "sovran Presence" (X, 144), the "Paternal Deitie" (VI, 750), the "Supream of heav'nly Thrones" (VI, 723), the "Eternal King . . . Author of all being, / Fountain of Light" (III, 374–75) are all descriptions expressing a true and perfect part of God as perceived in the human imagination, all different and freely so according to the situation. Freely knowing and naming were, for Milton, appropriate for human dignity, as a reflection of God's love, and as a part of "daily work of body or mind . . . which *declares* his Dignitie" (IV, 618–19; our emphasis).

DREAM VISION

Ways of knowing, as distinct from what may be known, must be under-stood both by the category to which they belong and by their place within a hierarchy of value that indicates, but does not replicate, the Great Chain of Being. The categories of knowing in the Miltonic cosmos, in descend-ing order of value, are

1. Epiphany, in which a shining moment, etymologically a "showing forth" of the efficacious grace of God, illuminates the soul, thus changing it forever by adding the understanding of redemption.

---

trans. William Arrowsmith, in *The Complete Greek Tragedies* (4 vols.; Chicago, 1955–92), IV, 542–608. For a more extensive conception of the visionary than ours, see Michael Lieb, *Poetics of the Holy: A Reading of "Paradise Lost"* (Chapel Hill, N.C., 1981), and Joseph A. Wittreich, *Visionary Poetics: Milton's Tradition and His Legacy* (San Marino, Calif., 1979). Without disputing Milton's "prophetic" calling, we here explore and reassert the utility of separating that from *dream* vision as a way of knowing.

2. Bennett, although she does not discuss naming or generativity at length in *Reviving Liberty,* persuasively finds Milton's convictions on liberty no less radical than we do. Her demarcations by similarity (with Richard Hooker) and contrast (with almost everyone else) are particularly rich. See *Reviving Liberty,* Chap. 1.

2. Body, in which direct physical experience, such as sleep, bird-songs, rainbows, or "conjugal Caresses" (VIII, 56), can communicate when words fail.

3. Dreams, vision, intuition, in which one knows as a whole and as completely as mankind can, though the analysis of meaning may be delayed or withheld.

4. Discourse of reason, in which all the defects of signification, equivocation (philosophically meant), and incorrect inference arise, as well as the inherent problem of learning linearly and in part.

Within this Augustinian (and Platonic) hierarchy of knowing, the categories of dream, vision, intuition and of body occupy the intermediate rungs. They provide understanding more immediately and completely than does verbiage, but not necessarily in a way that is less confusing. In the first place, dream vision can lead down as well as up, away from God as well as toward him. Eve's first dream in *Paradise Lost* is a demonic vision, an instantaneous and confusing view of the varieties of evil. What is more, dream vision can be and usually is ironic, ambiguous, and Delphian; what is most clearly seen may be "hard to understand."[3] Thus, an intermediate level of knowing does not signify truth, nor does it mean that higher or more important things are being communicated. The way of dream, vision, intuition is higher and better solely because it enables us to transcend the limitations of space-time, to see comprehensively. With it, it is not necessary to wait until the end of an argument to grasp meaning; it is possible to be liberated from the linear, one-thing-at-a-

3. See McColley, "Eve's Dream." Attentive not to dream but to Milton's knowing and naming of all Eve's doings, Janet E. Halley argues for a partnerlike "heterosexual design" nonetheless governed by a "homosocial function." See her ironically titled "Female Autonomy in Milton's Sexual Politics," in *Milton and the Idea of Woman*, ed. Julia M. Walker (Urbana, Ill., 1988), 230–53. See, in the same volume, Marshall Grossman's closely woven argument of textuality and sexual difference as *différance*, in "Servile/Sterile/Style: Milton and the Question of Woman," 148–68. See also William Shullenberger, "Wrestling with the Angel: *Paradise Lost* and Feminist Criticism," *Milton Quarterly*, XX (1986), 69–85. For two psychoanalytic arguments differing from this and from each other, see Roger B. Rollin, "Milton's 'I's': The Narrator and the Reader in *Paradise Lost*," in *Renaissance and Modern Essays in Honor of Edwin M. Moseley*, ed. Murray J. Levith (Saratoga Springs, N.Y., 1976), 35–55; and Shari A. Zimmerman, "Milton's *Paradise Lost:* Eve's Struggle for Identity," *American Imago*, XXXVIII (1981), 247–67.

time constrictions of knowing discursively.[4] The way of dream, vision, intuition gives a hint of our fate, a moment of insight into the moral and intellectual meaning of our lives. But the moment is brief, the glimpse is ambiguous, the hint ironic. We hardly know what to think.

Dream vision, by the time of the Age of Iron, had become a tradition of Western culture in both sacred and secular learning. Within Holy Scripture, the visions of Revelation, Daniel, and Jacob, along with the cosmogony of Job, come readily to mind. In the secular tradition, there were Cassandra, the oracle at Delphi, Plato's vision of Er, the dream of Scipio in Cicero's *De re publica* and discussed in Macrobius' *Commentarius,* the *Roman de la rose,* and *A Midsummer Night's Dream*—and these are but a sample of the ubiquity of the dream vision in the Western intellectual tradition. Milton himself regarded the classical tradition as a dark glass and its poets as at best mere acolytes in the service of the revealed word of God, but the classical dream vision provides a clearer ingress for analysis than the scriptural, since it is unencumbered by the massive weight of chiliastic and messianic prophecy.[5]

Recall Cassandra in *Agamemnon,* crying out her vision of doom and ruin, not only for herself but for everyone. She sees at once the entire curse of the house of Atreus from first malefaction to final expiation. No one else can see it this way, of course, and so the leader and the chorus are confused by her ravings. They assume she is talking about her own death, but we in the audience, who have learned discursively what she understands intuitively, know better. More is meant; in a vision more is always meant.

---

4. On this point, see Augustine's theological view of multiple and simultaneous and overlapping dimensions of time, a view that demands an acute sense of hierarchy and is obviously compatible with the doctrine of the Great Chain of Being. See *The Confessions of Saint Augustine,* Bk. XI, Chaps. 13–28. See also Augustine, *Enarrationes in Psalmos,* XXXVIII, 7, in *Patrologiae Cursus Completus . . . Series Latina,* ed. J. P. Migne (221 vols.; Paris, 1844–1903), XXXVI, 419: "Isti ergo dies non sunt: ante abeunt pene, quam veniant, et cum venerint, stare non possunt: iungunt se, sequuntur se, et non se tenent. Nihil de praeterito revocatur: quod futurum est transiturum exspectatur; nondum habetur, dum non verit; non tenetur dum venerit. 'Numerum' ergo 'dierum meorum qui est.'" (Therefore these days are not, they are gone almost before having come and when they have come they cannot continue; they press upon and follow one another and cannot remain. Nothing of the past can be recalled and the expected future will pass; it is not yet had when not yet come, and when it has come cannot be kept. "What is the number of my days" [Ps. 39:4]).

5. See Cohn, *The Pursuit of the Millennium,* esp. Chaps. 5, 10, 11, 12.

Cassandra begins by calling on the source of her vision, Apollo:

> Aieeeeeee! Earth—Mother—
> Curse of the Earth—Apollo!
> . . . the house that hates god,
> an echoing womb of guilt

She goes on to describe the Furies, seen only by her in an interior vision that is superior to mere seeing or mere telling:

> These roofs—look up—there is a dancing
> troop that never leaves.
> . . . the Furies!
> They cling to the house for life. They sing,
> sing of the frenzy that began it all

From there, she turns to Agamemnon:

> so blind, so lost to that detestable hellhound
> who pricks her ears and fawns . . .
> No, he cannot see
> the stroke that Fury's hiding

Beyond the present murders, Cassandra sees that there

> Will come another to avenge us,
> born to kill his mother, born
> his father's champion. A wanderer, a fugitive
> driven off his native land

All this is told with expressions of pain, of rending and fire, of terror and compassion. The vision must give the sense of being direct experience, as Milton understood for Eve's first dream:

> If dream'd, not as I oft am wont, . . .
> But of offence and trouble, which my mind
> Knew never till this irksom night
>
> (V, 32, 34–35)

It is appropriate, thus, that Cassandra be described as "mad with rapture," and she herself shouts, "I know that odor. I smell the open grave."[6] The raw power of Hellenic tragedy was inappropriate for the philo-

---

6. Aeschylus, *Agamemnon*, trans. Robert Fagles (London, 1977), 1075–76, 1189–90, 1195–96, 1237–39, 1302–1305, 1333, pp. 145–57.

sophical treatises of Plato and Cicero, but the device of dream vision retained its usefulness. Ironically, systematic logical exposition may yield confusion, which analogy may attempt to resolve. Plato closed the *Republic* with the vision of Er, and his example was copied by Cicero in the "Somnium Scipionis," the final section of *De re publica*. In common with virtually all philosophical schools of antiquity, both Plato and Cicero viewed nature as a unity, clear when writ large, though often confusing and hidden in detail. The unity and fixity of nature underlay assurance about the consequent unity of knowledge and of the good, the cosmos possessing therefore the dual qualities of order and comprehensibility. Such a conclusion was certainly not incompatible with Milton's view of the entirety of being, in relation to God: "Immutable, Immortal, Infinite, / Eternal King; thee Author of all being" (III, 373–74).

Prophecy and philosophical explanation by story and analogy were also compatible with Christianity, in both its biblical and its extracanonical theological manifestations. In the late classical period, as intellectual life gradually assumed a Christian complexion, dream vision as prophecy and as auxiliary to philosophical explanation became largely fused with allegory. The philosophical basis for this was provided by Macrobius, in the *Commentarii in somnium Scipionis,* and by Fulgentius, in the *Mitilogarium libri tres*. In the first treatise the significance of dream vision was affirmed, and in the second the technique of giving a Christian allegorical gloss to pagan myth and story was advanced and its importance urged. Both passed into the general medieval culture, and the prophetic, philosophical, and allegorical dream vision became a Christian genre.[7]

The full flower of this genre can be seen in the *Roman de la rose,* by Guillaume de Lorris and Jean de Meun, which told the story of the fall of man in a way so vastly different from *Paradise Lost* that it requires an effort of scholarship to make the connection.[8] Through the *Roman de la rose,* we

---

7. See Kathryn L. Lynch, *The High Medieval Dream Vision: Poetry, Philosophy, and Literary Form* (Stanford, Calif., 1988), esp. Chaps. 2, 4. This book is essential for dealing with dream vision prior to Milton. On the dream of Scipio, see Marcus Tullius Cicero, *De re publica,* ed. K. Ziegler (Tübingen, 1969), 126–36. See Ambrosius Theodosius Macrobius, *Commentarii in Somnium Scipionis,* ed. Jacob Willis (Tübingen, 1953). See also *Macrobius, Commentary on the Dream of Scipio,* trans. and ed. William Harris Stahl (New York, 1952).

8. We have used the modern French translation: Guillaume de Lorris and Jean de Meun, *Le Roman de la rose,* trans. André Larly (2nd ed.; 4 vols.; Paris, 1973–75). See Edward Sichi, Jr., "Milton and the Roman de la Rose: Adam and Eve at the Fountain of

can see the Miltonic use of dream vision illuminated by contrast. In the earlier work, save for incidental reference, Adam and Eve do not appear. They, and their disobedience, are understood to be present, hidden behind the envisioned discourse of imaginary characters, who are allegorized virtues, vices, and characteristics undergoing a symbolic fall in the presence of a dreamer who is not within the dreamscape, which like other psychological settings has no "where."[9] At the level of *anagogia*, Eve is in the *Roman de la rose* as that element of *cupiditas* which may be described as an excess of ardor in the delight of the heart. She is not the rose but a wrongful—sinful—attitude toward the meaning of the rose, and thus has stronger affinities with Eve's dream (IV, 800–809) than to Eve herself in Milton's epic. Adam is in the *Roman de la rose* as the overthrow of reason that a consent to falling requires, not totally outside the Miltonic view, but theologically impoverished. The *Roman de la rose* belongs, of course, to a different age and a different view of the faith. With the earlier romance we are in the midst of the full richness of multilevel Catholic symbol and allegory, in which biblical themes are described in terms that are at once abstract, Platonic, metaphorical, and complex with multiple meaning. In such an intellectual environment, the biblical becomes theologized.[10]

Narcissus," in *Milton and the Middle Ages,* ed. John Mulryan (Lewisburg, Pa., 1982), 153–82. See also *The Romance of the Rose by Guillaume de Lorris and Jean de Meun,* trans. and ed. Charles Dahlberg (Princeton, 1971); Maxwell Luria, *A Reader's Guide to the "Roman de la rose"* (Hamden, Conn., 1982); John V. Fleming, *The Roman de la Rose: A Study in Allegory and Iconography* (Princeton, 1969); John V. Fleming, *Reason and the Lover* (Princeton, 1984); Heather M. Arden, *The Romance of the Rose* (Boston, 1987); Pierre Yves Badel, *Le Roman de la rose au XIVe siècle: Etude de la reception de l'oeuvre* (Geneva, 1980), esp. Chap. 7; Jean Batany, *Approches du "Roman de la rose"* (Paris, 1973), esp. Chap. 2; David Hult, *Self-Fulfilling Prophecies: Readership and Authority in the First Roman de la Rose* (New York, 1986); Joseph R. Davos, *A Concordance to the Roman de la Rose of Guillaume de Lorris* (Chapel Hill, N.C., 1975); and G. Paré, *Le Roman de la rose et la Scholastique courtoise* (Paris, 1941).

9. See the Introduction by Charles Dahlberg to *The Romance of the Rose,* trans. and ed. Dahlberg.

10. The visual metaphorical theology is as important for medieval Catholic culture as the literary. See Emile Mâle, *The Gothic Image: Religious Art in France of the Thirteenth Century* (1913; rpr. New York, 1958); Erwin Panofsky, *Studies in Iconography* (New York, 1939); Erwin Panofsky, *Abbot Suger on the Abbey Church of Saint Denis and Its Art Treasures* (Princeton, 1946); Otto von Simson, *The Gothic Cathedral: Origins of Gothic Architecture and the Medieval Concept of Order* (New York, 1956); and A. Katzenellenbogen, *The Sculptural*

For Protestant Christians drawing more inspiration from Scripture than from other literary or philosophical traditions, the appearance in the Bible of dreams and visions gave validity to the whole genre. What was biblical was, by its nature, anagogic, and the secular conventions were uncertain, even dim, reflexions of the Word. The Bible was full of dream visions, from the dreams of Pharaoh interpreted by Joseph, through the vision of Daniel, to the temptation of Jesus and the entire book of Revelation. Religious authority thus reinforced both a long Western cultural tradition and vivid and unforgettable psychological experience.

There are other explanations, beyond established literary and philosophical usage and biblical authority, for the appearance of the dream vision in *Paradise Lost*. There is the aptness dream visions have for representing boundlessness, and there is also the theatrical ambiguity characteristic of them. Both boundlessness and dramatic ambiguity typify the large, the complex, the important, and the transcendent. Since these are the stock stuff of literature and theology, the dream vision is always in style. That was particularly true during the Renaissance, when debate about metanarratives, such as those concerning salvation, love, or kingship, was combined with a continuing examination of the nature of reality, as, for example, in Don Quixote's experiences at the court of the duke and duchess.[11] In such an environment, the boundless and theatrical dream vision was practically perfect in every way.

The boundlessness of the dream vision has two complementary aspects: it consists of a culturally understood virtually infinite expansion of space-time and an equally expansive number and variety of things to fill space-time. In a dream vision, the absolute linearity of ordinary time is ruptured decisively, and the rupture is equally true of the continuity of space. In a

---

Programs of Chartres Cathedral: Christ, Mary, Ecclesia (Baltimore, 1959). Collectively, these fundamental studies have informed our view of medieval dream, vision, and allegory as represented spatially and taxonomically.

11. See Miguel de Cervantes Saavedra, *Don Quixote,* trans. J. M. Cohen (London, 1950), Pt. II, Chaps. 30–47. We see here the plasticity of reality. Does treating the Don as a real knight-errant make him one? Is Sancho a real governor? Do the enchanters really change things when we see them changed and acting upon the new appearances? There is no absolute answer to such questions, first raised by the Sophists—at least no answer that remains solely on the human level of the Great Chain of Being and ignores the salvific journey and divine grace. See also Jackson Cope, *The Theater and the Dream: From Metaphor to Form in Renaissance Drama* (Baltimore, 1973).

dream vision, it is not necessary to be somewhere and somewhen; it is possible to be everywhere and everywhen. The potential can be seen in *A Midsummer Night's Dream* as fairy time, dream time, and real time juxtapose themselves, overlap, and intermingle. The night in the woods is expansive, both synchronically and in terms of the events and images that fill it. Love, hate, pursuit, rejection, enchantment, merriment, mistake, wrath, envy, good luck, and human and transhuman bungling fill the varieties of time and dream. The effect is breathtaking. Time, that most implacable reality, is folded and stretched in order to make available the most delicate thing of all, good social order. Love, that most violent of human conditions, is affirmed, denied, parodied, and dramatized while modernity's increasing commodification of time is reversed, all to good effect. If the notions of time, order, and love that the play avails itself of were put to us in a straightforward narrative, we would rebel; in a dream vision they seem almost heartbreakingly charming and plausible.

The boundless is, as boundless, also ambiguous. We constantly ask, "Is the dream in us or are we in the dream?" [12] In the realm of reason we cannot tell; the dream state is always equivocal. In ordinary theater, with a willing suspension of disbelief, it probably does not matter; the play is the same either way. But in questions of theology it does matter. In the transfiguration of Jesus there is a serious difference between seeing a spectacle and participating in the naming of the Christ. The former is an act of human sensation, or perhaps, imagination; the latter, like participating in the Eucharist, is an act of grace. An analogous distinction pertains to Eve's first dream vision. Was it merely spectacle, or did Eve participate fully in the dream? Uncomprehending, Adam offers comfort and rationalization instead of prayer:

> be not sad.
> Evil into the mind of God or Man
> May come and go, so unapprov'd, and leave
> No spot or blame behind: Which gives me hope
> That what in sleep thou didst abhorr to dream,
> Waking thou never wilt consent to do.
> Be not disheart'nd then . . .
> So cheard he his fair Spouse, and she was cheard
>   (V, 116–22, 129)

12. José Ortega y Gasset, *Ideo del theatro* (Madrid, 1958), 69 (quoted by Cope in *The Theater and the Dream,* 16).

So ambiguous and so theatrical is the dream vision, so hard to understand, that interpretive help is needed. For Augustine and for Milton, there was only one thing that could bring order to disordered dream vision and lead to the narrow way and the strait gate. That was grace.

EVE'S VISION OF EVIL

Eve's way of knowing, in its native capacity, should be understood as having been the same as Adam's. Since she existed on the same level of being as he, it could scarcely have been otherwise. Raphael indicates that discourse was the normal way of knowing for both. But Eve's manner of knowing, like galaxies red shifted, was more concentrated at the higher levels, particularly in dream vision. Through this medium, Eve learned the most important things, most important to her and Adam, to us, to Satan, and perhaps (we in the Bard's audience are invited to consider) most important to God. Within the epic, Eve has two crucial dream visions, the first, in Book IV, when Satan introduces her to "offense and trouble" (V, 34), and the second, in Book XI, when Michael describes human futurity to Adam and Eve's eyes have been "drencht" (XI, 367) so that "dreams advise" (XII, 611).

In a necessary imitation of the Bible and Augustine's *Confessions*, we begin at the end and "return to the Origin," examining the second dream vision first.[13] It barely receives direct mention in the text. Eve is "let . . . sleep below" (XI, 367–68) and is "with gentle Dreams . . . calm'd" (XII, 595) until Michael is finished telling Adam about the checkered course of mankind. When Adam has taken in all he can, he utters one of his weightiest lines: "I now / Acknowledge my Redeemer ever blest" (XII, 572–73). Michael thereupon congratulates him and instructs him to wake Eve and tell her what he knows. But Eve already understands perfectly:

> Whence thou returnst, and whither wentst, I know;
> For God is also in sleep, and Dreams advise,
> Which he hath sent propitious
>
> (XII, 610–12)

---

13. We are indebted to Robert McMahon, in *Augustine's Prayerful Ascent*, for the term "return to the Origin" (p. 118). Like him, we adopt Said's distinction between transcendent *origin* and worldly *beginnings*, as reflected in Said's title *Beginnings*.

She instructs Adam to "lead on" (XII, 614); in her there "is no delay" (XII, 615). She accepts both blame and redemption:

> though all by mee is lost,
> Such favour I unworthie am voutsaft,
> By mee the Promis'd Seed shall all restore.
> (XII, 621–23)

Her composure is impressive. Her knowledge is complete. The "Redeemer ever blest" has spoken to her as surely as he did to Adam. She understands it all without knowing every detail.

One is left by the text to speculate on just what Eve does know, exactly. To be thus reduced to imprecise speculation is theologically appropriate, however, for dream visions can never be fully explained or communicated. At least, they can never be fully communicated *now*, after the Fall, after sin has clouded vision and grace prevenient is necessary even to know that one is supposed to turn to God. All of this was obvious to Milton. When the Son came to judge humanity, he found our "Grand Parents" were "discountinanc't" by looks of "hate, and guile" (see p. 48 above). Communication, possible only with love, can hardly penetrate that. But if we cannot know the details of Eve's second dream, it does not matter. We, at least, stand equal with Adam, and he, like us, can only be "Well pleas'd," even if he "answer'd not" (XII, 625). In the realm of postlapsarian redemptive grace, the dream vision, at its fullest, is the instrument of faith, and faith—many of the Reformers insisted—is the ground of obedience as love, and thus of salvation.

Eve's first dream vision is given far more extended treatment in the text. The dream vision is prelapsarian, and humanity is in a different state with regard to grace and communication. Before the *infelix culpa,* communication was open, with God, with angels, with nature, with each other.[14] Compare Adam's conversation with God and that of poor Job:

> Author of all this thou seest
> Above, or round about thee or beneath.
> This Paradise I give thee, count it thine
> To Till and keep, and of the Fruit to eat:
>
> .   .   .   .

---

14. For an extended discussion of the implications of the *culpa,* see pp. 80–91 above.

> But of the Tree whose operation brings
> Knowledge of good and ill, which I have set
> The Pledge of thy Obedience and thy Faith,
> Amid the Garden by the Tree of Life,
> Remember what I warn thee, shun to taste
>
> (VIII, 317–20, 323–27)

Could anything be clearer than that, or more unlike postlapsarian communication with God, which must pass through the filter of sin and be seen "through a glass darkly"? That clarity, as Satan quickly realizes, is vulnerable to mystification.

Moreover, Eve's dream vision occurs in the precise theological center of the epic, at that moment when the possibility of downward movement away from God and his love is opened to humanity. Eve is, with her dream vision, literally pregnant with history; if she does not taste the fruit, the instruction of Michael and the second vision will be unnecessary, to say nothing of all that follows. Her dream vision means that humanity's free will is to be genuinely tested, not merely by *ethos* and *logos* but by *pathos* as well, in a test of love. Will humanity really be "Sufficient to have stood" (III, 99), will man and woman be able to say, with Raphael,

> freely we serve,
> Because wee freely love, as in our will
> To love or not; in this we stand or fall
>
> (V, 538–40)

The importance and centrality of Eve's first dream vision is apparent from comparisons with the Bible. Of biblical dream visions, the temptation of Jesus bears the closest resemblance to the dream of Eve. In both dream visions, Satan is the tempter; in both, only grace permits an adequate defense, though right reason and obedient action give form to the defense. In both, too, the whole is shown all at once, but to fraudulent purpose. Dream vision is, apparently, a prized technique of Satan, both in what it presents and as a stratagem, the false coin of pretended love. We find Satan saying, "If thou be the Son of God, command that these stones be made bread" (Matt. 4:3). The devil, "taking him up into an high mountain, shewed unto him all the kingdoms of the world *in a moment of time.* And the devil said unto him, All this power will I give thee, and the glory of them" (Luke 4:5–6; our emphasis). Satan challenged Christ, saying, "If thou be the Son of God cast thyself down: for it is written, He shall give his angels charge concerning thee" (Matt. 4:6). This was not hard to understand, nor was it a philosophical summation or an allegory of the fall of humanity or of death in any form. The temptation, though adapted to the human capacity for knowing, as was right for the human nature of Jesus, still differed fundamentally from all other dream visions. It involved, proved, and ultimately confirmed a condition of sinlessness and obedience that could not be damaged. The temptation is redemptive, and thus a symbol of the gracious restoration of intuitive knowing to humanity. There is also in the temptation of Jesus the unmistakable implication that discursive knowing will be healed. For biblical Christians, the healing of words by the Word was unquestionably betokened. On Milton, as particular heir to the line, the idea of the Son's redemptive obedience in response to "all temptation" (*Paradise Regain'd*, I, 5) made so forcible an impression as to occasion his last epic, and we shall consider his concluding elaborations on the theme in Chapter Seven.

The similarities between the temptations and techniques practiced on Jesus and those employed on Eve in her first dream vision are remarkable. That is theologically appropriate, for Eve was still untouched by sin and Christ was by nature sinless. Power, the prospect of improving on God's work, and the acceptance of something lesser to love ahead of God all figure in what is offered to Eve. They are offered as truth, which they are not, and the sin is therein artfully concealed. Both dream visions are the perfect picture of sin: fraud, a power coup masked as love, and abandonment concealed behind pretended gain.

This is all made perfectly clear by the Bard in his narrative description of Eve's dream vision. Satan sat,

> Squat like a Toad, close at the ear of *Eve*,
> Assaying by his Devilish art to reach
> The Organs of her Fancie, and with them forge
> Illusions as he list, Phantasms and Dreams,
>
> . . . .
>
> At least distemperd, discontented thoughts,
> Vain hopes, vain aimes, inordinate desires
> Blown up with high conceits ingendring pride.
> (*Paradise Lost*, IV, 800–803, 807–809)

He, like "L'Allegro"'s *Zephir,* "Fill'd her" ("L'Allegro," 23). Although interrupted by Ithuriel, Satan is still able to impart his essential message, introducing Eve to imaginative pride and discontent and to the consideration, though not yet the enactment, of evil.

The consideration is terrifying enough, even if, in Milton's view, it is not yet sin itself: terrifying to Eve on waking, to the Bard, potentially to readers as well. The next morning, when Eve recounts the dream to Adam, he is sympathetic yet essentially uncomprehending "of offence and trouble, which [Eve's] mind / Knew never till this irksom night" (*Paradise Lost,* V, 34–35). It would verge on spatializing to say that the angelic discovery in Book IV and Eve's complaint to Adam *frame* the dream as she tells it. A better description is that the dialogue in heaven, the description of unfallen paradise, and Eve's remonstrance against "offence and trouble" offer hermeneutically successive redefinitions of the dream—as do the dispatch of Raphael, his message, the Fall in Book IX, and the dispatch of Michael and his message, subsequently. Satan, who will not acknowledge that, like the moon, he can shine only by reflected light, employs to quintessentially sinister purpose the fallen human literary *topos* of the *locus amoenus.* And he characteristically reveals himself to be fallen, if not to Eve: Is a love song properly "labor'd"? (V, 41). Does *sweetest* herald decay? Does the allegedly "more pleasing light" (V, 42) that "Shadowie sets off the face of things" (V, 43) highlight those things or obscure the truth? Within Christianity, beauty is not the same as truth: grace fills that role, whereas beauty, Janus-like, faces both ways. Satan, who lacks all innocence and beauty himself, is clearly able to recognize both in others, as Uriel has discovered. Eve, thus trusting, cannot tell the song from the shadow.

Eve's dream vision moves her swiftly to the "Tree / Of interdicted Knowledge" (V, 51–52), which she recalls as seeming "Much fairer to my Fancie then by day" (V, 53). Again there are the interrelated themes of concealment, the seeming rational plausibility of sin, and its affective attractiveness, including the appearance of safety. Concealment and even olfactory plausibility extend to Satan himself, "shap'd and wing'd like one of those from Heav'n / By us oft seen; his dewie locks distill'd / *Ambrosia*" (V, 55–57). Her naïve word *like* arrests us: exactly alike, yet no longer very like, not morally. For Milton's Bard, the *like* of simile in fallen naming always insists on the possibility of baneful or grace-filled difference.[15]

---

15. See MacCaffrey, *"Paradise Lost" as "Myth,"* Chaps. 4, 5. In *Naming in Paradise,* Leonard provides many acute readings of particular speeches which we see as supportive.

There is nothing so far in the dream vision that might reasonably have alerted Eve to the true nature of her imaginative, and proleptic, experience.[16] Untutored by sin, she discerns no hypocrisy. Moreover, things, even shadows and night, are not in themselves evil, though they may have unlovely metaphorical connotations for us. Their role as metaphorical holders of evil comes from the experience of fallen mankind, not from the object itself. It is attributed, not inherent. The things of nature, as Psalm 19 and many another biblical text instructed Milton, are the products of God's love and generativity.

Everything is to change quickly, of course, as we know but Eve does not. Within the dream vision, Satan spends no time on the unessential. He immediately addresses the tree and Eve, praising both with discourse proper only to the divine, and therefore, *in se,* blasphemy and an invitation to pride:

> is Knowledge so despis'd?
> *Or* envie, *or what* reserve forbids to taste?
> Forbid *who* will, *none* should from me withhold
> Longer thy offerd good, *why else* set here?
>
> . . . .
>
> O Fruit Divine,
> Sweet of thy self, *but* much more sweet thus cropt,
> Forbidd'n here, it seems, *as onely* fit
> For Gods, *yet* able to make Gods of Men:
> *And* why not Gods of Men, *since* good, the more
> Communicated, more abundant grows,
> The Author not impair'd, *but* honourd more?
> (V, 60–63, 67–73; our emphasis)

After the prideful equation of man to God in eating the fruit comes the apostrophe to Eve, who is already declared "Angelic" (V, 74), someone who could be a "Goddess" (V, 78), and to power more than human. Here and in what follows, the theological appeal to pride—"Gods of Men,"

But the names Satan (from the Hebrew verb "to bear a grudge, to cherish animosity") and Lucifer ("light bringer," to God rather than to himself, despite himself)—*both* subsequent, as Leonard observes, to Satan's erased name—are likely names; Leonard has the bad news without the good news.

16. For our purposes, the indispensable article on Eve's first dream is McColley's "Eve's Dream."

"angelic" Eve—has political and psychological dimensions. There is the invidious and activist appeal to power—"none shall from me" (V, 62), "Ascend" (V, 80)—as well as the political and rhetorical appeal to it, in which linear, analytic syntax is a power game of marshaling conditionals, disjunctions, and concessions for intellectual control and coercion. Love of God—expressed as obedience—is to be set aside in favor of power. The same is true for the love of Adam. Psychologically, any love is to be turned inward, toward narcissism, as Satan's has been. Perhaps Milton conceived the existential turn from love to self-empowerments like narcissism as a quasi-Aristotelian formal cause of falling:

> Here, happie Creature, fair Angelic *Eve,*
> Partake though also; happy though thou art,
> Happier thou mayst be, worthier canst not be:
> Taste this, and be henceforth among the Gods
> Thy self a Goddess, not to Earth confind
> But somtimes in the Air, as wee, somtimes
> Ascend to Heav'n, by merit thine, and see
> What life the Gods live there, and such live thou.
>
> (V, 74–81)

Here is an echo of Eve's first narcissism, the sight of her reflection in a pool, where she had seen

> answering looks
> Of sympathie and love; there I had fixt
> Mine eyes . . . and pin'd with vain desire
> (IV, 464–66)

This innocent incident gave Satan, with "jealous leer maligne" (IV, 503), a hint of just which weakness to probe for in Eve.

Satan's speech contains an appeal to Pelagianism, a doctrine that denied original sin, the human necessity of grace, and affirmed that man might achieve salvation by his own efforts.[17] This doctrine, condemned at the Council of Orange in 529, is clearly contrary to life as we live and observe it, but Satan's enunciation of it cannot be taken as unequivocal evidence

---

17. See Pagels, *Adam, Eve, and the Serpent.* An older treatment can be found in B. B. Warfield's *Studies in Tertullian and Augustine* (New York, 1930), Chap. 5. The relevant Latin is "libertas ad peccandum et ad non peccandum."

of his capacity for lying and his intent to deceive.[18] At the time when Satan declares that Eve might achieve her own salvation, this is true, as Raphael shortly informs Adam:

> And from these corporal nutriments perhaps
> Your bodies may at last turn all to Spirit,
> Improv'd by tract of time . . .
> If ye be found obedient
>
> (V, 496–98, 501)

Satan, as Pelagian, and therefore heretical, is presenting darkness, but only proleptically. The Fall and *nox* can occur and have meaning only if Eve eats the fruit.

Eve's dream vision takes a sharp and radical turn when, on the point of tasting, which in a dream vision she could not really do, she is suddenly whisked into the sky, where Satan opens to her a "prospect wide / . . . this high exaltation" (V, 88–90). When the dream vision ends, Ithuriel appears and Eve falls asleep, later to awaken and tell Adam, who can worry and attempt to comfort but cannot comprehend.

The final incident of the dream vision brings us back to the theological starting point, the biblical presentation of the temptation of Christ. Both Eve and Jesus were carried to a high place and shown the world. Both were offered power on a condition that was utterly inappropriate. And everything connected with the offer was false. The world was not Satan's to give, nor did he have any power, nor was Eve a goddess, nor was the Son of Man supposed to be a secular king or a magician. The prophecy read, "He is despised and rejected of men; a man of sorrows, and ac-

---

18. The decision of the Council of Orange in 529, which emphasized and enlarged the teaching of the Synod of Arles, of 473, provided a definitive and Augustinian critique of the Pelagian doctrine. A report on the Synod of Arles can be found in Faustus of Rhegium's *Epistola ad Lucidum,* in *Patrologiae . . . Latina,* ed. Migne, LIII, 683. For the Council of Orange, see J. D. Mansi, *Sacrorum Conciliorum Amplissima Collectio* (31 vols.; Florence and Venice, 1759–98), VIII, 712–20. Although the synod and the council were largely forgotten as historical events, the Augustinian doctrines, as Pagels has pointed out, entered the basic Christian moral and theological culture. The sharply defined Augustinian doctrines of fallenness, total human depravity, and the absolute need for grace—as seen in the TULIP of the Canons of Dort, for example—formed a fundamental part of the Puritan faith that many critics have attributed to Milton. Milton, we argue, changed the emphasis within this theological context from punishment to love and salvation, while retaining the Augustinian emphasis on grace.

quainted with grief: and we hid as it were our faces from him; he was
despised, and we esteemed him not. Surely he hath borne our griefs, and
carried our sorrows: yet we did esteem him stricken, smitten of God,
and afflicted" (Isa. 53 : 3−4). In both temptations the technique of falsity
and the emptiness of Satan are similarly described. Milton thus reconsti-
tutes the biblical doctrine that the ways of the Lord may be infinite but
deception is the same always.

If the similarities between the temptation visions are remarkable, the
large differences between Book V and Scripture in the treatment of Eve's
temptation are also striking. In Genesis, there is much talk of death and
no hint of dream vision. The knowing and the selective attention to what
one knows are entirely discursive. The dream vision appears to be a Miltonic refinement in understanding, representation, and ontology. The explanation lies in Milton's theological position, which separates uncommit-
ted thought from sin. For him, imagination is not sinful, though it may
well be troubling. Evil lies in the doing, which may include embracing
the fantasy, as Adam sees in Book V but takes too blithely, as Book IX
shows. The distinction in culpability between imagining and doing is
implicit in Adam's phrase "so unapprov'd" (V, 118). The dream vision is
the perfect vehicle for making that distinction. Satan is doing evil, Eve
is only imagining and relating it. In a dream vision, imagination can
include the fullness of feeling, the whole sense of horror, the entire dimension of pathos. It can also include the act of Satanic deception entire
and immediate. Thus for Milton, dream vision, at the edge of the human
capacity for knowing and hard to understand, stands at the origin of the
infelix culpa and at the end of innocence.

ADAM'S EPIPHANY

Eve's dream vision is not the only one in the epic. There are two others,
one experienced by the Bard himself and the second an epiphany to Adam.
These dream visions, though less central to the unfolding of human disobedience than Eve's, are no less important to the epic or to our proper
understanding of it as members of the fit audience.

Adam's epiphanic dream vision is difficult to analyze, or even describe,
since the poetic boundaries of the event are hard to find. Nonetheless,
within its limits, liberally set, several important things occur. The dream
vision begins with God speaking to Adam:

> thy mansion wants thee, *Adam,* rise,
> First Man, of Men innumerable ordain'd
> First Father, call'd by thee I come thy Guide
> To the Garden of bliss, thy seat prepar'd.
> So saying, by the hand he took me rais'd,
> And over Fields and Waters, as in Air
> Smooth sliding without step, last led me up
> A woodie Mountain; whose high top was plain,
> A Circuit wide, enclos'd, with goodliest Trees
> Planted, with Walks, and Bowers, that what I saw
> Of Earth before scarse pleasant seemd. Each Tree
> Load'n with fairest Fruit that hung to th' Eye
> Tempting, stirr'd in me sudden appetite
> To pluck and eat; whereat I wak'd
>
> (VIII, 296–309)

The call of the dreamer for guidance in this dream vision is in sharp and total contrast to the picture of evil painted for Eve by Satan. Adam is not given an alluring picture of evil, which is the repudiation of the "Garden of bliss," but is rather shown the garden itself. The comparative *seemd* of "scarse pleasant seemd" contrasts poignantly with seemings in fallen-world Miltonic settings, as with those of Spenser and Shakespeare. This seeming is innocent: valid revaluation in retrospect. Adam, here, is raised to an inner height, and can see paradise whole, as only a dream vision can allow. It is a vision of comfort.

At this point the dream vision appears to end, though the epiphany continues. Speaking again, God warns Adam of dearth and death:

> Knowledge of good and ill, which I have set
> The Pledge of thy Obedience and thy Faith,
> Amid the Garden by the Tree of Life,
> Remember what I warn thee, shun to taste,
> And shun the bitter consequence: for know,
> The day thou eat'st thereof, my sole command
> Transgrest, inevitably thou shalt dye
>
> (VIII, 324–30)

This dread caution was delivered to an apparently wakeful Adam, for our "First Father" goes on to name animals and ask for Eve. God replies that he is pleased to find Adam "Expressing well the spirit within thee free" (VIII, 440), and he agrees to Eve's creation, in the biblical fashion, from

Adam's rib. The creation of Eve, Adam's other self, occurs within a second dream vision:

> Mine eyes he clos'd, but op'n left the Cell
> Of Fancie my internal sight, by which
> Abstract as in a transe methought I saw,
> Though sleeping, where I lay, and saw the shape
> Still glorious before whom awake I stood
>
> (VIII, 460–64)

In Adam's case, unlike Eve's, the line between wakefulness and dream vision is indistinct and difficult to find. We assume that Adam moves easily back and forth between waking and dream states, the difference between the two being psychologically blurred by the fact of epiphany. The ultimate reality is, of course, God; both faith and experience, such as baptism by the Holy Ghost, combine to confirm this. The Bard has, thus, poetically put us within Adam. We are invited to experience through description, albeit in an impoverished way, what Adam felt: the overwhelming presence of God that obliterates merely mundane differences.

If Adam's exact state—of wakefulness or of sleep—is unclear, the message from God is not. God's message to Adam is love. Divine love is shown in the very talking with Adam, in the great gift of paradise, in the greater gift of the creation of Eve and through her of humanity itself, and in the warning against disobedience. The outpouring of God's love and grace in Adam's dream vision and epiphany makes his experience the polar opposite of Eve's. Eve experiences *nox* in the form of malign and devilish hate, whereas Adam is given a glimpse of *lux* in the form of God's generativity. Theologically and psychologically, it is Adam's disobedience that is truly monstrous, for he is much better prepared than Eve to obey, yet he falls willingly, miserably and consciously. Eve is tricked; Adam bungles. Milton does not say this explicitly. His presumptively Christian readers are left to ferret it out themselves, left to liberate themselves from the prevailing views of the moral inferiority of women, left to overcome the psychological consequences of the Pandora legend, and the line of Jerome through Rome, and any more localized antifeminisms apparent to Milton or to them. The striking qualitative disparity between the dream visions of Adam and Eve indicates to us that Milton saw a disparity in the capacities of the two, and that Eve's was the greater.

BARDIC SEEING AND SAYING

We as readers may catch, and reflect upon, what Adam and Eve say to each other, what is explicit and implicit in that. But that is rarely possible for long, because the Bard repeatedly reminds us that their utterances are situated in a framing context of knowing and naming: they are naming, and they come to us by Bardic or Bardic-Uranial transmission. Hence, the reader of *Paradise Lost* is constantly redirected from passages of text to questions about the conditions of saying what they say, from the culturally and straightforwardly lexical to the theoretical and, hence, problematical. The text exhibits, and invites us to, hermeneutic recirculation.

The Bard's own dream vision, which he twice describes briefly, carries the inspiration for the entire epic. Bardic speech, as we have been calling it—hitherto with little justification—reminds us of the need to communicate, a need familiar and difficult here in the middle of the fallen world of "evil dayes . . . and evil tongues . . . darkness, and . . . dangers . . . And solitude" (VII, 25–28). Fallen neediness begets the familiar questions intrinsic to life: Where is the good in our days? What illumination of truth can be had? How may tongue rightly proclaim the good and the true? And, first and last, Wherein is love? These questions may be thought to imply or at least require answers, but they do not necessarily yield any that are satisfactory or encouraging. Even a Bard who convincingly asserts eternal providence and decisively justifies the ways of God to man, thereby transcending solitude, has no answers that are conclusive like the solutions to chemical equations. Milton, in creating the most commanding Bard in the English language (in, but enlarging, that language) achieves answers that by the constraint of fallen worldliness are hermeneutic and dialogic subtotals, indefinitely successive, never monologically conclusive.

To put it more explicitly in terms of the literary tradition, he pushes the status of epic bard and the question of theodicy to a point extreme as dialogic, even as he amplifies and extends other epic possibilities or conventions, especially the convention of beginning in the middle of things, *in medias res*. The middleness, as we have argued, is of several framing sorts, and the paradox is necessary. The Bard is, by reason of the inconclusive and dynamic nature of fallen living, in the middle between question and answer for his fit audience. He has composed in the middle, not only between question and answer, but with Platonic awareness of being between birth and death, with Christian awareness of being between personal birth and rebirth, and with cosmic awareness of being between primordial origin (*arche*) and the end of the world as both *telos* and *eschaton*. His own strongest affirmations, moreover, by the nature of the historicity informing them, imply newly aware and accordingly readjusted reiterations of the "Name . . . the copious matter of [his] Song / Henceforth" (III, 412–14). And so it must be with the engaged reader or auditor experiencing the Bardic dialogue and rearticulating it in the contexts of new experience. For "Knowledge is as food," Raphael insists (VII, 126), and it must hence be partaken as long as life is to last.[19] Bard and audience, at table or between meals, are always in the middle of the human feast of understanding. The Bard, moreover, engages the audience with himself and Urania in the middle of the tradition of epic *historicized* by textuality, and in a *generic* middle: inspired epic—notwithstanding from mouth of fallen Bard—between a prelapsarian Edenic pastoral of transcendent fulfillment and the ironic simplifications of fallen pastorals.

It is another transcendence of literary precedent, of course, that the Bard's "Song . . . with no middle flight intends to soar / Above th' *Aonian* Mount" (I, 13–15), and so to rise above the classical middle style and pagan subject matter and, indeed, above classical heroic style and matter. Milton moves in the vaster middle between highest heaven, where "Dark with excessive bright" (III, 380) the skirts of God appear, transcending even the Uranially inspired imagination, and the ever deteriorating pit of "bottomless perdition" (I, 47) with "no light, but rather darkness visible" (I, 63). Doing so, he answers the questions about eternal providence and God's ways within time. He answers these questions in terms of love. If theodicy could not be understood in terms of love, it would be understood in terms of harshness or abuse, and returned in kind. Even more desperately, it would be understood as absence, as some hideous myth of Moloch or Belial or Mammon or Beelzebub—some disgraceful myth of power. The transcendence of epic convention and the need to understand and

19. Raphael's insistence on "Temperance over Appetite" (*Paradise Lost*, VII, 127) is an interesting but subordinate point. For a delectable exploration of it, see Maggie Kilgour, *From Communion to Cannibalism: An Anatomy of Metaphors of Incorporation* (Princeton, 1990), esp. Chap. 3. See also Jacques Derrida, *Writing and Difference*, trans. Alan Bass (Chicago, 1978), 228.

communicate meet at love, and thus give the Miltonic dialogue its sense of the presence of the Logos.

We conceive Miltonic dialogue as voice, that is, as presence, and as text, that is, as persistence, and as both together. That duality is meta-dialogic in two senses: as being about dialogue, and *as* participating in the transcendent and endless resonance of grace that makes a unity out of the welter of petty text—oral, written, or otherwise material—constitutive of dialogue.[20]

With regard to speech and writing, there is the mysterious figure of Urania, who visited Milton in "slumbers Nightly" (VII, 29), and who sang "Celestial Song" (VII, 12) with her sister "Eternal wisdom," the *hagia sophia* (VII, 9). She occasions the confluence in a single passage of all of the voices in *Paradise Lost,* from God to that analogously unheard and unseen chorus, the fit audience:

> Descend from Heav'n *Urania,* by that name
> If rightly thou art call'd, whose Voice divine
> Following, above th' *Olympian* Hill I soar,
> Above the flight of *Pegasean* wing.
> The meaning, not the Name I call:
>
> . . . .

---

20. For particularly relevant elaborations and alternatives, see Anne Ferry, *Milton's Epic Voice: The Narrator in "Paradise Lost"* (Cambridge, Mass., 1963; rpr. Chicago, 1983); Ong, *Orality and Literacy;* and Ong, *The Presence of the Word.* For the by now current poststructuralist argument, see, for notable example, Jacques Derrida, *Of Grammatology,* trans. Gayatri Spivak (Baltimore, 1976); Derrida, *Writing and Difference;* Jacques Derrida, *Dissemination,* trans. Barbara Johnson (Chicago, 1981); and Jacques Derrida, *Margins of Philosophy,* trans. Alan Bass (Chicago, 1982). Not primarily concerned with textuality but provocative with regard to a Bard "freed by defeat to assume the prophet's posture of divinely inspired alienation" between God and the alien people is Richard Helgerson's *Self-Crowned Laureates: Spenser, Jonson, Milton, and the Literary System* (Berkeley and Los Angeles, 1976), esp. 250–80, p. 254 quoted. And see Martz, *Poet of Exile,* esp. 79–94. For a provocative dark offshoot of this line of reflection, see William A. Sessions, "Abandonment and the English Religious Lyric of the Seventeenth Century," in *Bright Shootes of Everlastingnesse: The Seventeenth-Century Religious Lyric,* ed. Claude J. Summers and Ted-Larry Pebworth (Columbia, Mo., 1987), 1–19. For a very substantial version of the argument, less dependent on alienation, see William Kerrigan, *Prophetic Milton* (Charlottesville, Va., 1974). See also George de F. Lord, "Milton's Dialogue with Omniscience in *Paradise Lost,"* in *The Author in His Work: Essays on a Problem in Criticism,* ed. Louis L. Martz and Aubrey Williams (New Haven, 1978), 31–50; and E. R. Gregory, "Three Muses and a Poet: A Perspective on Milton's Epic Thought," *Milton Studies,* X (1977), 35–64.

> Standing on Earth, not rapt above the Pole,
> More safe I sing with mortal voice, unchang'd
> To hoarce or mute, though fall'n on evil dayes,
> On evil dayes though fall'n, and evil tongues
> (VII, 1–5, 23–26)

She "inspires / Easie [his] unpremeditated Verse" (IX, 23–24) by giving illuminated significant sights or even written signs, articulated by eyes planted inwardly (III, 53), verse that is then to be sung in the theater of our minds. Voice is summons to belief, as Walter J. Ong has put it for our generation, and any poetic or discursive text carries compelling suggestions of voice.[21] As John Donne expressed it in a letter to the countess of Montgomery, accompanying a sermon he had preached before her, and at her "commandment" written out,

> I know what dead carkasses things written are in respect of things spoken. But . . . the Spirit of God that dictates them in the speaker or writer, and is present in his tongue or hand, meets himself again (as we meet ourselves in a glass) in the eies and eares and hearts of the hearers and readers: and that Spirit, which is ever the same to an equall devotion, makes a writing and a speaking equall means to edification.[22]

Thus, more fundamental than distinctions between speech and writing for serious seventeenth-century writers were grace, presence, and persistence. Presence is a function of love, as common experience attests. For Milton, love is identical with grace at the divine level and intimately related to grace at the human level of *devotion,* and it may be opposed by the lies, disdain, obscurity, and indifference associated with the absence of grace—to which common experience likewise attests. But lies and indifference, though obscuring the divine voice and muting its presence, are, for Milton, ultimately powerless. The dialogue continues anyway:

21. Walter J. Ong, "Voice as Summons to Belief," in *Literature and Belief,* ed. M. H. Abrams (New York, 1965), 80–105. On the feminine aspects of Urania, see Stevie Davies' excellent and provocative *The Feminine Reclaimed: The Idea of Woman in Spenser, Shakespeare, and Milton* (Lexington, Ky., 1986), 186–90. See also Eleanor Cook, "Melos Versus Logos; or, Why Doesn't God Sing? Some Thoughts on Milton's Wisdom," in *Re-Membering Milton: Essays on the Texts and Traditions,* ed. Mary Nyquist and Margaret Ferguson (New York, 1987), 197–210; and Walter Schindler, *Voice and Crisis: Invocation in Milton's Poetry* (Hamden, Conn., 1984). But Maureen Quilligan has argued that the Miltonic Bardic position entails female submission, in *Milton's Spenser,* 218–26.

22. Donne, *The Sermons,* II, 179. Our emphasis.

macrocosmic history moves toward redemption, and the individual has always the choice of hearing the Word and feeling the love.

Persistence is a function of power, power as well to commission audible repetition—for instance, by heralds or in trentals for departed souls—as to promulgate statutes, texts, inscriptions, or other persisting physical meaning bearers that may yet be overpowered by the broils of war or by iconoclasm. What Milton composed, we might put it, falls thematically in between Spenser, whose text mourns the subjection to mutability of all things here below, and Shakespeare, whose "leaves" ("On Shakespear," 11) may provoke "wonder and astonishment" (line 7) longer than the marble and gilded monuments of princes. On the other hand, Milton would scarcely have been surprised by Pope's somber prediction that "such as Chaucer is, shall Dryden be." Milton's own attitude, from the early commendation of Shakespeare to the panorama of history presented to Adam, was consistent: all fallen nature and culture decays, and persistence beyond the briefest comes not through power but only through love, insofar as that love partakes of the grace of divine, eternal love.

Milton's request to himself, his question in the form of a petitionary prayer, his Bardic invocation addressed to Urania, is to compose something his countrymen will not willingly let die. The possible persistence of print is obviously an insufficient material cause: the writing must engage but not coerce. Monologue risks coming moribund from the press.[23] "Communication" in that pejorative sense is precisely antidialogic, a manipulative or coercive effort to secure not collegial rejoinder and accord but purchase, seduced approval, and supine acquiescence. Milton understood his true neighbor to be like the true neighbor in the parable of the Good Samaritan. He invites that neighbor by presenting a Bardic self in dialogue. The dialogue he offers is more fundamental than that of (call them) the characters in the epic, with whom readers may or may not feel kinship. The Bardic self is privately and publicly dedicated in dialogue with Urania, with itself, and with its audience. It thereby contrasts with various other sorts of self, meditative, say, or celebratory or elegiac or

23. Iconoclasm has of late received rewarding critical attention. See, for particularly notable example, James R. Siemon, *Shakespearean Iconoclasm* (Berkeley and Los Angeles, 1985), esp. Chap. 1; and Ernest B. Gilman, *Iconoclasm and Poetry in the English Reformation: Down Went Dagon* (Chicago, 1986), esp. Chaps. 2, 6. On the idea that Milton's theology and poetic were iconoclastic—to which we say yes and no—see Michael Murrin, *The Allegorical Epic: Essays in Its Rise and Decline* (Chicago, 1980), Chap. 6.

efficient, engrossed in solicitude on the one hand or in play on the other. But it is in the fit audience of those in whom the epic cannot die that the Bardic dialogue finds its conclusion and its justification. For Milton, the dialogue is aways the vehicle of grace.

Indeed we can scarcely avoid metadialogic stocktaking as we replay in our minds the Bard's own resituatings of himself: revisiting light, having been taught to "venture down" (*Paradise Lost,* III, 19) and "to reascend" (III, 20); reflecting that "Half yet remains unsung" (VII, 21) or that he "now must change / Those Notes to Tragic" (IX, 5–6), for example. We must, as part of the fit audience remind ourselves that all is movement in *Paradise Lost.* Satan is ever falling; mankind is ever in movement within grace and away from grace, through mishap and mayhap; history is ever marching away from the good yet toward redemption; and the reader is, possibly, turning from sin to life. The bard shifts to accommodate himself to these acquists of his, and to our knowledge, in a respectfully communicative manner.[24]

We might rather speak of Bardic communion than communication if we recall Allen Tate's "man of letters," for whom communion stands against and above the imprinting efforts of the media of communication employed as tools of power. Communion, by contrast, invites charitable and reciprocal presence, even if the charity entails negative judgment. So it is when the Bard comments to himself on behalf of his readers, in rejoinder to Urania's disclosures. Consider how he answers, "Let none admire / That riches grow in Hell" (I, 690–91), and remarks, "O shame to men! Devil with Devil damn'd / Firm concord holds, men onely disagree" (II, 496–97). It is similar when he says that Adam and Eve

> eas'd the putting off
> These troublesom disguises which wee wear,
> Strait side by side were laid, nor turnd I ween
> *Adam* from his fair Spouse, nor *Eve* the Rites
> Mysterious of connubial Love refus'd:
> Whatever Hypocrites austerely talk
>
> (IV, 739–44)

---

24. A generation ago, Martz celebrated this "voice of the bard" against then-current objections to it, but with an emphasis on "renewal of human vision." See his *The Paradise Within,* 105–10. For "haps," as in *happenstance,* and receptivity to them, see Weinsheimer, *Gadamer's Hermeneutics,* esp. Introduction.

And in the same vein, he asks, "O when meet now / Such pairs, in Love and mutual Honour joyn'd?" (VIII, 57–58), and laments, "O much deceav'd, much failing, hapless Eve / Of thy presum'd return! event perverse!" (IX, 404–405). We can reflect that Milton's composing is not so much an aestheticizing as a dialecticizing, indeed, a hermeneutic circling to know the end by the beginning and the beginning by the end.[25] In the exclamation about hapless Eve in Book IX, he evinces dismay at the actual consideration of some tragic notes he himself announced four hundred lines earlier. Hence, when he arrests us, as for a picturesque epic simile, he often modulates very quickly into dynamisms of affective experience or of history: from fair field of Enna, to Ceres' search in pain (in Book IV); from the vast trajectory of Mulciber's fall, to rebuttal of that "Erring" pagan notion of sacred history (I, 747); from autumnal leaves where Vallombrosan "shades / High overarch't imbowr" (I, 303–304), to waves overwhelming "*Memphian* Chivalry" (I, 307) and angels springing up like capitally negligent sentries (I, 331–34).

Such instants of aesthetic contemplation become the fulcrums on which hermeneutic epicycles turn. The Bard's great spiral of hermeneutic exposition, of assertion and justification, which we recapitulate in our own effort to know the beginning and the end by the middle, takes us from the middle of hell to the middle of heaven, with its anticipation of history, to midgarden and therein back in Raphael's dialogue to creation, on to postlapsarian garden and Michael's account of history and its fulfillment, and downward with Adam and Eve to midworld unevenly positioned between unfallen state and redemption.

But the recirculation of the Bard in dialectic with himself, with fit audience, and—in rebuttal—with more or less unfit sectors of the human line, is in some sense constituted of metadialogue with Urania. Not to be neglected are the celebrated invocations of the muse with which the Bard inaugurates Books I, III, VII, and IX. *Paradise Lost* is a book of names—approving or partial or tendentious names. Urania mysteriously exceeds her name, and is like God in that respect. She is so closely asso-

25. This is to go a third way with regard to that earlier "Milton controversy" that had Ezra Pound, T. S. Eliot, F. R. Leavis, *et al.*, discounting Milton as a *rhetorical* "bustuous rumpus," and the New Criticism mounting defenses. See Ezra Pound, *Literary Essays,* ed. T. S. Eliot (London, 1954), esp. 201–202; Cleanth Brooks, "Milton and Critical Re-Estimates," *PMLA,* LXVI (1951), 1045–54; and W. B. C. Watkins, *An Anatomy of Milton's Verse* (Baton Rouge, 1955).

ciated with light (coeternal beam?) and wisdom and godhead as to be the more mysterious for that. She must be invoked but seems desirous of being called and is *disponible,* like grace.[26] She answers in more than one way, a

> Celestial Patroness, who deignes
> Her nightly visitation unimplor'd,
> And *dictates* to me slumbring, or *inspires*
> Easie my unpremeditated Verse
> (IX, 21–24; our emphasis)

Such references to the Sister of "Eternal wisdom" (VII, 9), if not indeed of the *hagia pneuma,* may once have seemed to some readers merely genuflections to epic convention, devoutly witty accessories. But recent critics have taught us to recognize that these invocations are essential.[27] There would be no epic without the transactions they partly report, partly enact, even on the assumption that what as final cause and as efficient cause moved Milton's mind can be specified independently of such transactions. The ostensible final cause, "to justifie the wayes of God to men" (I, 26) in epic "Argument" (I, 24) is too high for merely human invention, formally and ontologically too high, even if it is granted that many theologians contrive to "assert Eternal Providence" (I, 25) in prose. Only with the constant guidance of Urania is it possible, poetically or theologically, for the Bard to tell the right tale. On his own, without divine help, he must fall into sin—idolatry, pride, aimlessness, all the conditions generic to *aversio.* For Milton, nothing was more certain. Accordingly, he gives us

26. The term *disponible* is from Marcel's *Creative Fidelity.*

27. See Davies, *The Feminine Reclaimed;* Cook, "Melos Versus Logos"; and Noam Flinker, "Courting Urania: The Narrator of *Paradise Lost* Invokes His Muse," in *Milton and the Idea of Woman,* ed. Julia M. Walker (Urbana, Ill., 1988), 86–99. Flinker reads Milton as, among other things, anti-Petrarchan. On Milton's ambivalent relation to classical convention more generally, see Barbara Pavlock, *Eros, Imitation, and the Epic Tradition* (Ithaca, N.Y., 1990), Chap. 5. For elaboration upon Milton's correspondingly enterprising recuperation of biblical motifs of poetic origin, see Virginia R. Mollenkott, "Some Implications of Milton's Androgynous Muse," *Bucknell Review,* XXIV (1978), 27–36; and David Quint, *Origin and Originality in Renaissance Literature: Versions of the Source* (New Haven, 1983), Epilogue. See also William G. Riggs, *The Christian Poet in "Paradise Lost"* (Berkeley and Los Angeles, 1972), which, however, alleges the education of Adam (p. 101); and Donald Bouchard, *Milton: A Structural Reading* (London, 1974), which posits a narrator's unsuccessful poem and a muse's successful poem to be read simultaneously (pp. 108–14).

his ultimate *bona fides*, the inspiration of Urania, who comes in a continuing dream vision partaking of epiphany, the only appropriate form of visitation for a power so high. The poem belongs as much to feminine Urania, who guarantees its truth in mediating between God and Milton, as to masculine Milton, who Bardically mediates between her and this middle world. Without the Bard's dialogic dream vision, we could have only error, the dismal vaporings of the usual suspects, of old priests and new presbyters.

Moreover, as Eleanor Cook has shown, Milton goes out of his usual way to associate the enabling Urania with play and song, in contrast to discursive saying.[28] That is, he departs from the King James Version's "rejoicing" at Prov. 8:30–31 and the corresponding *laetificans* in Tremellius, in favor of the Vulgate's *ludere*, "to play." That more properly translates the Hebrew, as Cook explains. It is deeply suggestive regarding Urania's relationship with transcendent Deity, and regarding the Bard's relationship with her revelation. In perhaps the most telling instance of playfulness, she with both utmost seriousness and utmost solemnity translates patrifilial dividuality in Heaven as dialogue, and the Bard is moved to pledge that the Son's "unexampl'd love" (III, 410) will make his

> Name
> . . . the copious matter of my Song
> Henceforth, and never shall my Harp thy praise
> Forget, nor from thy Fathers praise disjoin.
>
> (III, 412–15)

The vocalist-harpist will realize himself in patrifilial descants—one is tempted to say in patrifilial jazz improvisations—on all the matters and motifs of prelapsarian and postlapsarian history to follow. This is possible because simultaneous divine justice and mercy are played out as dramatic dialogue. Supersolemn Raphael reduces rhetorical dialectic to grammar and logic in *his* famous accommodation by "process of speech" (VII, 178).

To put it another way, the *disponibilité* of Urania with sister wisdom in songful play before "th' Almightie Father" (VII, 11), like the analogous songful susceptibility of the Bard—always serious but not always solemn, like Chaucer himself—to visits of Urania "unimplor'd" (IX, 22), and his resultant verse "unpremeditated" (IX, 24), is as much a modality of love for God as is obedience. As such, it enacts love as the central Miltonic

28. Cook, "Melos Versus Logos," 197–210.

alternative to lust for power, and to modalities of control. And since dialogic presence and persistence are functions of love, for Milton, any Bardic talk of love is metadialogic, in the sense of being about dialogue.

Satan acknowledges as much from the dark side, the side of discursivity intended or apprehended as coercion and recurrently imaged in the linearity of gradation and debt (see pp. 66–79 above):

> I sdeind subjection, and thought one step higher
> Would set me highest, and *in a moment quit*
> The debt immense of endless gratitude,
> So burthensome still paying, still to ow;
> Forgetful what from him I still receiv'd,
> And understood not that a grateful mind
> By owing owes not, but still pays, *at once*
> Indebted and discharg'd
>
> (IV, 50–57; our emphasis)

A loving mind, which Satan characteristically cannot quite conceive apart from an onerous sort of gratitude, is a radical and immediately decisive alternative to the grinding, time-bound mechanism of unredeemed debt theology. Satan, a tower builder before Babel, a hunter of men before Nimrod, cannot ascend by power. On the other hand, the loving mind is already there, and insofar as linear at all, embodies the playful and songful linearity of antiphon. Urania dictates or inspires precisely in a dialogic mode of the unselfish absorption of unaggressive play—as the loving mind approaching the condition of music.

Presence and persistence, as well as hermeneutic progress itself and the measure of the contribution that dialogue can make to it, are, for Milton, dependent on grace. Metadialogue in this regard has to be ontologically different from mere dialogue, which has about it the inevitable and necessary imperfections of fallenness. Metadialogue here is not just a matter of understanding or knowing or perceiving, of epistemology or phenomenology; it goes rather to the ultimately fundamental level of being. Hence, metadialogue is not adequately defined as dialogue *above* dialogue, in the way metahistory might be described as an examination of the ideas informing or explaining history. Nor can metadialogue be adequately thought of as dialogue about dialogue, in the manner of Aristotle's *Rhetoric* or classical invocations of the muse. Such conceptions of metadialogue confine themselves to the realm of immanence, which for Milton can only be fallen. Such conceptions suffer not from any quasi-Manichaean undecidability between presence and absence but rather from some alteration or perversion of presence. For Milton, metadialogue has to transcend dialogue and exist at a higher position on the Great Chain of Being.

The Miltonic ontological distinction between metadialogue and dialogue does not render dialogue useless or valueless, but it does entail limits upon it. The limits apply wherever dialogue occurs, in the conversations between Adam and Eve, in the monologues of Raphael and Michael, in the utterances of the Bard to the audience, and in the demonic anti-Symposium in hell. In every case, whatever the state of grace of the speaker—something that varies widely—the dialogue is damaged by it. Even to a fit audience, language will, *ex natura rerum,* be both understood and expressed inexactly, incompletely, and imperfectly. But imperfection and flaw are not total disability. For Milton, dialogue is one of God's instruments in the instruction and salvation of mankind, and it is an instrument chosen for its suitability to fallenness. Even though the immediate effect of dialogue is frequently confusion and distance from God—as three centuries of misreading Book III attest—the ultimate effect can be salvation. If dialogue does not enable precisely communication at once, it makes plain that there exist more than precision and more than the moment. Thus, dialogue can

> What in me is dark
> Illumin, what is low raise and support;
> That to the highth of this great Argument
> I may assert Eternal Providence,
> And justifie the wayes of God to men.
>
> (I, 22–26)

In short, through the "wandring mazes" (II, 561) of dialogue we move restlessly within the hermeneutic progress from God to man, from end to beginning, from the whole to the part and back again, with "new acquist" (*Samson Agonistes,* 1755) of knowledge.

With grace there is no movement; all is stationary, transcendent, and eternal. Here dwells the pure story of Urania, which the Bard dialogically and imperfectly transmits through the work of grace to us. We can only glimpse the right tale, and this applies to the Bard as well, who tells it better than we could but who recurrently comes to the limits of his inspired understanding, being human and fallen as are we. Metadialogue in *Paradise Lost* may be compared to that in the *Divine Comedy,* which Milton admired, but it is strikingly different from similar critical commentary for the *Aeneid,* the *Argonautica,* or the *Odyssey* or *Iliad. Paradise Lost* does not sing with the *"Orphean* Lyre" (*Paradise Lost,* III, 17) or "nocturnal Note" (III, 40), and the muse is heavenly, Urania, the *lux sancta* or *hagia sophia,* she who is by definition ontologically separate. But dialogue and metadialogue are not merely ontologically different; they also communicate differently. Grace is not the same as process of speech, and dialogue is a series of successive subtotals while metadialogue is the wholeness of the divine presence and persistence.

PROCESS OF SPEECH

Process of speech, by which Milton meant what we would call discourse, differs not only in degree but also in kind from dream vision, especially in respect of the process itself rather than its purpose. Indeed, the sole serious similarity between the two may be regarding purpose; they are both forms of communication for humanity and are thus part of human naming and knowing. Beyond that all is difference. If it is argued that both dream vision and process of speech are divinely inspired, the rejoinder must be that in linguistic communication the divine element is so attenuated as to be generally and ordinarily unrecognizable. Moreover, dream vision, with its intensity, its short duration, and its glimpse of knowing the whole, hardly resembles formally the meandering, repetitive, and exclamatory hunter-gatherer habits of colloquial speech, or the imperious monologue of both strict narration and logical argument. Too, the immediacy of dream vision contrasts sharply with the mediative nature of speech. Common purpose, formal disjunction—we assert both. But since the general purpose of speech and dream vision is both obvious and tangential to the argument, primary attention must be to the formal nature of the process of speech.

The essence of linguistic communication is distance, which may be understood partly in terms of the elemental gap between what is meant and what is understood. As for the gulf between what is said and what is meant, the at least formal assumption must be that Milton's poetic voice, his Bard, as inspired by Urania, both says what he meant and means what he said. Beyond meaning and understanding, there is the increased distance added by equivocation, words having vitally different meanings across different levels of being. There is the additional distance added by cultural elaborations in more or less idiosyncratic usage: the tropes of metaphor, metonymy, synecdoche, irony, and formality. And there is the distance added by time. We speak and live moving forward through time, or with time a current bearing us "into the past," as Nick Carraway would have it. But we understand retrospectively, looking back upon our experiences in order to find meaning. Thus distance informs process of speech in various ways, each occluding immediate but not necessarily ultimate comprehension. Knowing, and naming rightly, and knowing another's naming word by word, step by step, is a journey, perhaps not unlike that leading to salvation. Milton's Jesus proceeds to his encounter with Satan in the wilderness, "Thought following thought, and step by step led on" (*Paradise Regain'd*, I, 192) by the Spirit and his own "deep thoughts" (I, 189).

In *Paradise Lost,* knowing and naming through process of speech, with all its formal distance and its hope of progressive and, perhaps, salvific understanding, is directed toward Adam. He is instructed by Raphael and Michael, who tell him of the origins of the cosmos, the war in heaven, and the nature of his enemy, all before the Fall, as well as the ultimately graced path of fallen history. The horror of anticipated evil, which can be felt immediately only in dream vision, is reserved for Eve. Adam is exposed to the results of grace and disruptions of evil, with both seen at the distance of one remove. (With Adam, the bad educationist metaphor of *exposure* sadly applies.) A scientific analogy holds. Our weight is the result of gravity, but it is not gravity itself. With words, unlike the Word, there is always the shadow of incomprehension.

But what of Edenic speech, the "prompt eloquence" (*Paradise Lost,* V, 149) of pure language? [29] Surely here words infused with grace, carrying the Word, would be perfectly understood. Milton gives a qualified affirmative answer to that proposition. Adam, when dealing with nature as he immediately perceives it, fuses knowing and naming into a single cognitive act. A gracious simultaneity makes knowing the same as naming, and so both primal parents can discourse fully on what they perceive per-

29. In dealing with discourse and the "process of speech," it is essential to examine Robert L. Entzminger's clear and cogent *Divine Word: Milton and the Redemption of Language* (Pittsburgh, 1985), esp. Chaps. 1–3. More particularly, Leonard, in *Naming in Paradise,* presents a rich panoply of close readings illustrating what we call distances, but he frames them largely in terms—going back to F. R. Leavis and Christopher Ricks—of inclusion and exclusion rather than hermeneutics.

fectly. Adam's naming of the animals is his unfallen work; he identifies their nature. Upon waking in paradise, Adam possesses the capacity for that as a condition of unfallen nature. Nothing can be defamiliarized; everything is understood:

> Hill, Dale, and shadie Woods, and sunnie Plains,
> . . . all things smil'd,
> With fragrance and with joy my heart oreflow'd
>
> (VIII, 262, 265–66)

Joyful understanding here is personally as intimate as fragrance and a smile, and is perfect; such knowing and naming already lie in the heart, ready for pure discourse in a pure language.

Nonetheless, "prompt eloquence" seems not always to apply. What comes so easily with terrestrial nature, that joyous knowing and naming, seems to fall short when applied to astronomy. Adam asks for help in the form of archangelic discourse:

> something yet of doubt remains,
> Which onely thy solution can resolve.
> When I behold this goodly Frame, this World
> Of Heav'n and Earth consisting, and compute,
> Thir magnitudes, this Earth a spot, a grain,
> An atom, with the Firmament compar'd
> And all her numberd Starrs, that seem to rowl
> Spaces incomprehensible
>
> (VIII, 13–20)

Raphael's reply is not altogether reproving, but the benevolent archangel is clearly dubious about the value and utility of inquiring after "secrets to be scann'd by them who ought / Rather admire" (VII, 74–75). When Raphael does explain, though vaguely, and repeats his admonition to leave certain matters to God, Adam pronounces himself satisfied and "cleerd of doubt" (VIII, 179), though, from the text, it is hard to see how this could be completely true. Certainly Adam is not asked to name the stars, and we may note that he has retrogressed from his wiser sense of the stars' place in creation which he expressed instructively to Eve (IV, 660–75).

If the distance inherent in discourse, even in unfallen paradise, is apparent in Raphael's comments on astronomy, it is also evident by inference in other passages dealing with the ostensible instruction of Adam. Adam is often told how to live, and often asserts that he understands. Raphael, after telling Adam of the war in heaven, concludes with a moral lesson:

> let it profit thee t' have heard
> By terrible Example the reward
> Of disobedience; firm they might have stood,
> Yet fell; remember, and fear to transgress.
> (VI, 909–12)

Once is not enough. Even perfect discourse lacks the power and immediacy of dream vision, and Adam's response to the archangel indicates the need for reinforcement. Raphael obliges, and concludes his exposition with further moral advice:

> Be strong, live happie, and love, but first of all
> Him whom to love is to obey, and keep
> His great command; take heed least Passion sway
> Thy Judgement to do aught . . .
> And all temptation to transgress repel.
> (VIII, 633–36, 643)

As it turns out, of course, Adam is unable to do this. Transgression is not something he understands, and pure language and unfallen discourse, even at some length and repeated, are not able to close the distance to complete understanding that discourse must involve.

Adam, however, says he understands, and gives assurances. The words at least are right. Adam tells Raphael,

> Yet that we never shall forget to love
> Our maker, and obey him whose command
> Single, is yet so just, my constant thoughts
> Assur'd me, and still assure
> (V, 550–53)

Unfallen assurances in unfallen language are followed by a fallen pledge in an impure tongue. Once again Adam is "Greatly instructed" (XII, 557) by Michael, and once again he promises:

> Henceforth I learn, that to obey is best,
> And love with fear the onely God, to walk
> As in his presence, ever to observe
> His providence, and on him sole depend
> (XII, 561–64)

The irony of that promise, like the ambiguity of *as in,* between *just as in* and *as if in,* can hardly be lost on anyone, as it comes after two books describing the utter inability of Adam and his descendants to keep it. Yet both assurances are honestly meant and freely given. The problem lies not in Adam's failure of analysis or prophecy but in language itself. Linguistic distance in *Paradise Lost* is not only in the gap between what is said and what is understood but also between one's words and oneself. One's words, *pace* Eliot, do not bend, sometimes break; one may oneself do so. Humanity speaks and hears in metaphor, ironically and with formality, because that is all there is. Adam understands only as far as is possible.

The sense of the inadequacy of language in *Paradise Lost,* even under ideal conditions, is reinforced by Adam's idolatrous regard for Eve and hers for him. A general admonition against transgression is clearly noteworthy but is somewhat divorced from experiential reality. Warnings to have due regard for Eve are not. These are well within Adam's capacity to understand, not only by faith but also by measurement and memory, and his wisdom should bring Eve to a just regard for him, avoiding idolatry. We as readers have been proleptically alerted to the point by the mention of the "uxorious King" (I, 444). But linguistic communication fails here as well. Raphael reminds Adam that Eve is

> fair no doubt, and worthy well
> Thy cherishing, thy honouring, and thy love,
> Not thy subjection . . .
> In loving thou dost well, in passion not,
> Wherein true Love consists not; love refines
> The thoughts, and heart enlarges, hath his seat
> In Reason, and is judicious
> (VIII, 568–70, 588–91)

Adam is "half abash't" (VIII, 595) at being bluntly told what he half knows and half does not know. Again, the linguistic separation from self appears, compounded in this instance by the contradiction between what is known and named by process of speech and what is known—is it yet named?—by the body.

To the warning from Raphael is added the reproof of the "sovran Presence" (X, 144). Adam is asked, "Was shee thy God, that her thou didst obey / Before his voice, or was shee made thy guide" (X, 145–46). There is no answer convincing to God on that question. Adam had been told, by process of speech, and in a presumably pure language, that he should not confuse Eve with God. Love is not to become idolatry—a difficult thing for language to convey. And passion, for all its ferocity, would seem like any other form of idolatry to contrast by its *fixity* with the Miltonic notion and language of love, love expressed most decisively in the language of divine generativity.

Ironically, the limitations of the process of speech are seen anew in the one area where linguistic communication is, apparently, perfect. Adam can name the animals because he "understood / Thir Nature" (VIII, 352–53). True knowledge and true naming of the animals are easily within Adam's grasp, although astronomy and Eve are not. How is it that one true knowledge is attained and the other missed? The type of knowledge is less important than the method of communicating it. Adam's knowing and naming the beasts are not the result of his being told about them by archangels but come instead from an epiphany. What is learned in this manner, though not free from the consequences and opportunities of free will, is nevertheless perfectly understood within the state of grace and adequately understood afterward.

Not everything can be learned by epiphany, or humanity would not be human. Although unmediated communication with God is certainly desirable for immediate and complete comprehension, it is also unique and sublime and unnerving and exhausting, as Job found out: "Where wast thou when I laid the foundations of the earth? declare, if thou hast understanding. Who hath laid the measures thereof, if thou knowest? or who hath stretched the line upon it? . . . Wilt thou also disannul my judgment? wilt thou condemn me, that thou mayest be righteous?" (Job 38:4, 5, 40:8). Adam can hardly receive such an answer, at least not yet, but he can experience the exaltation and exhaustion of epiphany. Adam relates to Raphael,

> I heard no more, for now
> My earthly by his Heav'nly overpowerd,
> Which it had long stood under, streind to th' highth
> In that celestial Colloquie sublime,
> As with an object that excels the sense,
> Dazl'd and spent, sunk down, and sought repair
> Of sleep, which instantly fell on me
>
> (VIII, 452–58)

The comic line "We can't keep meeting this way" takes on new meaning when applied to the Miltonic sense of epiphany. Mankind simply cannot take this sort of experience very often or very well, no matter how perfect the communication.

Two general categories of explanation concerning the imperfection of linguistic discourse suggest themselves, both related to time. Adam lacked the time, and thus the experiences, necessary to judge the import of what he was told, whether by the archangels, by Eve, or by the "Universal Lord" (VIII, 376). Not only did he lack experience, he also lacked memory. All of this is true of Eve as well, who, although better instructed than Adam about the meaning of sin, is no better prepared than he to avoid it. Both are virtually without a past, and thus essentially unable through their own capacities to imagine a future. Being extrinsic to time is a fundamental characteristic of God, but for humanity the passage of time is the matrix within which wisdom, knowledge, and understanding develop. Compare the incipiently falling angels, who "know no time when we were not as now" (V, 859).

The absence of the effects of time on Adam and Eve can be dealt with in at least two rather different ways: by recourse to psychoanalytic analysis, focused on the time of beginnings, and by an examination of time as related to the salvific journey, particularly as understood in the *Confessions* of Saint Augustine.

With regard to the time of beginnings, what does it mean that Adam and Eve have—to put it very mildly indeed—no familial past, no conventional mothering or fathering?[30] It means, of course, that Milton was respecting his biblical source—a point too important not to state, obvious though it is. Moreover, Milton reinforces the biblical source in its tendency to distance, even defamiliarize bodily knowing, the as-if-unmediated sensory perceptions and feelings and "primary process" psychic inscriptions, with displacement and condensation, which we have partially considered as recited dream vision. We say as-if-unmediated and put Freud's term *primary process* in apologetic quotation marks because for Milton anything human is always already mediated, as we have been ar-

---

30. That Adam and Eve have a godly father who in turn has an invisible, first-person-of-the-Trinity Father is patent. That these points are more fruitfully considered as analogical and psychoanalytically suggestive than as doctrinal and implicative of the heresy of adoptionism has been richly argued by Kerrigan in *The Sacred Complex,* esp. 97–102, 155–57, 186–88. But Kerrigan's focus, despite efforts to socialize it and to escape psychic determinism, remains schematic and psychogenetic—usefully so—in comparison with a focus on ontology and process.

guing. Serious dreams are divinely or angelically inspired, and the very matters of dream vision and sensoriums are gifts that may mediate between the self and a transcendent creator. Milton's practice is glossed aptly by the brilliantly revisionary Freudianism of Julia Kristeva, who distinguishes between, on the one hand, the *symbolic* utterance—in the language of discourse, even psychoanalytic discourse—which is "tributary to the system of language" in that it foregrounds the public order of signifiers (grammatical, syntactic) and the public order of signified (lexical), and on the other, the *semiotic* utterance, which is less tributary to the public orders in foregrounding "psychic inscriptions" more privately "controlled by the primary processes" of affective displacements and condensations.[31]

By honoring the biblical prototype, Milton can exempt Adam from any melancholy or nostalgia—real or supposed—for a lost maternal plenitude, which for poet and reader can be displaced to and diffused in unfallen paradise. Adam's need for bodily knowing can be distanced for theological as well as psychological inspection—whether the categories of the theological and the psychological are construed as significantly overlapping or not. Eve is not another *self* but an *other* self, different, and Adam's recognition of the need for a differing other to complete his life remains one of his finest moments. After all, God responds positively. What stronger endorsement could Milton give? Although Adam's expression of need, his near argument with God, may depart happily enough from complete solemnity, it gets none of the sardonic framing attendant on his pretensions to adequacy with regard to Eve's dream, his cosmological question to Raphael in Book VIII, his dysfunctional rescue of the separation of Eve in Book IX, and his presumption in Book X to fix the Fall by suicide. Unfallen Adam and Eve in their garden are distanced—made

31. See Julia Kristeva, "The Speaking Subject," in *On Signs,* ed. Marshall Blonsky (Baltimore, 1985), 210–20; and Julia Kristeva, *Desire in Language: A Semiotic Approach to Literature and Art,* trans. Thomas Gora, Alice Jardine, and Leon S. Roudiez (New York, 1980), 36–91. Kristeva is thus opening out and making dynamic—in a way vital for understanding Milton—the quasi-Saussurean notion of the sign: the familiar emblematic oval with bar, dividing signifier above and signified below. The static taxonomy is deathly, as Colin Falck has argued in *Myth, Truth, and Literature: Towards a True Post-Modernism* (New York, 1989). It has also tended to oversimplify Saussure, as Harris has shown in *Reading Saussure,* 219–37. Compare also Augustine's distinction between *ratio* and *intellectus*—for example, in *De trinitate,* XII, xiv, 22. See also Janet Adelman, "Creation and the Place of the Poet in *Paradise Lost,*" in *The Author in His Work,* ed. Martz and Williams, 51–69.

other—by Bardic exclamation, by their nudity and extemporaneous hymnody, and as Louis Martz has noted, by bursts of mythological imagery.[32]

What of Eve's motherlessness? As with Adam, the unprecedented newness of bodily knowledge in sexual love comes to the fore. The founding and fundamental quality of the wedded love so famously hailed (IV, 750) is rendered theologically and psychologically more plausible.

Less obviously, the incestuous hellish family of Satan, sin, death, and Hell-hounds defines and is defined contrastively by its redemptive opposite, the family of Christ, Eve, Adam, and humanity. This typological contrast stands alongside the more familiarly noted—but asymmetrical—contrast with the heavenly Trinity, and the more compelling one with Christ, church (bride and mother), clergy, and communicants.[33] Eve is fashioned by divine agency—should we way semiotically?—in response to Adam's sense of lack. That sense can come only from within him, like his sense of her once she is incarnate, however markedly either may be defined by contrast with exterior nature and its animal life. But Adam's lack is precisely not narcissistic, nor is Eve narcissistically regarded, as is the image of sin that breaks as if abortively from the prideful and self-idolatrous temple of Satan. Adam and Eve's children-to-come accord with the prelapsarian promise of hands to help foster the generativity of Eden. Something of that noble end and vocation remains, however greatly the Fall has damaged the lineage and the garden. Adam and Eve's line will, the poet reminds us, eventually include a second Adam, whereas Satan's line can only extend to what an omnipotent God permits as a noisome

32. See Martz, *The Paradise Within*, 117–21; and Martz, *Poet of Exile*, 136–37.

33. The typological and structural symmetry was pointed out over twenty years ago by S. E. Roberts in "A Phenomenological Approach to Milton from Typology to Existentialism" (Ph.D. dissertation, State University of New York at Buffalo, 1970). For a provocative alternative interpretation in terms of Satan, Moses, and Mosaic law, see Samuel S. Stollman, "Satan, Sin, and Death: A Mosaic Trio in *Paradise Lost*," *Milton Studies*, XXII (1986), 101–20. For an interpretation that has Milton rectifying Hesiod, see Philip J. Gallagher, "Real or Allegoric: The Ontology of Sin and Death in *Paradise Lost*," *English Literary Renaissance*, VI (1976), 317–34. See also Judith E. Browning, "Sin, Eve, and Circe: *Paradise Lost* and the Ovidian Circe Tradition," *Milton Studies*, XXVI (1990), 135–58. On narcissistic sins, with reference to the Satanic trinity, see Jean Hagstrum, *Sex and Sensibility: Ideal and Erotic Love from Milton to Mozart* (Chicago, 1980), 41–46. On the Augustinian grounding, see especially Stephen M. Fallon, "Milton's Sin and Death: The Ontology of Allegory in *Paradise Lost*," *English Literary Renaissance*, XVII (1987), 329–50. On the specific biblical rationale, see Mary Ann Radzinowicz, "Psalms and the Representation of Death in *Paradise Lost*," *Milton Studies*, XXIII (1987), 133–44.

and terminal cleanup crew of scavengers. Careful comparison of Eve's re-action to her reflection with Milton's source in Ovid's account of Narcissus reveals a sensitive and affectionate but not a narcissistic new consciousness, as Robert McMahon has shown us.[34] The essence of Adam and Eve's situation was newness, a defining contrastive condition to the Bard's and reader's in the middle of time and history.

For Saint Augustine, time is the measure of the salvific journey that turns humanity (*retorqueo*) from the darkness of being that is pointed away from God (*aversio*) toward the light of salvation from the true God, a complete reorientation (*conversio*). This might involve baptism by the Holy Ghost, as described in Book VIII of the *Confessions,* but that would be the work of a moment, and the journey is more complex than that. Augustine illustrates the nature of the journey by comparing it to the reading of a psalm:

> Suppose I am about to recite a psalm which I know. Before I begin, my expectation (or "looking forward") is extended over the whole psalm. But once I have begun, whatever I pluck off from it and let fall into the past enters the province of my memory (or "looking back at"). So the life of this action of mine is extended in two directions. . . . It is true also of the whole of a man's life, of which all his actions are parts. And it is true of the whole history of humanity, of which the lives of all men are parts.[35]

We think and act forward, as Adam and Eve did when they "did eat," but we understand backward, as memory sorts life into significant patterns. The past and the future, though separated by what is now, are tied together in a single fabric of obedience, the more so by the weaving of a *textus,* and neither can exist without the other. For Adam and Eve, as Milton clearly saw, pastlessness lent incomprehension to all they thought they understood, even when most plainly presented. Thus, Milton often

34. Robert McMahon, "Eve's Reflection, and Ovid" (Typescript, n.d.). We are grateful to the author for letting us see this. It is perhaps obvious that we intend *narcissism* throughout in the conventional sense of "preoccupation with oneself or with a self that is scarcely other." This is *unlike* Adam's desire for a maintained—albeit diminished—self when he eats the fruit in Book IX of *Paradise Lost.* The point holds, whether or not there are Freudian or Lacanian emphases on fixed or futural or fictional elements in the beloved image; the beleaguered woman's welfare is not in focus for Adam in Book IX or, in *A Mask,* for Elder Brother in the rescue of the Lady from Comus (see pp. 154–58 below).

35. *The Confessions of Saint Augustine,* Bk. XI.

describes innocence by associating it with newness. Theology and psychology come together here. We ourselves conventionally describe newness as innocent, and myth does as well. Comparison with the myth of Pandora is obvious. As the chest is opened, so the fruit is eaten, and newness disappears, innocence vanishes. Humanity is suddenly endowed with both a past and a future.

With past and future, the looking forward and looking back at of Augustine, words are inescapably and substantially differentiated from the Word. Linguistic tropes, such as formality or irony or metaphor, merely add to distance, because they add to the burden of human past and future. Language can never be pure, because humanity can never be new again. And even when humanity was new and innocent, pastlessness made discourse, in fundamental ways, incomprehensible. Without the saving grace of God's love, it is literally, for the Augustinian Milton, damned if you are and damned if you aren't.

BODILY KNOWING

Knowing involves more than dream vision and discourse; it includes the body. But knowing with and through the body provides an immediacy and vividness of experience that is much more akin to dream vision than to linguistic discourse. Knowing through the body privileges quality and degree of intensity but occludes ambiguity and obviates equivocation, irony, and other linguistically derived tropes.[36] As with discourse, though, knowing through the body may be difficult to interpret exactly, but the body seldom makes mistakes in major categories—for example, exactly why one hurts. Milton articulates dysfunctionality in naming and knowing as the peculiar province of Satan, whose "foul descent" (IX, 163) is "Into a Beast, and mixt with bestial slime, / This essence to incarnate and imbrute" (IX, 165–66). The reduction, clearly not to nerveless apa-

---

36. It is possible to work up cases of ambiguity in bodily knowing: a very hot drink both welcome and painful to someone chilled, a crushing hug upon relief from danger, the too vigorous tickling of a child by a playful sibling. The elaborate specifications make plain how much working-up is necessary to contrive cases that can override the ordinary immediacy and unambiguous vividness of bodily knowing, as against linguistic knowing. We draw support from, rather than discover opposition in, John C. Ulreich's "Milton on the Eucharist: Some Second Thoughts About Sacramentalism," in *Milton and the Middle Ages*, ed. Mulryan, 32–56.

thy, seems to approximate the primal polarity of pleasure and pain. But for fallen humanity, knowing and naming through the body are one of several contacts with grace and truth, as common as speech, as immediate and total as dream vision, but experienced always through the medium of fallen will, damaged memory, and vulnerable reason—vulnerable reason because Milton may not have disagreed with the Thomist precept that the intellect by itself is inerrant, though he certainly never expected to find it acting in the fallen world "without dust and heat" (as he had written in *Areopagitica*), however grace might lead it.

Some ordinary physical knowing and naming, both in paradise and afterward, appear to Milton to be mechanically indifferent to a state of grace. The body knows, in its natural way, such things as heat, cold, thirst, fatigue, and repletion regardless of the presence of sin—an obvious point, perhaps, but critical for Milton as for earlier Renaissance writers such as Thomas Nashe, Ben Jonson, and Shakespeare. Disobedience may have prevented the children of Eve from knowing the real names of the animals, but they were always able to give some sort of name to the beasts of the field, however arbitrary the names in the age of Babel. In the same way, the pure and grace-dependent meaning of physical experience may be lost, but not all meaning, and thus not all knowing and naming, is. This is taken for granted in *Paradise Lost*. What is essential to an epic of grace and disgrace is the capacity of the body to know as generativity. Here two things are involved: on the one hand, the sexual union of wedded love or its alternative, the lustful embrace, "joyless, unindear'd" (IV, 766), of casual intercourse, and on the other, the ultimately salvific incarnation of the Christ within a daughter of Eve. At both ends of meaning, in the purely human and in the anagogic metanarrative, the generativity is overwhelmingly feminine. That commonality is a fundamental illustration of Milton's connection of knowing and naming with grace, by which knowing through the body is given a meaning both momentary and eternal.

The transfiguring role of grace in knowing and naming through the body appears in Milton's contrast between married love and "casual fruition" (IV, 767). The same act is transformed by grace from something merely erotic, and hence directed away from God, into the generativity of love. That is so whether or not the generativity of children is a consequence: wedded love has been hailed irrespective of Eve's future pregnancies. Mary Nyquist has acutely pointed out a frequently misread definition by contrast. Adam and Eve are *both* compared (IX, 1060) to "Sampson in the act of discovering he has lost his strength. . . . Eve and Adam, in becoming conscious of their loss of sexual innocence, experience sensuously and immediately the loss of that most immaterial of theological goods, divine grace."[37] Nyquist adds that the polarity in Milton's disposition of allusions to Bible, *Iliad,* Platonic commentary, and his own prelapsarian Adam and Eve of Book IV is not a patriarchal one of male and female but rather one of sacred and profane. So it is here and throughout. Married love, as opposed to lust in and out of marriage, is basically holy and biblically sanctioned: "Marriage is honourable in all, and the bed undefiled" (Heb. 13:4). Building on that premise, Milton described married love using terms appropriate for sanctification: "mysterious law" (IV, 750), "all the charities" (IV, 756), and "holiest place" (IV, 759). The bodily knowing, clearly graced, of what Milton means by "wedded love" (IV, 750) stands at the heart of all bodily knowing and human love and creativity in *Paradise Lost.* Bodily knowing in the lesser "Charities / Of Father, Son, and Brother" (IV, 756–57) and of citizen, and in uncharities—such bodily knowing is peripheral. Milton integrates variously corporal, especially kinesthetic, elements into many an epic simile and into the description of Satan moving (with little learning) and of the amenities of paradise, but they and the significance they have there always remain subordinate to the wellspring of "Relations dear, and all the Charities" (IV, 756), on the one hand, and to what he does with respect to defining contrasts in bodily knowing, on the other, in *Paradise Regain'd* and *Samson Agonistes.* A union of wedded love is, if nothing else, a continuing defiance of Satan, sin, and death. It must be understood—as also in *The Doctrine and Discipline of Divorce*—as yielding more and more extended love, not merely offspring.

In this passage critical for the meaning of the entire epic, two unobviously significant words appear. One is *holiest,* a term used in *Paradise Lost* only here (IV, 759) and at line 724 of Book VI, and in *Paradise Regain'd,* of and by the Son at line 110 of Book II and at line 349 of Book

---

37. Mary Nyquist, "Textual Overlapping and Dalilah's Harlot Lap," in *Literary Theory / Renaissance Texts,* ed. Patricia Parker and David Quint (Baltimore, 1986), 341–72, pp. 345, 365 quoted. Nyquist's concluding characterization of the passage as "radically dialectical . . . casting a Platonic doubt on . . . its own mimesis" (p. 367) accords with the insistence on fallenness and with the attendant matter of hermeneutic process that we have introduced and shall reengage in the following chapters. Nyquist might not agree.

IV. It is, certainly, impossible for fallen mankind to be holy in any literal sense of the word, any more than it is possible to be whole, nor are places in and of themselves holy (see, for example, XI, 837), but inclinations and attitudes and prayers, and acceptance of God's law, may justly be so described. Among such, wedded love is described as the holiest. The exaltation of married love is reinforced by the second crucial word of the passage, and that is *all,* metrically stressed. *All,* a word frequently found within the epic Miltonic precincts, often has implications of the absolute, especially when metrically stressed as it is in "all the Charities" (IV, 756). Its power in this instance is heightened by the word it modifies.[38] Saint Paul wrote, "Though I speak with the tongues of men and of angels, and have not charity, I am become as sounding brass, or a tinkling cymbal. And though I have the gift of prophecy, and understand all mysteries, and all knowledge; and though I have all faith, so that I could remove mountains, and have not charity, I am nothing" (1 Cor. 13:1–2). Wedded love, that holiest state and condition, is the Miltonic matrix of all *caritas.* This is one of the strongest affirmations of the epic.

Milton also describes wedded love less generally, with more attention to particular detail, in examining the proper relationship between Adam and Eve. The poet casts the graced relationship between man and woman in terms of love, of knowing the body and more than the body through the body, and of difference and union. For Adam the essence of his bond to Eve is completion: with "Part of my Soul I seek thee, and thee claim / My other half" (IV, 487–88). The sense of personal incompleteness, of being only half of what one ought to be, is repeated when Adam tries to console Eve for her bad Satanic dream:

> Best Image of my self and dearer half,
> The trouble of thy thoughts this night in sleep
> Affects me equally
>
> (V, 95–97)

Nor is such attachment confined to pleas and reassurance. When faced with the ultimate decision whether or not to eat the fruit, Adam thinks less about the consequences of the Fall than about Eve:

---

38. Our point is the word's sense *in connection with* the central Christian concept of charity; its metrical stress is a secondary point. William Empson seems to us hopelessly idiosyncratic on this as on much else about Milton. See his *"All* in *Paradise Lost,"* in *The Structure of Complex Words* (London, 1951), 101–104.

O fairest of Creation, last and best
Of all Gods works, Creature in whom excell'd
Whatever can to sight or thought be formd,
Holy, divine, good, amiable, or sweet!
How are thou lost, how on a sudden lost

. . . .

Certain my resolution is to Die;
How can I live without thee, how forgoe
Thy sweet Converse and Love so dearly joyn'd,
To live again in these wild Woods forlorn?
Should God create another *Eve,* and I
Another Rib afford, yet loss of thee
Would never from my heart; no no, I feel
The Link of Nature draw me: Flesh of Flesh,
Bone of my Bone thou art, and from thy State
Mine never shall be parted, bliss or woe.

(IX, 896–900, 907–16)

With this ironic anticipation of the marriage vow, Adam, even if confusedly or wrongfully, affirms that he cannot return to incompleteness.

Eve's view of the bond differs from Adam's, because she differs from Adam. Although the union of woman and man in the love of God alone provides completeness, the resulting whole is not composed of two partners who are exactly the same. They are different, and as the French deputy noted, it is the differences that matter. At least Milton thought so, in emphasizing not the similarities but the differences between masculinity and femininity, and beyond that their complementarity, not their interchangeability. We inhabit a world where the emphasis on similarity or even interchangeability is both a powerful and a needful lever against injustice ("equal pay for equal work"). Milton's emphasis on complementarity instead can make it very difficult to recognize him as a herald and champion—with regard to Urania, a mediator and advocate—of womanhood.

For Eve, the union involves differences in function. She describes her relationship to Adam in terms of his authority over her:

O Thou for whom
And from whom I was formd flesh of thy flesh,
And without whom am to no end, my Guide
And Head, what thou hast said is just and right.

(IV, 440–43)

Adam, as we have seen, is virtually to no *beginning* without Eve. She repeats the theme of authority and subordination, addressing Adam:

> My Author and Disposer, what thou bidst
> Unargu'd I obey; so God ordains,
> God is thy Law, thou mine: to know no more
> Is womans happiest knowledge and her praise.
>
> (IV, 635–38)

Another voice earlier enforced the view of different functions in a hierarchy of authority. The Bardic voice describes the cruising Satan's sense of Adam and Eve as

> Not equal, as thir sex not equal seemd;
> For contemplation hee and valour formd,
> For softness shee and sweet attractive Grace,
> Hee for God only, shee for God in him
>
> (IV, 296–99)

Is one to take these obvious and dramatic and powerful differences within unity in a reductively literal manner, regarding Eve as inferior in law to Adam? Certainly she is not inferior in beauty and grace, nor in virtue, for the Bard describes here in the same terms Adam used: "Truth, Wisdom, Sanctitude severe and pure" (IV, 293). But what about in law? What about the plain meaning of the text? That cannot be ignored, and Thomas Aquinas did not despise it. At the Marburg Colloquy, Martin Luther insisted on the literal meaning of the biblical text in this regard, and our reliance on hermeneutic analysis compels us to begin at the same place. Milton could scarcely disregard the biblical authority for the husband's superiority in the law of marriage. Saint Paul wrote, "Wives, submit yourselves unto your own husbands, as unto the Lord. For the husband is the head of the wife, even as Christ is the head of the church" (Eph. 5:22–23). He also wrote, "But I would have you know, that the head of every man is Christ; and the head of the woman is the man" (1 Cor. 11:3).

Such presumptively inspired biblical texts would be part of the eternal providence to be asserted, the ways of God to men to be justified. But not only literal meaning matters. Saint Augustine argued in *De doctrina christiana* that where difficulties of interpretation arise, the true Christian ought to take that meaning "which leads to the reign of love (*cari-*

tatis)."[39] Milton was not unmindful of this, of interpretation of the spirit rather than of the letter. He includes descriptions of Eve incompatible with subordination, descriptions having to do with knowing through the body, as in Raphael's salutation to her:

> Hail Mother of Mankind, whose fruitful Womb
> Shall fill the World more numerous with thy Sons
> Then with these various fruits the Trees of God
> Have heap'd this Table.
>
> (V, 388–91)

Eve's generativity is lauded here, a capacity that belongs to her alone. Raphael is echoing God, who made Eve the same incarnational promise, that she would "bear / Multitudes like thy self" (IV, 473–74). Eve is, quite literally, the womb of the future. She is also the "Daughter of God and man" (IV, 660). Eve is twice addressed in this fashion by Adam while he is still in a state of grace and thus able to name correctly. The description is in terms of her origins. But it is her destiny that matters most. She is not only the "Daughter of God," she is also, indirectly, the *theotokos,* the mother of God. Eve's knowledge of the body is ultimately incarnational. Her level of redemptive worth through the body, which is entirely feminine, alters the meaning of the line "Hee for God only, shee for God in him" (IV, 299). An appropriately theological reading, one that regards the incarnation as at least as important as everyday life, would understand the line as meaning that she is formed for the God that is in Adam. Eve is always, though indirectly, the *theotokos.* Adam is merely the first man. A hermeneutic reading of that notorious line, a reading that seeks to understand the past in terms of the future, the ordinary in terms of the ultimate, thus produces a new understanding of Milton's view of the nature of gracious marriage. Eve's duty to Adam, woman's duty to man, is generativity and generosity, not law and obligation. Adam's duty to Eve, man's duty to woman, is supporting strength and—the trickier part—loyalty to the God in her while well and truly providing the medium of the God she seeks in him. Milton's triangulation by the beginning in hell, the ascent to heaven, the recourse to the fallen world and to

39. "Ad regnem caritatis interpretatio perducatur" (Augustine, *De doctrina christiana,* III, xv, 23, in *Patrologiae . . . Latina,* ed. Migne, XXXIV, 157). See also Lee A. Jacobus, *Sudden Apprehension: Aspects of Knowledge in "Paradise Lost"* (The Hague, 1976).

its myths by way of simile, and the hermeneutic recirculation in the sub-sequent fallen life in history firmly anchor in unfallen paradise, not else-where, the version he offers of Saint Paul's affirmation that man is woman's law (IV, 637). Readers and even critics overlooking the larger context may miss the point.

WILL

Ineluctably, a hermeneutic analysis of the human capacity for knowing and naming in *Paradise Lost* comes eventually to the topic of liberty and free will.[40] Milton departed sharply from the conventional Calvinism of his day by advancing a doctrine of radical free will that supposed there to be freedom even to reject saving grace. Milton's initial comment on the nature of humanity makes that clear, by the very words of God:

> I made him just and right,
> Sufficient to have stood, though free to fall.
> Such I created all th' Ethereal Powers
> And Spirits, both them who stood and them who faild;
> Freely they stood who stood, and fell who fell.
> Not free, what proof could they have givn sincere
> Of true allegiance, constant Faith or Love
>
> (III, 98–104)

To give true allegiance requires full freedom not only in everyday choice but in the choice of accepting grace and participating in redemption or refusing it. Milton was alive to the inherent psychological and ministerial contradictions within predestinarian Calvinism: if one is predestined for salvation, what is the use of obedience and what "constant Faith or Love" can be shown? The Bard gives unfallen reiteration to the belief in free will. Adam tells Eve, "But God left free the Will, for what obeys / Rea-son, is free, and Reason he made right" (IX, 351–52). "Reason also is choice," God says to the Son (III, 108). We may doubt that Adam under-stands exactly what he is telling Eve, but no comparable doubt about God's comprehension is possible. Beyond this, Milton specifically rejected the rigorism implicit in predestinarian Christianity by declaring Eve "yet sinless" (IX, 659) before eating but after being tempted and imagina-tively committing the sin in her heart. For Milton, knowing, even know-

40. On this, see Joan S. Bennett, *Reviving Liberty*, esp. Chap. 1.

ing the temptations and possibilities of evil, could never be sinful *in se,* though it might lead to sin at a later time. For him, like Augustine, it was the will that had been fatally damaged by the Fall, not reason, though reason was left subject to limit and distraction. Nonetheless, knowing and naming, operating through reason, always has a capacity for good, for *conversio,* for leading the fallen sinner to the "knowledge and love of God," in the prayer book's formula. That is, indeed, the very purpose in knowing and naming, and Raphael's and Michael's discourses are directed to that end, both for Adam and for us. After all, God is not defective in his love for humanity, humanity is short in love and obedience for God. The commandment given to Adam in his dream vision and conversation with the Presence Divine—to "shun to taste" (VIII, 327), as a pledge of obedience—is literal for Adam and metaphorical for us. It is too late to avoid tasting the tree; we can never be "new" and pastless, but it is not too late to be obedient. Obedience comes from love and love from knowledge, for us as it did for Adam and Eve. But knowledge, though a necessary condition of obedient love, is never a sufficient condition. And knowledge, considered in purely human terms, is inadequate for salvation. Equally inadequate is the subjective experience that attaches to knowing. Not a Manichaean, Milton was not a Gnostic, either. The imaginative horror of Eve's dream vision is no better at reinforcing obedience than the work—should we say habitual work, or merely accustomed?—that the pair did in the garden. A purely human capacity has to be insufficient for a divine purpose. In the theological universe of Milton's Protestantism, anything else would have been inconceivable. Fallen knowing and naming can lead even to further fall, as with Satan. It is all within the choice of the individual, in the realm of free will. When Adam desired to know about astronomy, about the battle in heaven, about the history of the universe, he was told these things, but they availed him not. Eve was given a vivid awareness of sin and disobedience, but her knowing was not transformed into faith in grace. Warnings were given concerning temptation, disobedience, and transgression, but . . .

For Milton, obedience given by a free act of the will is the true "constant Faith or Love" (III, 104) owed God. Free will justifies both the person and freedom itself, gives meaning to naming and knowing, and stands at the core of Milton's view of humanity. With the educated reason's choice of obedient love, the ways of God to man are justified: without it eternal providence is merely asserted. For Milton, indeed for any Christian, a definition of humanity is insufficient if couched in terms only of humanity. Faith through grace can alone give that knowledge force, make the knowledge real. Full faith in the grace of God is the element missing in the knowledge Adam and Eve have. As both so dramatically show, without grace we live but do not learn. Augustine put the point succinctly in Sermon 43: "Believe that you may understand."[41] In Milton's treatment of freedom in naming and knowing, Protestant theological truth is complemented by the sudden sting of psychological recognition.

41. "Crede ut intelligas" (Augustine, *Sermones ad populum*, XLIII, iii, 4, in *Patrologiae . . . Latina,* ed. Migne, XXXVIII, 255). See also Hans Georg Gadamer, who has in effect rendered the Augustinian idea in terms that pay their dues to, though not exclusively to, a latter-day naturalism: "It makes a difference whether a limit is experienced from out of the subjectivity of the act of meaning and the domineering character of the will or whether it is conceived in terms of the all-embracing harmony of beings within the world disclosed by language. . . . Metaphysics once taught . . . the original harmony of all things created, especially as the commensurateness of the created soul to created things" (*Essays in Philosophical Hermeneutics,* 81). For Gadamer, naming in the fallen world tends to be an impaired ability, like fallen knowing. But faithful, and accordingly graced, naming can designate a part in the dynamic and limitless—because eternal—harmony. "Harmony" is, of course, Milton's (and Donne's) metaphor as much as it is Gadamer's. For a provocative argument that Milton is *inter alia* fulfilling a Vergilian model, see Stella P. Revard, "Vergil's *Georgics* and *Paradise Lost:* Nature and Human Nature in a Landscape," in *Vergil at 2000: Commemorative Essays on the Poet and His Influence,* ed. John D. Bernard (New York, 1986), 259–80.

Six

Youth to Maturity: Journey's Early Perils

Paradise Lost did not suddenly appear de novo and ex nihilo. The work has biblical, secular literary, and patristic forebears, among others. We think the hermeneutic loop of analysis is most enriched by what we take to be Miltonic ideas of hermeneutic, by biblical and Augustinian theology, not least in its liturgical manifestation, and by an analysis of Milton's earlier poetic works. Each body of poetry illuminates the other, and the poems of 1645 and A Mask show us the Miltonic journey as surely as does the fall of humanity, though in terms of vagaries of personal development and early choice.

We would emphasize the fundamental continuity of Milton's early and late poetic concerns—continuity and interrelationships more fundamental than whatever differences in emphasis or even differences in genre exist between Paradise Lost and the other works. In A Mask, which Milton published in 1637, 1645, and again in 1673, substantially as he had written it in the Trinity manuscript, the themes of love and an ordered human community appear with greater poignancy than they do in Books XI and XII of Paradise Lost. The same themes appear in acrid contrast in Samson Agonistes. Still, the themes have equivalent force in the several works. The differences in tone, so much more marked than the differences of intellectual substance, owe, we think, chiefly to differences in genre and time, for Milton's regard for a morally and graciously ordered human community remained even as his expectations flagged.

Moreover, "Reason also is choice" (Paradise Lost, III, 108). In A Mask, Milton dramatizes external and internal obstacles to such loving choices as lead to communal wholeness, even salvific abundance of life, with emphasis on the external—as represented in part by Comus—and on the given, as represented, inter alia, by the stages of life and their relation to cultural, familial, and political circumstance. In the shorter works in Poems, Milton illuminates external and internal dilemmas of choice—including hermeneutic choice, with emphasis on the internal and the grace assisted. The early poetry deals with the same concerns, both social and theological, that are conspicuous in *Paradise Lost*. Milton's early journey was not a separate road but a stage on the same hermeneutic loop. It is worthwhile to look back to something like Milton's beginnings after having ourselves begun in something like the middle—*Paradise Lost*—and before considering Miltonic endings.

A MASK AND TIMELY TRIALS

In the dark a bit ourselves, we may all recognize the two boys in *A Mask* groping in unfamiliar surroundings, speaking at length not so much to each other as each to revive his own distracted spirits. The first speech by Elder Brother—like the earlier and more familiar entry speeches of the Spirit and the Lady—sketches a great deal of the realm of discourse and general dramatic situation:

> Unmuffle ye faint stars, and thou fair moon
> That wontst to love the travailers benizon,
> Stoop thy pale visage through an amber cloud,
> And disinherit *Chaos*, that raigns heer
> In double night of darknes, and of shades
> (*A Mask*, 331–35)[1]

It was no faint personage from "Before the starry threshold of *Joves* court" (*A Mask*, 1) we see unmuffled as the action begins. Before long we will see neither fair moon nor allegorical Cynthia but the better and more remarkable Sabrina lovingly earning "travailers benizon." But the boys' terms, their perplexity, the inadequacy of their apprehension, and the changefulness of their situation from antecedent action to conclusion all invite us to scrutinize what is going on and to frame an appraisal in terms literal, semiotic, symbolic, and hermeneutic.[2]

---

1. *A Mask* (based on the text of 1645), in *The Complete Poetry of John Milton*, ed. John T. Shawcross. All quotations are from this edition.

2. R. H. Bowers has emphasized an appropriate starting term, in "The Accent on Youth in 'Comus,'" in *SAMLA Studies in Milton*, ed. J. Max Patrick (Gainesville, Fla., 1953), 72–79. For a variety of more recent emphases, see C. L. Barber, "*A Mask Presented at Ludlow Castle:* The Mask as a Masque," in *The Lyric and Dramatic Milton*, ed. J. H. Summers (New York, 1965), 35–63; Thomas O. Calhoun, "On John Milton's *A Mask at Ludlow*," *Milton Studies*, VI (1974), 165–79; John G. Demaray, *Milton and the Masque Tradition: The Early Poems, "Arcades," and "Comus"* (Cambridge, Mass., 1968); Angus

For all the illuminations of recent scholarship, the seventeenth-century masque can be an uncongenial artifact for us, both in form and in theme. This masque poem appears to be animated by an accessible ideal of community, however, community that must constantly reinforce itself by a significantly precarious process of recruiting children who will accept communal commitment, responsibility, and love. The ideal of community, lying in the social action—never in the perfected achievement—of grace and *philos* in the fallen world, is accordant with the Bard's themes in Books X to XII of *Paradise Lost,* in *Paradise Regain'd,* and in the definitions by contrast of *Samson Agonistes.* This ideal, capable of actuating speech and action everywhere, appears to be an emergent conviction that the true earthly fulfillment of individuals is in free participation in loving, God-seeking society. Loving concord, permitting orientation and aspiration toward the "palace of Eternity" (line 14) would seem to be the cosmos to "disinherit *Chaos*" (line 334). And both chaos and eternity appear to offer themselves, never standing farther apart than the *civitas terrena* and the *civitas Dei.* Indeed the Lord President's house, at which the masque was first performed, teeters between chaos and the palace.

Some such description of this masque seems indispensable if we are to assimilate the thematic sense of the boys' large roles, of lines reading "Mortals . . . Love vertue, she alone is free" (line 1019), instead of "Girls, love chastity, she alone is wise," or of why Thyrsis "Longer . . . durst not stay" (line 577). Moreover, this masque, so much less given to tableaux vivants than earlier instances of the genre, possesses a striking dynamism. The substance of the action sees three young people moving from the relative existential isolation and passivity of early youth to responsible activity and charitable commitment attending "thir fathers state" (line 35). They are, like everyone, "Confin'd and pester'd in this pinfold" (line 7) but are equal to their exemplary role partly because they are "nurs't in princely lore" (line 34) to become mindful of crowns and partly because they have their own aspiration "by due steps . . . To lay thir just hands on that golden key / That opes the palace of Eternity" (lines 12–14).

Since the young Egertons were only nine, eleven, and fifteen years old in 1634, when they played the two brothers and the sister, it is tempting to

Fletcher, *The Transcendental Masque: An Essay on Milton's "Comus"* (Ithaca, N.Y., 1971); Maryann Cale McGuire, *Milton's Puritan Masque* (Athens, Ga., 1983); Cedric C. Brown, *John Milton's Aristocratic Entertainments* (New York, 1985).

think of the masque's principal characters as children. But the seventeenth century tended to regard children as compact adults, and this poem treats them as youngsters with burgeoning powers of reason and choice. They move out of early childhood and the tutorial closet into the woods and a rising awareness of sexuality, and finally to a postlapsarian earthly counterpart of the heavenly mansion.[3] In doing so, they learn needful lessons that are complex, mysterious, and above all communal, and they learn them as recruits to a free world's work. Since most travelers through the woods of Comus taste his cup "through fond intemperate thirst" (line 67), the three appear a surviving minority in a tremendously costly battle. Those who perish represent a qualification upon Elder Brother's touchingly premature declaration that "Virtue may be assail'd but never hurt" (line 589).

The Spirit initially defines the danger impending from Comus as a breach not only of reason—or of virginity—but also of charitable community: the beguiled ones "all thir freinds and native home forget / To roul with pleasure in a sensual stie" (lines 76–77). Hermeneutic circulation of recollection and anticipation is aborted for a bestially reduced present. Appropriately, the figures who succumb are made visibly alien to us and to each other by being given heads resembling disparate beasts. With

---

3. Cleanth Brooks and John E. Hardy, "Essays in Analysis," bound with *Poems of Mr. John Milton: The 1645 Edition* (New York, 1951). See also Sears Jayne, "The Subject of Milton's Ludlow *Mask,*" *PMLA*, LXXIV (1959), 533–43. On Jayne's view, the earl has to be less an agent of than a figure of God (p. 542), but his article continues to offer the most substantial argument for the masque as a Platonic allegory of chastity. Mindele Treipe's "*Comus* as 'Progress'" (*Milton Quarterly*, XX [1986], 1–12) reinforces our explication of the metaphoric aspects of the youthful journey by an altogether persuasive reading of the Bridgewater manuscript's implication of a metonymic "artistically retarded procession: through dusk and nightfall from grounds to courtyard to castle hall" (p. 11). Provocative oscillations between what may be taken as these extremes of theoretic concept and praxis continue. See, notably, David Norbrook, *Poetry and Politics in the English Renaissance* (London, 1984), Chap. 10; Jeanne S. Martin, "Transformations in Genre in Milton's *Comus,*" *Genre*, X (1977), 195–213; Kathleen M. Swaim, "Allegorical Poetry in Milton's Ludlow Mask," *Milton Studies*, XVI (1982), 167–99; Guillory, *Poetic Authority*, Chap. 4; Richard Halpern, "Puritanism and Maenadism in *A Masque,*" in *Rewriting the Renaissance: The Discourses of Sexual Difference in Early Modern Europe*, ed. Margaret W. Ferguson, Maureen Quilligan, and Nancy J. Vickers (Chicago, 1986), 88–105; and John Creaser, "'The Present Aid of This Occasion': The Setting of *Comus,*" in *The Court Masque*, ed. David Lindley (Manchester, Eng., 1984), 111–34.

more orthodox Christian conviction, the Spirit notes that the sinners' sins are self-blinding, even ludicrously so.[4] They "Not once perceave thir foul disfigurement, / But boast themselves more comely then before" (lines 74–75). That irregular things had occurred in the household of the rapist brother-in-law of the earl of Bridgewater's wife—in the Castlehaven scandal—makes the Spirit's description simultaneously immediate and appalling. And the sensational trial and conviction of the earl of Castlehaven, Mervyn Touchet, for sexual abuse of the lady's young cousin left no doubt that such things might threaten the three young actors of *A Mask,* were they ever so virtuous.

The community from which the three actors came was centrifugal, idiosyncratic, and vulnerable. The Welsh border neighborhood, as some in the first-night audience certainly knew, had been the setting of the crime of rape and had experienced a corruptly collegial malfeasance of justice in the aftermath even prior to the earl of Bridgewater's appointment.[5] The symbolic and psychological landscape of the masque permits the unfolding action to show very quickly the relationships of the three

4. Don Cameron Allen has observed that some of *A Mask's* "characters are uncertain about their theology and their chronology" ("Milton's *Comus* as a Failure in Artistic Compromise," *English Literary History,* XVI [1949], 117–18). We agree. How steadily does youth feel any connection between the daily and the transcendent realm of being, or the extension of the daily into a thick and living history? For a richly rewarding article on learning by ear more than eye or establishmentarian authority, see Donald M. Friedman, "*Comus* and the Truth of the Ear," in *The Muses Common-Weale: Poetry and Politics in the Seventeenth Century,* ed. Claude Summers and Ted-Larry Pebworth (Columbia, Mo., 1988), 119–34.

5. See Barbara Breasted, "Comus and the Castlehaven Scandal," *Milton Studies,* III (1971), 201–24; and Rosemary Mundhenk, "Dark Scandal and the Sun-Clad Power of Chastity: The Historical Milieu of Milton's Comus," *Studies in English Literature,* XV (1975), 141–52. On the failure to convict the rapist Philbert Burghill despite the earl's best efforts, and on *A Mask* as an admonitory mirror for magistrates, see Leah S. Marcus' partial but essential "Justice for Margery Evans: A 'Local' Reading of *Comus,*" in *Milton and the Idea of Woman,* ed. Julia M. Walker (Urbana, Ill., 1988), 66–85. See also Leah S. Marcus, "Milton's Anti-Laudian Masque" in *The Politics of Mirth: Jonson, Herrick, Milton, Marvell, and the Defense of Old Holiday Pastimes* (Chicago, 1986), 169–212. Marcus' argument builds toward an application to Miltonic epic, but it is also appropriate to mention here, as another pole of reference, Anna Nardo's discussion of discourse in the Italian academies, in "Academic Interludes in *Paradise Lost,*" *Milton Studies,* XXVII (1991), 209–41; and, not least, Robert Wilcher's "Milton's Masque: Occasion, Form, and Meaning," *Critical Quarterly,* XX (1978), 3–20.

not only to one another and to other characters but also to various features of local reality.[6]

Elder Brother begins authoritatively with his adjuration to stars and moon to "disinherit *Chaos*" (line 334) and the "usurping mists" (line 337), or in the event of the heavenly bodies' being shrouded, to "a rush candle" to provide at least a "long levell'd rule of streaming light" (line 340). *Disinherit, usurping,* and the doubly meaningful *rule* bespeak a lively sense in the speaker of the issues animating the action.[7] These appear to him in a categorical, rational fashion that lets him sanely caution Second Brother against "over-exquisite" (line 359), if valid, conjectures "Of Savage hunger, or of Savage heat" (line 358). But he quickly betrays a quasi-philosophical egotism that partly disables him for dealing with the world around him, an unawareness that the real world may not accord with his abstractions. But more than that, his style as he thinks he appraises the real world veers from distortion to distortion in a way that may seem at first simply to jumble abstraction and concreteness. Always, though, his style depersonalizes his subject and favors the conceptual. He dismisses what he takes to be only literal and material: the "single want of light and noise" (line 369) should indeed not "stir the constant mood" (line 371) of his sister's thoughts—*if* light and noise are totally unsymbolic, that is, if she is a stone. But as her situation, like modern brainwashing and experiment, shows, sensory deprivation usually disorients a person and provokes unsettling fantasy, with figures from memory and the imagination. Elder Brother magnifies the conceptual: he speaks of virtue seeing "to do what vertue would" (line 373), as if automatically, as a

6. We might expect from the young poet who proclaimed his admiration for Spenser that characters in the woods will be ethically or at least perceptually in the shade. Readers who have the *Faerie Queene* fresh in mind will readily see kinships between *A Mask* and elements in the stories of Florimell (besieged by Proteus), Amoret (by Busyrane), Belphoebe, even Britomart, or Acrasia's bower, but readers who do not have it in mind would be helped not at all by comparisons that in any case would take more space. William Madsen made the basic point about the landscape, in "The Idea of Nature in Milton's Poetry," in *Three Studies in the Renaissance* (New Haven, 1958), 197. For provocative points in both agreement and disagreement, see Guillory, *Poetic Authority*, Chap. 4; A. Kent Hieatt, *Chaucer, Spenser, and Milton: Mythopoeic Continuities and Transformations* (Montreal, 1975); and Quilligan, *Milton's Spenser*.

7. For an additional example, see John D. Cox, "Poetry and History in Milton's Country Masque," *English Literary History*, XLIV (1977), 622–40. Or consider the notorious ship money case: roughly, realm and rule versus thick local history—and the king won.

quasi-personified or Scholastic virtue might see, but less diversely than the Lady or any whole person does see. He refers to "wisdoms self" (line 375), with "nurse Contemplation" (line 377) pluming "ruffl'd" feathers (line 380), and to an unspecified *he* with a by now symbolic light "within his own cleer brest" (line 381). By the time Elder Brother comes to "'Tis chastity, my brother, chastity" (line 420), he is taking his somewhat Platonized conceptual heritage of more or less biblical traditions about the armor of righteousness and finding in virtue "compleat steel" (line 421) and "sacred rayes" (line 425) more substantial than the material world. Accordingly, we are given in a dependent clause of logical concession— "Be it not don in pride, or in presumption" (line 431)—what is a major concern of the masque, as it is of Milton's career. Milton could not have been unaware of the late-Renaissance sense that both male and female chastity were concrete personal goods, and that chastity was conventionally metonymic for prudence and good stewardship.

Elder Brother executes dramatically a kind of rising turn toward inanity, continuing full circle into the interchange with Thyrsis before subsiding into step with that guide's wisdom. In the speech beginning with the soberly practical—"Peace brother, be not over-exquisite" (line 359)— he quickly launches into elevations, circumlocutions, slippery equivalences, and quasi-philosophical verbosities as if words were magic enough without community association. In this context, even if wisdom "lets grow her wings" (line 378), the growth becomes the less than natural fecundity of mere verbal profusion. The "ruffl'd" feathers are a signifier with scarcely any shareable signified, their condition "sometimes impair'd" (line 380) a generality without particulars. Within a few lines come a catalog of static counters—*virgin purity* (line 427), *unblench't majesty* (line 430), *congeal'd stone* (line 449), *rigid looks* (line 450), *a soul . . . found* (line 454)—and then the building-block construction of a romance landscape, charming in its overexquisiteness: "defilement to the inward parts . . . clotted by contagion . . . shadows damp . . . in charnel vaults" (lines 466–71).[8] By another half-turn in a later speech he reaches a prac-

---

8. Platonic bookishness, perhaps, as Demaray urges in *Milton and the Masque Tradition,* 134. But surely Elder Brother's recollection from the *Phaedo* has become uncannily phantasmal. For persuasive advocacy of the relevance of Scholastic theology in understanding *A Mask* as a whole, see James Obertino, "Milton's Use of Aquinas in *Comus,*" *Milton Studies,* XXII (1986), 21–43. James Andrew Clark elaborates on the Scholastic background particularly with regard to nature, and argues that Sabrina reconciles the divergent

tical suggestion about the immediate situation which by its arbitrary and fanciful impracticality—it is a quasi-epic boast—puts Thyrsis to his best courtesy and tact: "Ile . . . drag him by the curls and cleave his scalp / Down to the hipps" (lines 606–609). On the other hand, there could be no heroic tradition or legacy of philosophy such as those genuflected to in the masque without something like the words and verbal structures Elder Brother relishes. Milton does not *satirize* children, here or elsewhere.

Second Brother's style generally complements his elder's. He deals in materiality. His sense of the outside world does not assess realities welling from within that have directed it or might redirect it. In a variation on the masque's pervasive themes of community and freedom, he is apprehensive of an external, material "dungeon of innumerous bows" (line 349). Elder Brother's apprehensions concern an internal, negative "dungeon" (line 384), prisonlike because unfurnished with his compendious abstractions virtue and wisdom. If Elder Brother discounts the "single want of light and noise" (line 369), Second Brother avers, "Of night, or lonelines it recks me not, / I fear the dred *events* that *dog* them both" (lines 404–405; our emphasis). Second Brother has his abstractions—beauty, incontinence, danger, opportunity—but they sink in a redolence of depersonalizing *things:* "her blossoms" (line 396), "her fruit" (line 396), "rash hand" (line 397), and the like. And what dare we expect from the lad who indirectly labels the virginity of the prim Lady "unsun'd heaps / Of misers treasure" (lines 398–99) though she speaks of "Faith . . . Hope . . . Chastity" (lines 213–15), and yet more impressively of the "Sun-clad power of Chastity" (line 782)? But he rises to a new style, a change of heart, personal and humbly concerned: "I fear . . . Lest som ill greeting touch attempt the person / Of our unowned sister" (lines 405–407). And in any case *A Mask* does insist that those who would go to heaven must tread on the ground. The very genre suits Milton's incarnationism.[9]

---

attitudes toward it of Comus and the Lady. Clark's argument illuminates much (although Second Brother nearly disappears), not least in the implicit suggestion of a hermeneutic loop back to the attendant Spirit's view—rearticulated at the end. See Clark, "Milton Naturans, Milton Naturatus: The Debate over Nature in *A Mask* . . . ," *Milton Studies,* XX (1984), 3–27.

9. Demaray reminds us that Milton's "early verse introduces allusions to masque spectacle" (*Milton and the Masque Tradition,* 129), and he cites as examples the more or less liturgical passages of "On the Morning of Christs Nativity," stanzas XIV–XV, "L'Alle-

Elder Brother needs external prompting. Thyrsis, by voice and person and associations with madrigals, chastens him slightly with benign reminders of aesthetic, graceful communication in a natural and humane world. The shepherd's greeting invokes relationships of affection, civic order, lineage, and calling, in almost checklist order: "O my lov'd maisters heir, and his next joy" (line 501). He asks, "O my virgin Lady, where is she?" (line 507). She is in trouble, we know. For her, neither Elder Brother's conceptualizing detachment nor Second Brother's unassimilated outwardness: she has the strength of both tendencies with little of the related weakness. Moreover, her predicament has acute poignancy. Her opening lines are surely no simple rehearsal of a Renaissance hierarchy of the senses: "This way the noise was, if mine ear be true, / My best guide now" (lines 170–71). A word stressed by metrics and situation is *now*. Her eye may have been a better guide before, but the whole poem asks whether it either was or is now adequate. She has moved out of the study and into an orally immediate world of "riot" (line 172) and conversation and summons. She continues scornfully on themes of "ill manag'd merriment" (line 172) by "loose unlettr'd hinds" (line 174) who "in wanton dance" (line 176) "thank the gods amiss" (line 177). The masque seems to hold that what she contends is too limited and partial in its nature. Shepherd and "swain" (line 852) certainly carol and dance acceptably enough in the description by Thyrsis late in the play (line 849), and at the festival at the Lady's "Fathers residence" near the end (line 947).

Her soliloquy in this peculiar landscape unfolds more of her misorientations and indispositions toward the world. Milton has formulated a domain that shows good and ill partly by externalizing them and that tends to make material those things taken to be real. In this landscape, chastity manifests itself to Comus as a "different pace" (line 145) or "footing" (line 146) on a purposeful journey, in contrast to his "fantastick round" (line 144). The comparison seems to be not so much one of the order of grace versus the order of nature as between less and more *inclusive*, less or more orderly, modes of reality in nature. "Good is as visible as green," Donne said in a differently ironic context.[10] Goodness and greenness have a rough parity of materiality in two ways: within the mind, as

---

gro," 128, 136–37, and "Lycidas," 180. (On the other hand, the speaker of "Il Penseroso," 97–100, would *reduce* tragedy to the costume parade of weak masque.)

10. John Donne, "Communitie," 14.

notions, and in the external world, in some of their consequences. The Lady has not coherently internalized, engaged, or integrated good and ill. But her Augustinian journey is not averse . . .

She errs, even if somewhat winningly, in thinking the woods "kind" and "hospitable" (line 187), though, of course, if *kind* carries its other sense, of having blood relationship, her belief is ironically true. She errs in thinking the sylvan world, at evening in seeming "palmers weeds" (line 189), will provide for her and her brothers in the way she herself would prescribe, the naïvely flashy way of "golden wings" (line 214) and "glistring" guardians (line 219). When Comus appears, his "quaint habits" (line 157) are supposed to look "glistring" to the audience, but not to her bleared and beguiled eye. The poignancy in this deepens presently in her plaintive comment on eye and ear at odds:

> mirth
> Was rife and perfet in my list'ning ear,
> Yet nought but single darknes do I find.
> (Lines 202–204)

Her egotism is apparent when she attributes to "envious darknes" (line 194) and "theevish night" (line 195) a "fellonious end" (line 196), as if the travelers, "misled and lonely" (line 200), were merely passive victims of nature's scariness.

Darkness here is neutral, of course, save insofar as it is *nox,* a projection of the observer's self. When it appears in that character, "A thousand fantasies / Begin to throng into my memory . . . pure-ey'd Faith, white-handed Hope . . . And thou unblemish't form of Chastity, / I see ye visibly" (lines 205–16).[11] The Lady's disproportionate concern with the negative—with unblemished chastity, instead of, say, resplendent charity, with faith pure-eyed but not explicitly viewing anything, with white-handed hope not explicitly offering or receiving, with a "supreme good" (line 217) noteworthy for "officers of vengeance" (line 218), with even "love-lorn nightingale" (line 234)—comes out of her own mind. That it comes naturally in the dramatic situation is just the point: showing and educating her natural self and applying her educated self to a newly challenging nature constitute the double work under way. Something must integrate the elements of her being and of the world which she takes—

---

11. In this sense, relatively "local" new historicist readings have been needed correctives.

comically or fatally but all too crisply—as separate, like thoughts and walking mind (lines 210–11) or "mind" and (jarring jingle) "corporal rind" (lines 663–64). She briefly figures as the Manichaean in the group.

If Second Brother is in an inchoate sense the perennial Lucretian, and hence the most novelistic character, Comus stands farther in that line as the being who has committed his will to the materialistic, deterministic round. Comus is thereby demonic and closer to a character of romance or tragedy. And Elder Brother's will churns actively enough so that the possibility of tragedy, like that of burlesque, just begins to show—as in his arrogant proclamation "if this fail, / The pillar'd firmament is rott'nness" (line 598). But whereas his naïve variation upon the perennial conviction that "the world is my idea" offers entry to redemptive ideas, Comus' representation of reality to himself and the Lady appears in diction and image a tissue of reductive ideas. In his first speech he offers "Joy and feast" (line 102) and "shout" (line 103) and "dance" (line 104), promising exemption from "Rigor" (line 107), "Advice" (line 108), "age" (line 108), and "severity" (line 108). Light and dark are for him less cosmic than appetitive alterations:

> gilded car of day
> His glowing axle doth allay
> . . . slope sun his upward beam
> Shoots against the dusky pole
> (Lines 95–99)

These in turn control values: "'Tis only daylight that makes sin" (line 126). In his second speech, he expresses surprise, after the Lady's song, that "somthing holy" (line 246) might lodge in "Earths mould" (line 244) and master brute nature, as testified by "vocal air" (line 247), but he immediately longs to subdue such a strange mixture to the brute nature of his will. His seduction speeches proffer imagistically an interior life dominated by naturalistic, exterior forms: "all the pleasures / That fancy can *beget* on youthfull thoughts" (lines 668–69; our emphasis). His exterior life puts the goddess Natura in charge: "dainty limms which nature lent" (line 680). It lets "mortal frailty" (line 686) subsist along with "shops" (line 716) and consumption and something like a death wish (lines 715–36), but not mortal strength, still less immortality.

Comus does not simply personify a sexual license antithetical to a narrowly, negatively conceived chastity; his remarks point toward a rejection of the work of daylight, of nature, nurture, and the *polis,* toward dynamism as chaos. The brothers and the Lady have made no such rejection, but only by the end have they moved and been moved to harmonious commitment to night, day, nature, nurture, and *polis.* [12]

Misdirection and Fixity

Movement and a journey dramatic, literal, and hermeneutic loom large in *A Mask.* [13] "Where els / Shall I inform my unacquainted feet," asks the Lady (line 180), who later speaks of "this leavy Labyrinth" (line 278). The spirit begins by adverting to due steps in the image of a bird alighting and regaining the air:

> I knew the foul inchanter though disguis'd,
> Enter'd the very lime-twigs of his spells,
> And yet came off
>
> > (Lines 645–47)

At the end he says, "follow me, / *Love* vertue . . . She can teach ye how to clime" (lines 1018–20; our emphasis). In a similar vein are various references to the travels of wise Ulysses. Comus participates in the pattern of describing the human condition as movement, but with a difference. He attempts to lie, but ironically speaks the truth:

> I can conduct you Lady . . .
> . . . where you *may* be safe
> Till furder *quest.*
>
> > (Lines 319–21; our
> > emphasis)

12. David Wilkinson asserts that the poem concerns itself primarily with chastity and secondarily with family solidarity, but denies that the subtheme works independently of the special factors involved in the first performance. See his "The Escape from Pollution. A Comment on *Comus,*" *Essays in Criticism,* X (1960), 32–43. See the rejoinders by Geoffrey Rans, in *Essays in Criticism,* X (1960), 364–69; and by William Leahy, in *Essays in Criticism,* XI (1961), 111.

13. For a richly illustrated compendium on the journey as a commonplace in Renaissance art and literature, see Samuel C. Chew, *The Pilgrimage of Life* (New Haven, 1962), esp. Chaps. 6, 7. Chew's emphasis on visual art makes his book an appropriate resource for considering Milton's elaboration on the Augustinian journey in this masque.

Or he introduces a relatively inharmonious note, as in the fruitless circularity of "Com, knit hands, and beat the ground, / In a light fantastick round" (lines 143–44).

All this is as it should be for aesthetic and thematic unity. Milton is no Manichaean, and Comus cannot create, work, or even propose things, ex nihilo. He testifies to cosmos over chaos sometimes even when trying to lie, as Chaucer's Pardoner does: "It were a journey like the path to Heav'n, / To help you find them" (lines 303–304). He self-disqualifyingly pictures as bad (even if it were possible) something clearly good in Renaissance iconography (if only it were possible): "To gaze upon the sun with shameless brows" (line 736).

Comus participates in the reciprocal definition of outer and inner life (see p. 161 above). The Spirit later proclaims that "unbelief is blind" (line 519), a kind of interior night, *nox,* akin to that externalized on stage as a setting for the young three's set of ignorances, nonaffiliations, misbeliefs, and presumptions. In a way daylight does make sin, in making it apprehensible to a dawning or enlightened awareness. To describe hearing the Lady's song, the Spirit invokes "drowsie frighted steeds" (line 553) that seemingly figure languid rhythmic progressions alike of night and sleep, as well as a "breathing sound" (line 555) like perfumes (which engage possibly the most internal and intimate of sense modalities) and a creaturely "silence" that is soothed and "took e're she was ware" (line 558). He "took in strains that might create a soul / Under the ribs of Death" (lines 561–62). Silence is "took" rather than ended, and the fulfilled union of song and silence "might create a soul" by an impregnation of spirit, not sport. Comus hears the song as a like fusion of externality and internality, and activity and passivity, but he orients the experience hedonistically; of "these raptures" (line 247) he exclaims,

> How sweetly did they float upon the wings
> Of silence, through the empty-vaulted night,
> At every fall smoothing the raven down
> Of darknes till she smil'd
>
> (Lines 249–52)

Darkness, not an element of social communication, is merely titillated; silence buoys up speech, but not in any dialogic or dialectical manner—no generativity there. The whole configuration diverges markedly in coordination, purposiveness, and fertility from the analysis proposed by the spirit. Elder Brother's ears might be presumed to have taken in the strains had his tongue not been so engaged in spinning out variations on the figures of birds and communication [14] and of daylight and virtue:

And wisdoms self
Oft seeks to sweet retired solitude,
Where with her best nurse Contemplation
She plumes her feathers, and lets grow her wings
That in the various bustle of resort
Were all to ruffl'd, and somtimes impair'd.
He that has light within his own cleer breast
May sit i'th center, and enjoy bright day
(Lines 375–82)

But although the Lady herself comes to sit fixedly "i'th center," where she is "freez'd . . . to congeal'd stone" (line 449), that is, astounded, despite her contrary expectation (line 210), while her foes remain mobile, neither she nor her brothers enjoy bright day. Her trial and her brothers' constitute the second phase of the action. The opening three hundred lines or so of the play show in the main an apparently close-knit group that disintegrates. The phase after that shows what happens when nurture already seen to be strong but not strong enough for a menacing world is put under trial.

The Lady goes offstage, beginning the part of the journey that is to be in the company of Comus, with remarks that are an overture to the trial. She speaks in terms that subsume and go beyond even a large concept of chastity:

Shepherd, I take thy word
And trust thy honest offer'd courtesie,
Which oft is sooner found in lowly sheds
With smoaky rafters, then in tapstry halls
And courts of princes, where it first was nam'd,
And yet is most pretended: In a place
Less warranted then this, or less secure
I cannot be, that I should fear to change it;

14. It is worth reiterating in this connection that the Lady sings of a "love-lorn nightingale" (*A Mask,* 234) and the Spirit characterizes her as "poor hapless nightingale" (line 566). She likens the brothers to Narcissus. And the "spungy air" (line 154) that is the medium for Comus' "dazling spells" (line 154) seems significantly unfit for graceful flight or sound.

Eye me blest providence, and square my triall
To my proportion'd strength. Shepherd lead on. —
(Lines 321–30)

Her imagery restlessly implies one kind of sensory experience after an-other, as if pointing up the question of what will be paramount in reveal-ing the truth.[15] Will it be the primarily auditory taken word or named name of courtesy, the primarily visual "tapstry" or eyeing, the odorous, eye-smarting, tactile smoky rafters, the bodily kinesthetic squared trial or proportioned strength or lowliness of the sheds or the shepherd who leads on? She shows naïve overconfidence in her basic assumption that her fallen and bodily apprehension will be adequate. Her conventional paean to uncertainly confused georgic pastoralism shows irony both general and immediate, ending as it does in a misplacement of trust as ironic as Oth-ello's "Honest Iago." If she is right about the location of true courtesy, what is to fear in woods most likely peopled with low shed dwellers? The masque moves ultimately by song, dance, and story to learn and enact the stylistic, aesthetic, intellectual, and moral primacy of something contrast-ing with the pastoral and broader than the courtly: the superior civic, or communal.

If we find the three young people's situation, speech, and action a bit wide of the full truth, in an uneasy mix of emotional and evaluative im-plications, we have smelled out irony. But the irony is not dependent on a motley parade of knaves and fools. Clearly Milton has not drawn an Egerton child parallel to Shylock exultantly croaking, "A Daniel, come to judgement," nor to a Malvolio, cross-gartered in his inordinate hopes, nor to a cynical manipulator of language like Mark Antony in the Forum. Milton has presented the brothers and the Lady as never quite oriented toward a bad or self-seeking cause, and mistaken in outlooks that often would be less mistaken in a better world. The ironies invite the wry or rueful chuckle that is kept from condescension by the knowledge of hav-ing been there, or the twinge of recognition of how naïve missteps can lead to hurt that seems unfairly large in proportion to what produced it. And we, the viewers of the masque, do not want the heroes and heroines

15. Similarly Second Brother has implored that an earful of mobile associations amid appropriate frames of order serve in the place of habitual vision (lines 342–49; see Fried-man, "Comus and the Truth of the Ear"). For a quite different and radically allegorical argument, see Alice-Lyle Scoufos, "The Mysteries in Milton's *Masque*," *Milton Studies*, VI (1974), 113–42.

we are watching hurt at all, although in line with the expectations of comedy we may want them reformed or married.[16]

Within the broad, partly ironic scope of the communal, the largeness of Comus' challenge and of the Lady's faulty response should be remembered. His wand is a threat not just to her but to the boys. That which in the normal course of things can "unthred . . . joints, . . . crumble . . . sinews" (lines 613–14) and chain up nerves in (monumental?) alabaster (line 660) would seem to be the familiar Renaissance natural triad of time, decay, and death. The threat to the brothers if they do not employ "Farr other arms and other weapons" (line 612) and the command to the Lady, to be "as *Daphne* was / Root-bound" (lines 661–62) both work to the same end.[17] The wand is a symbolic condensation of natural processes in their brutal and mechanistic, graceless aspects. To live by them would be to die by them, as the Spirit in effect warns; to retreat into their lesser consciousness and vegetable determinism would come to much the same thing. Hence, Comus has unobtrusively been made to pose a dilemma that reveals his own plight: Be in tune with nature by joining me, or be in tune with nature as punishment. The two choices look alike because neither sex nor anything else in nature can ever be more than natural for him, can ever be articulated and oriented by something larger or of transcendent value. He must hold that being alive and conscious always involves sexual consciousness without ever involving faith, hope, and charity, or community or patience. Indeed, in his extraordinary vivid lines about "green shops" (line 716) and the like, he views the whole cosmos in consumerist and technocratic terms, and sees no ruling Father or genuinely nurturing Mother, nor any such pairing of lovers as Cupid and Psyche, but only a weltering race between appetites and the gratifications and fruits of appetite—the fueling of a loveless machine.

The Lady's rejoinders to all this are apt to amaze: "none / But such as are good men can give good things" (lines 702–703). This variation of the Pauline notion that the good man from the good treasures of his heart brings forth the good can be derived only by formally invalid logic. Moreover, its congruence is uncertain with the disparagement of integrity

16. E. M. W. Tillyard, for example, affirms that "she must take her place in society" (*Studies in Milton* [New York, 1951], 95). We cannot agree that for the Lady to mention marriage to Comus "would be a dangerous digression" (Demaray, *Milton and the Masque Tradition*, 139).

17. On the "Root-bound" lady, see Kerrigan, *The Sacred Complex*, Chap. 2.

seemingly involved in rejecting the cup *even* "Were it a draught for *Juno* when she banquets" (line 701). Shaky logic paradoxically allies with acute psychology in the Lady's first, fragmentary recognitions—a precarious one of saving division, "Thou canst not touch the freedom of my mind" (line 663), and the immediately telling one of a damning division, "false traitor" (line 691).[18] Her constructive destiny develops, not surprisingly, in an intermittent note, a counterpoint of humble tones: "while Heav'n sees good" (line 665); "Mercy guard me!" (line 695); "swinish gluttony / Ne're looks to Heav'n amidst his gorgeous feast" (lines 776–77). With the humility goes a developing sense of ongoing process, of life as more dynamic than categorical. The Lady herself dramatizes this by acting in response to Comus' challenge, even if sometimes presumptuously or erroneously, to style her role and self as representative of a chastity now associated with virginity but—she has yet to understand—also "Sunclad" (line 782) and thus associated not only with enlightenment but with creativity and the works of daylight.[19] Not unlike the Son in *Paradise Regain'd,* but less consistently, she confesses divine love.

The counterforce endowing her movement with dramatic vitality and with some of its symbolic resonance appears not only in the externalized and rationalized element of Comus' argument but, as Cleanth Brooks and John E. Hardy have understood, in the subrational but not unnatural sexual instinct suggested by "this marble venom'd seat / Smear'd with gumms of glutenous heat" (lines 916–17) and by her numbed-out or fearful or traumatized fixity, a state counteracted by Sabrina's "chast palms moist and cold" (line 918).[20]

The fixity exemplifies captivity, which everywhere in the poem is insisted upon as besetting any life not sufficiently graced by love. Comus

18. For the Lady (as for Eve), see Joseph Wittreich's telling exposition of the once widely current and now reemergent feminist Milton in *Feminist Milton* (Ithaca, N.Y., 1987).

19. That the doctrine of virginity has not yet "entered fully into her experience" and become a "positive virtue, or principle of action," A. S. P. Woodhouse long ago urged as a reason for her fixity. See his *"Comus* Once More," *University of Toronto Quarterly,* XIX (1950), 218–23, p. 221 quoted. But his treatment seems to us overshifted in the direction of static category and abstraction. In any case, for emphatic dissent, see Rans's rejoinder to Wilkinson, in *Essays in Criticism,* X (1960), 367. On Sabrina as reconciler, see William A. Oram, "The Invocation of Sabrina," *Studies in English Literature,* XXIV (1984), 121–39.

20. Brooks and Hardy, "Essays in Analysis," 215–26.

himself feels that he does "fear" (line 800) her words to be "set off by som superior power" (line 801). He therefore "*must* dissemble" (line 805; our emphasis, but on a metrical stress). He remains master of the wood, but his rounds are compulsively and predictably patterned. As C. S. Lewis has observed about *Paradise Lost,* hell is locked on the inside. How the other characters' behavior bears on the themes of virtuous society, power, and liability, repays further attention.[21]

THE ACQUAINTANCE OF "UNACQUAINTED FEET"

The Lady's final deliverance, melodramatically begun with the onstage charge of the brothers, elaborates the action hermeneutically. The Spirit cannot completely effect her rescue, but that does not leave him simply a stage prop in the masque, nor does it run the masque aground on the difficulties that arise in presenting mystery. The Spirit's flight—"Longer I durst not stay" (line 577)—to find the brothers, and his lagging offstage until they have rushed on and "driven in" the rout (rubric at line 813), alike signal that the Spirit's gifts must work through the ties of human commitment and human relationship, as human nature comes to adequate and communal terms with itself. The dramatic facts stand as a corollary of Milton's incarnation-centered Christianity. In any case, the Spirit's gifts of discernment are godlike in a way that makes him look like an attendant on the Holy Ghost and makes his uncoercive comings and goings like inspirations in the mind. He "knew the foul inchanter though disguis'd" (line 645);[22] in *Paradise Lost,* hypocrisy walks "Invisible, except to God

---

21. *Ibid.,* 226. Madsen, after citing the passage on faith, hope, and charity from five hundred lines earlier in the play, asserts that "her Platonic idealist equipment is more than adequate to counter the all-dissolving skepticism of her tempter" ("The Idea of Nature in Milton's Poetry," 190). Apart from questions of whether Comus has the universal solvent or she the container for it, this shrewd judgment could be adequate only if the masque were merely a tableau. The study remains helpful, however, despite its neglect of Milton's dynamism.

22. That haemony signifies knowledge we take to have been convincingly shown by John Steadman in "Milton's *Haemony:* Etymology and Allegory," *PMLA,* LXXVII (1962), 200–207, whatever more concrete—even botanical—meanings it may be understood to have. John Arthos raises the question of conventions of magic, folktale, and romance but does not try to prove that we should demand perfect consistency in Milton's handling of these resources—any more than in his handling of epic conventions elsewhere. See Arthos, *On "A Mask Presented at Ludlow-Castle"* (Ann Arbor, Mich., 1954). Haemony can symbol-

alone" (*Paradise Lost,* III, 684). And his advice to reverse the rod and reorient natural powers parallels what must later be done by special agencies of God's grace.

The brothers cannot be any more efficacious than he, and their failure says things about broader concerns than boyish foibles. The heedlessness that, apparently, makes their apprehension of the Spirit's directions impatient and incomplete and their performance of them faulty seems an apt particular instance of ordinary self-absorption. Theologically it exemplifies the Augustinian dictum that to love someone not for God's sake is necessarily to love that person for one's own sake. If they at this juncture perfectly loved their sister for God's sake, with no trace of vainglory attending the rescue, they would necessarily resent the wand as much as any other element of the scene. Magic is evil. They can quite well recognize the rights and wrongs and desiderata in the situation intellectually, that is, in a way real and valid but as external to their living as the leaves of haemony. The anguish latent in the situation—which is indicated, and then displaced by thought of Sabrina's help—resides in the insufficiency of intellectually valid wishes, strongly felt by those who love her as well as they can, to make the Lady free.

There she sits, then, in a stasis of confused, immature, shocked, and fearful negation, becoming gradually conditioned and responsive—even if in distaste—to the obsessions of her adversary. "Shall I go on?" she asks (*A Mask,* 779), "Or have I said enough?" (line 780). Alas, she has said "false traitor" (line 691) quite enough, some forty of her own lines earlier, and had much better not "unlockt" (line 756) her lips further "In this unhallow'd air" (line 757). A not impossible she, the Lady is demure and chaste of upbringing, but her logic is unreliable and her instincts are no help. So far Milton might almost be giving in Comus and his wood the local habitations and names for depicting Martin Luther's thesis on Satan: "On earth is not his equal."[23]

But there would not be much satisfaction in citing Luther in connection with the Lady's redemption, which, in Hippolyta's words in *A Midsummer Night's Dream,* "More witnesseth than fancy's images / And grows to something of great constancy." Sabrina emerges from her pastoral river

---

ize knowledge—or something else—without the necessity arising for Comus' wand or glass to symbolize entities equally clear-cut.

23. See Kerrigan, *The Sacred Complex,* 48; and Canfield, *Word as Bond.*

as both a second-generation classical grace and a noncanonical saint, a combination precarious in a naturalistic external landscape, no doubt, but stable enough in an internal, imaginative, and psychological one, and a combatant there with various demonic forces and "shrewd medling" elves (line 846).[24] Not that she is wholly internal; the daughter of Locrine may in Milton's retelling be thought of generally as having experienced a transformation outside the realm of human life, yet a fulfillment in history. History is the simultaneously external and internal, public and private medium in which she can function as a species of grace, vivified by the Giver of all grace. She is associated with the "smooth Severn stream" (line 825), and the water imagery, pastoralism, and neo-Ovidian metamorphosis of that are tied to natural vitality, fertility, and mysterious process. Her own song emphasizes these things. The shepherds by their carol to her goodness, the Spirit by his "adjuring verse" (line 858) and effectively invocative "warbled song" (line 854), Sabrina herself by her sympathetic attention to him and her loving pronouncements to the Lady—all acquit her of bloodless abstraction and place her in the dynamic, mutually involved world of vocal communication.[25] The names in the Spirit's invocation involve Sabrina in a variously maternal company for all except four names, which are significant in other relevant ways: Ligea's presence in this context seems to accent beauty, Proteus' presence stewardship, the presence of Triton and Glaucus authoritative communication in groups. Sabrina leaves, hastening "To wait in *Amphitrite's* bowr" (line 921). No "huntress *Dian*" (line 441) is Sabrina. Service to the wife of the sea-god would seem a considerable endorsement of society and fertility.

The Spirit's two long final speeches, and the concluding action, illuminate Sabrina's role and the preceding action of the whole masque. The Spirit begins with a reminder of lineage, using diction that emphasizes the vitality of generation: "daughter of Locrine / *Sprung* of old Anchises line" (lines 922–23; our emphasis, with Milton's italics for names omitted). That leads, by a turn on due rule and order, to an anatomy of the perennial distortions, abstractions, and disorders afflicting her clear

24. Our focus is primarily though not exclusively on this masque's presence in print. But even a less "local reading" than Marcus proposes would want to note Demaray's intriguing suggestion that Sabrina may first have been played by Alice Egerton's older sister Penelope. See his *Milton and the Masque Tradition*, 77–78, 94–95. We are skeptical.

25. Juno, a relevant figure to whom the Lady alludes, never becomes so variously real as Sabrina.

"brimmed waves" (line 924): freezing, drying, turbidity, silt. Her crown is, on the contrary, to be abundance either biblically pastoral *or urban:* "many a towr and terrace round" (line 935).[26]

Thyrsis enjoins the three to fly, by the grace of heaven, "this cursed place" (line 939) which the Lady first thought benign. Their arrival at "holier ground" (line 943) means stepping into the festive paradigm of country, town, and the president's castle, with gabby brothers at last shaken into the heedful decorum of reinforcements for the godly *civitas.* The Spirit defines the dynamic situation of reunion, dance, familial initiation, and social responsibility by announcing his own destination as another kind of ideal, the world of noncyclical but benignly near-static, all but perfected labors of love. At the same time, his immensely associative and sensory description of the mysterious and accordingly paradoxical plenitude where "eternal Summer dwells" (line 988) provides the final, commensurately weighty answer to the sensory vividness of Comus. He dares, as Comus does not, to conceive the present and its means and parts relative to eternity and perfection. Now, more particularly, he can counterpoint closely and explicitly the complex and dominant motifs of love, reproduction, regeneration, and communication in an emblematic tableau of ideal integrity (lines 1003–11).

In this context his injunction to "List mortals, if your ears be true" (line 957) should make us surer than ever that the concern with noises, songs, and valid and reliable hearing throughout the poem has had to do with the harmonizing of appearance and reality, matter and spirit, vehicle and tenor, substance and structure, self and society. In a hermeneutic sense poignant in a fallen world of rape, intimidation, and subordination, and malfeasance in judicial office, his speech implies that we must know something of the truth to hear it, and hear it to know it better. He instructs,

> Love vertue, she alone is free,
> She can teach ye how to clime
> Higher than the spheary chime;
> Or if Vertue feeble were,
> Heav'n it self would stoop to her.
> (Lines 1019–23)

26. She thus connects two modes of life, as the Severn connects Welsh and English counties, perhaps suggesting, as Marcus notes, a pun on Bridgewater. See her "Justice for Margery Evans," 85*n*22.

Love, not merely follow; and as Milton would more explicitly insist in *Paradise Lost,* heaven stoops to the pilgrim by grace, heaven's own mode of love. The Spirit's mobility, from president's castle to the "green earths end" (line 1014) to the "corners of the Moon" (line 1017) is a figure for the freedom that in mortals attends love of virtue and only love of virtue. The Spirit directs his last speech forthrightly toward the conventional (and at the first performance literal) audience of the masque, which conventionally merged with the dramatis personae.

His formulation implies some decisive conclusion in any auditor who hears so intently as to engage in a dialogue of affirmation or dissent with the poet, hearing the self with the ear of internal reflection. That auditor must realize retrospectively that the Lady as fettered even after the flight of Comus must have been the Lady with virtue imperfect, if by no more than understandable fear and loathing. The auditor may infer that the touch of "chast palms moist and cold" (line 918) manifested to the Lady's consciousness some inclusive and positive ideal and that the Lady's release and status in her family and society are figures for an achieved love of virtue, a love of virtue achieved in not too closely specifiable part by the miracle of grace.

The play's extraordinary reach embraces a pastoral-romantic landscape that is both exterior and interior, proceeding from pastoral exclusions and simplifications in the leafy maze to the inclusions and possibilities and cosmic affinities of masque and godly *civitas.*[27] All this comes at us in a set of thematic cruxes that summon to hermeneutic dialogue and in a mode of comedy that stems from a vision of society as somewhat precariously viable—perhaps *narrowly* viable, if Milton's youthful Christian optimism is to be captured. The auditor may well arrive with the youthful three at some sense of not simply contemplating and celebrating a small miracle of threatened chastity retorqued from passive and negative to active and positive but, more intricately, of exploring large mysteries of freedom and necessity and grace elusively and inextricably bound, and large paradoxes of love in society as freedom in order.

27. We have an uneasy consciousness of Northrop Frye's remarks in "The Four Forms of Fiction," in *Anatomy of Criticism* (Princeton, 1957), and acknowledge a general debt to Ong's "Voice as Summons to Belief." The social rationale defined in this section, like the signification of *knowledge* adopted for haemony, would seem to agree in some particulars with the remarks about temperance by Robert Martin Adams in *Ikon: John Milton and the Modern Critics* (Ithaca, N.Y., 1955), 13–16.

Ultimately the human comedy Milton presents assumes the shape of a parable about society, about its tilth and husbandry and replenishment. Community is poignantly less simple and straightforward than the spirits accompanying it, and its catechumens—and hence its future—pass always through the valley of the shadow, handed on by care and forethought and a continuing miracle:

> yet O where els
> Shall I inform my unacquainted feet
> In the blind maze of this tangl'd Wood?
> (Lines 179–81)[28]

PREMATURE CELEBRATION: THE 1645 EDITION OF *POEMS*

The shorter English poems, in the order of Milton's presentation in the edition of *Poems* of 1645—from "On the Morning of Christs Nativity" to "Lycidas" constitute a sequence that is suggestive in much the way *A Mask* is, which was printed after *Poems*. In both, a fictive sequence with a thematic coherence verging on the dramatic is apparent. The Miltonic sequentiality has significance, we submit, and we are confident of the fruitfulness of considering individual poems with reference to their place within it.[29] In the English poems, Milton presents a self who by various

28. A preliminary version of this section was read by Gale H. Carrithers, Jr., to the English Institute, September, 1964, and appeared, slightly revised, as "Milton's Ludlow *Mask*: From Chaos to Community," in *English Literary History*, XXXIII (1966; reprinted in *Critical Essays on Milton from "ELH"* [Baltimore, 1971]). The present revision represents engagement with the publications of others since then, as well as dialogue between the present authors.

29. See especially Louis L. Martz, "The Rising Poet," in *The Lyric and Dramatic Milton*, ed. Summers, 3–33; and Arthur Barker, "The Pattern of Milton's 'Nativity Ode,'" *University of Toronto Quarterly*, X (1940–41), 167–81. See also Anna Nardo, *Milton's Sonnets and the Ideal Community* (Lincoln, Nebr., 1979). The 1645 edition is readily available in *Poems of Mr. John Milton: The 1645 Edition* (New York, 1951); it and the 1673 edition are less widely available in the facsimile *John Milton's Complete Poetical Works*, ed. Harris Francis Fletcher (4 vols.; Urbana, Ill., 1943). For elaboration on the Miltonic *ethos* and form, see Thomas O. Sloane, *Donne, Milton, and the End of Humanist Rhetoric* (Berkeley and Los Angeles, 1985), and John K. Hale, "Milton's Self-Presentation in *Poems* . . . 1645," *Milton Quarterly*, XXV (1991), 37–48. See also Annabel Patterson, "'Forc'd Fingers': Milton's Early Poems and Ideological Constraint," in *The Muses Common-Weale*, ed. Summers and Pebworth, 9–22. On postlapsarian, postpastoral, anti-imperial orientations even in the early poetry, see Anthony Low, "Milton and the Georgic Ideal," in *The Georgic*

steps and trials becomes a priestly poet in the priesthood of all believers, with the sophistication to frame the whole sequence in a book prominently displaying its date and to comment urbanely in Greek on the engraver's poor likeness of him.[30] He who hymns the infant God has scarcely met the problem of theodicy and is therefore—a bit like the young people in *A Mask*—somewhat uncertain, even vulnerable, in his sense of community. He must first discover in himself and the world that divine justice and providence are questionable or problematic, and then test the options. Don Parry Norford has commented that for representing a descent to a contrasting world and the subsequent transcendence in a resurrection, a "night-sea journey . . . is central in Milton's poetry."[31] The edition of *Poems* of 1645 begins with the incarnation and a new day, there is the night scene in the middle of the sequence, and the resurrection of Lycidas comes at the end. But the beginning, middle, and end of the sequence can harbor now one emphasis, now another, relating to vocation (what shall I do?), medium and genre (how shall I do it?), and communal context (what importance do our past and present fellows have for us, and where is God among us?).

The individual poems in the volume embody a great deal of literary history: long-established generic forms and conventional poetics and thematics. But there is also an internal sense in which these poems move toward history. The past is abundantly present to the speakers in the first half of the sequence, though mainly as an instrument or a medium for

---

Revolution (Princeton, 1985). See also Helgerson, *Self-Crowned Laureates*, esp. 254–70; and Raymond B. Waddington, "Milton Among the Carolines," in *The Age of Milton: Backgrounds to Seventeenth-Century Literature*, ed. C. A. Patrides and R. B. Waddington (Manchester, Eng., 1980), 338–64. On roles, see George W. Nitchie, "Milton and His Muses," *English Literary History*, XLIV (1977), 75–84. For a raking light on the earlier lyricism, see John R. Mulder, "The Lyric Dimension of *Paradise Lost*," *Milton Studies*, XXIII (1987), 145–63. See also William B. Hunter, "John Milton: Autobiographer," *Milton Quarterly*, VIII (1974), 100–104; and, especially for the Latin poems and "On the Morning of Christs Nativity," John T. Shawcross, "Milton's Shorter Poems" in *Intentionality and the New Traditionalism: Some Liminal Means to Literary Revisionism* (University Park, Pa., 1991). Unavailable to us as we wrote was C. W. R. D. Moseley's *The Poetic Birth: Milton's Poems of 1645* (Menston, Eng., 1991).

30. The analogy to drama holds most usefully for Shakespearean Elizabethan comedy and Middletonian (not Jonsonian) Jacobean comedy.

31. Don Parry Norford, "The Sacred Head: Milton's Solar Mysticism," *Milton Studies*, IX (1976), 61.

current work; later in the sequence there begins to appear a sense of human causality and vicissitude, and what a Bloomian would be bound to call an anxiety of influence.

Thus Milton comes to history both at large and in the individual poems. We see—if not quite a drama—a serious movement from ahistoric, youthful incompleteness to realized, adult selfhood. That has entailed finding vocation, what we might in an Augustinian sense call true love, and finding it implicated in history and oriented through the fallen world of persons and vicissitude. These considerations come abruptly into focus for the reader, who may have read stationer Humphrey Moseley's socially conscious preface, and who finds just below a printer's device with a crowned rose, on page 1, the title "On the Morning of Christs Nativity. Compos'd 1629."

The first poem of these "two books with a single cover" begins,

> This is the Month, and this the happy morn
> Wherin the Son of Heav'ns eternal King,
> Of wedded Maid, and Virgin Mother born,
> Our great redemption from above did bring;
> For so the holy sages once did sing
> ("On the Morning of Christs Nativity," 1–5)

That is as its author was later to begin the account of creation itself: with an originating distinction now born in human consciousness articulated as old wisdom differentiated by a new song. The old wisdom—from "holy sages" in this "nativity" ode, from Urania "with Eternal wisdom . . . In presence of th' Almightie Father" (*Paradise Lost,* VII, 9–11)—is like the new song in being a necessary but not sufficient condition of redemptive action. We must have divine help in conjunction with knowing and naming and acting by song; song is to be understood as the form loving action takes here, naming a "welcome," a hymnic ode. Language may be fallen for Milton at twenty-one as in later life, but not so sundered from effective action and from truth as it was construed to be by later poets and antipoets.

We are presented in the nativity ode, as in Book VII of *Paradise Lost,* and ironically at the end of *Samson Agonistes,* with a "new acquist" (*Samson Agonistes,* 1755) not so much of knowledge or virtue as of consciousness—of light out of dark, a new morn. There is a kind of history indicated in saying that "sages once did sing," as in mentioning the "Father, pleas'd / With thy Celestial Song" (*Paradise Lost,* VII, 11–12). But it tends to be the quasi history of myth: witness "sons of morning sung" ("On the Morning of Christs Nativity," 119) and "age of gold" (line 135). The heaviest emphasis falls on *newness.* Here is less Book VII's new creation of a human world between an angelic and a human fall than the new creation of the self in orientation toward the divine child—in keeping with biblical and prayer-book declarations of a new creation in Christ.[32]

The voice acknowledges "deadly forfeit" (line 6) but is confident of "release" (line 6), and acknowledges mysteries of the godhead in "Light unsufferable" (line 8) but finds them reassuringly "laid aside" (line 12) and in the end almost domesticated to "Handmaid Lamp" (line 242) and "order serviceable" (line 244). The young poet confesses that making a "present to the Infant God" (line 16) always implies a new welcome, but new sayings of the old redemptive truth come to him with relative ease. Would-be subverters of the long-promised, newly recognized "meek-ey'd Peace" (line 46) are also attended to in this poem, but they are more readily confounded or discounted than in *Paradise Lost:* vanity, sin, and "Hell it self" (line 139) in stanza XIV, Dragon, Oracles, Lemures, Baalim, brutish gods, Osiris, and Typhon in stanzas XVIII–XXV. Nature to this exuberant young poet in a new-world present of "holy Song" (line 133) appears "almost won / To think her part was don" (lines 104–105)—appears close to incorporation in a redemptive telos of "Heav'n and Earth in happier union" (line 107). Hence there is decorum to the jaunty assumption that the rising sun of this friendly nature, rising from bed as the infant Son will eventually do, "pillows his chin upon an Orient wave" (line 231). Fire and water and whatever they associate with are apparently reconciled.[33]

The trouble is not that Milton's control falters here, or even in the poem's extraordinary shifts of tense.[34] The informed and passionate

---

32. See Edward W. Said, "Notes on the Characterization of a Literary Text," in *Velocities of Change,* ed. Richard Macksey (Baltimore, 1974), 32–57; and Edward W. Said, "Narrative: Quest for Origins and Discovery of the Mausoleum," *Salmagundi,* IX (1970), 63–72 (reprinted in *Beginnings,* by Said). John Spencer Hill helpfully summarizes and persuasively argues from much previous scholarship in "Poet-Priest: Vocational Tension in Milton's Early Development," *Milton Studies,* VIII (1976), 41–69.

33. See Norford, "The Sacred Head."

34. For a summary of the debate on this poem, see *Variorum Commentary on the Poems of John Milton,* ed. A. S. P. Woodhouse and Douglas Bush (Additional vols. projected; New York, 1970–), Vol. II, Pts. 1, 2, 3. For "On the Morning of Christs Nativity," see

speaker, not unlike the wise virgins of the New Testament conjured up by the last stanza's reference to "Handmaid Lamp" (line 242), is not without celebratory spirit. True, in trying to make the known sacred history and recurring time sequence of the Christian year into the existential now of a new creation in Christ, he does not maintain a steady and constant hold on the sacred moment. The poet who relegates "Shepherds" (line 85) a little too distantly to the "Lawn . . . in a rustick row" (lines 85–87), who rhymes "wisest Fate says no, / This must not yet be so" (lines 149–50) a little too briskly, is to be understood as the appealing *ingénu*, whether chronologically young or not. It may be granted that personhood in this poem—whether of God, of speaker, or of others—lacks thickness. Milton wrote poems before this, and modern editors may choose to place them first. He decided to begin his book with this one, as if the book and its occasion permitted a hermeneutic placement of the poems. He seems to mean more than December 25, 1629, when his impassioned speaker proclaims,

> But now begins; for from this happy day
> Th' old Dragon under ground
> In straiter limits bound,
> Not half so for casts his usurped sway
> (Lines 167–70)

The remainder of the poems in English exhibit a deepening sense of the losses to be redeemed, of the bitterness of crosses, and of the lesser straitness in the Dragon's limits—deeper than the younger poet could have supposed or the older poet and audience have wished. Evasions of these trials are essayed but prove unsatisfactory (see pp. 185–91 below). But here the "Heav'nly Muse" (line 15) has created through the poet a "present," in both senses, to the "Infant God" (line 16), and the poet has

---

Vol. II, Pt. 1, pp. 38–63. See also George William Smith, Jr., "Milton's Method of Mistakes in the Nativity Ode," *Studies in English Literature*, XVIII (1978), 107–23; I. S. MacLaren, "Milton's Nativity Ode: The Function of Poetry and Structures of Responsibility in 1629," *Milton Studies*, XV (1981), 181–200; M. J. Doherty, "Salvation History, Poetic Form, and the Logic of Time in Milton's Nativity Ode," *Milton Studies*, XXV (1989), 21–42; and Patricia G. Pinka, "Timely Timelessness in Two Nativity Poems," in *Bright Shootes of Everlastingnesse: The Seventeenth-Century Religious Lyric*, ed. Claude Summers and Ted-Larry Pebworth (Columbia, Mo., 1987), 162–72. The two nativity poems to which Pinka's title refers are Milton's and George Herbert's. MacLaren includes a bibliography of modern criticism.

goldenly, and urbanely, enrolled us in what is finally "our tedious Song" (line 239).

In the 1645 edition of *Poems,* Milton includes versifications of Psalms 114 and 136, schoolboy exercises "don by the Author at fifteen yeers old" that owe something to other paraphrasers, as many have noted. But seventeenth-century eyes and ears could well detect significant contrasts with the King James Version and with the Bishops' Bible as preserved in the Psaltery of the Book of Common Prayer.

Milton's nature in Psalm 114 is more animate than it is in the Bibles his contemporaries were reading, even if in a quite conventionally pastoral way: only his sea that fled had "froth-becurled head" ("Paraphrase," 8), only his Jordan recoils "as a faint host" ("Paraphrase," 10), and only his skipping mountains are "huge-bellied" (line 11).[35] More tellingly, he changes the beginning. Compare

> When Israel came out of Egypt:
>> and the house of Jacob from among the strange people
>> [people of strange language, KJV],
> Judah was his sanctuary:
>> and Israel his dominion.
>>> (Ps. 114:1–2, Book of Common Prayer)

and

> When the blest seed of *Terah's* faithfull Son,
> After long toil their liberty had won,
> And past from *Pharian* fields to *Canaan* Land,
> Led by the strength of the Almighties hand
>> ("Paraphrase," 1–4)

From a Hebraic emphasis on divine doings and arbitrary power amid disparate societies, we have been moved to a rather cozy universe. The miraculous God-the-child Son of the nativity ode, the infant Hercules, has here a counterpart God the Father, who is powerful in a variously animate, handsome, and pleasant world and is paternally benign and reciprocally caring, although not prematurely so, for his generations of faithful. Only

---

35. William Riley Parker finds Joshua Sylvester's "manner . . . simple riming with ornate language" (*Milton: A Biography* [2 vols.; New York, 1968], I, 20). See Carolyn P. Collette, "Milton's Psalm Translations: Petition and Praise," *English Literary Renaissance,* II (1972), 243–59.

in this young poet's Jehovah do we find that this majestic explicability "ever was, and ay shall last" (line 16).

The paraphrase of Psalm 136 and "The Passion" lend themselves to consideration together. What are we as readers to make of Milton's inclusion of "The Passion" in the 1645 edition though "nothing satisfi'd with what was begun"? Milton presents us with a young poet who has not yet realized suffering in any depth, much less resolved it in a costly struggle.[36] He is a speaker who accordingly and not unbecomingly feels that the subject of the crucifixion requires the existential removal to "holy vision . . . pensive trance . . . ecstatick fit" ("The Passion," 41–42). Once there, so to speak, he is lost, turning uncertainly from Jerusalem's towers to "Sepulchral rock . . . Or should I thence" (lines 43–50) to "Mountains wild" (line 51). He asserts that "grief is easily beguil'd" (line 54), then belies that unbelievable sentiment by contorting himself into a neo-Spenserian gaucherie out of the metaphysical literature of tears, about his groans and tears begetting echoes and rain as if a "race of mourners on som pregnant cloud" (line 56).

Six years earlier in Miltonic biographical time, but only a page, a moment, earlier in the published poetic sequence is his version of Psalm 136. The bloodthirsty and vindictive gloating of the paraphrased psalm is tribally and boyishly unaware of what was really involved in the deific execution of the "first-born of Egypt land" ("Psalm 136," 39). This paraphraser is more intrigued with the physics of divine action: a "thunder-clasping hand" (line 38), a Red Sea the floods of which "stood still like Walls of Glass" (line 49), a "larg-limb'd *Og*" subdued (line 69). The language of Milton's version far exceeds what the biblical text requires. Almost ingeniously, too, Milton expands the refrain in the King James Version and the Book of Common Prayer, from "For his mercy endureth for ever" (Ps. 136:24) to "For his mercies ay endure, / Ever faithfull, ever sure" ("Psalm 136," 95–96).

If, consistently with our thesis, the 1645 edition of *Poems* is read as a hermeneutic exploration toward theodicy as love and self-commitment in history, these first four poems present themselves as the beginning of the quest. God is born into the young Milton's world, not without the poet's

---

36. Gregory F. Goekjian perceptively notes that "The Passion" cannot get from problems of poetry to its ostensible subject. See his "Deference and Silence: Milton's Nativity Ode," *Milton Studies*, XXII (1985), 119–35.

worshipful recognition. But his recognition of why that world needs the incarnate God scarcely extends beyond simple notice that there are enemies out there. Nor is there much sense that the action of God upon the world might be not just an exercise of power or a puzzling fact but a mystery, nor that human interrelationships and intersubjectivity might compound the problem, nor that, among other consequences of that, song itself might be compromised. Compare the uncritical relationship to pastoralism in his paraphrase of Psalm 114 with the action in "Lycidas."

The next few poems reify the poet's preliminary discoveries. "On Time" surprises by its curious distancing. *On time* means both "about time" and "set upon a clock case," as script, rather than voice, adorning a mechanical gauge of time, as the poem was originally intended to do. The distance is not lessened much by the poet's personifying time, for the personification is out there as an *other*. One might argue—as congenially to Renaissance Christianity as to Gabriel Marcel or José Ortega y Gasset—that the self and others are linked as mutual determinants. But that linkage seems obscured or attenuated here where the *I* becomes a vague corporate "our . . . us . . . we" and the personified Time simply an other, neatly vanquished.

The poems in the sequence begin to show provocative dichotomies. In "The Passion," commonplace glances at history—at, for instance, "Once glorious Towers, now sunk" ("The Passion," 40)—stand at odds with events transcending history.[37] "On Time" presents a more interrelated but largely static taxonomy of temporality opposed by eternity. "Upon the Circumcision" similarly presents both the redeemed and the unredeemed, and "At a solemn Musick" harmony and discord. But the differences between the poems merit attention too.

Milton's yearly vanquishment of Time as alien other is orthodox, though at a distance. So too are the notions of "meerly mortal dross" ("On Time," 6) and "Earthy grosnes quit" (line 20)—however impersonal. But this orthodox speaker remains somewhat childlike. He fancies dress-up: "Attir'd with Stars" (line 21). He could be vengeful: "sit, / Triumphing over" (lines 21–22). He lumps together as bogeymen the existentially incommensurable: "Death, and Chance, and thee O Time" (lines 21–22). He proposes alternatively that Eternity's "individual kiss; / And Joy shall

---

37. *Commonplace* in the semitechnical sense. See Ong, *Rhetoric, Romance, and Technology,* esp. Chaps. 2, 4, 11.

overtake us *as a flood*" (lines 12–13; our emphasis); the imagery betokens a kind of regressive hearkening toward lost maternal plenitude.

Yet there is ambivalence: the Time whose not *maw* but "*womb* devours" (line 4; our emphasis). No doubt we should not make too much of that, because the poem and the sequence alike go on to other things, leaving the image for *Paradise Lost,* where it is Belial (*Paradise Lost,* II, 150) and Satan (X, 476) who are swallowed. "On Time" artfully gives a somewhat mixed bearing toward life, which may be associated with adolescence but can persist indefinitely.

"Upon the Circumcision," though relatively labored in syntax, diction, and cadence—and listlessly conventional in imagery—claims some attention by its position after the nativity ode and "The Passion," on the way toward, but existentially far from, "Lycidas." The feast of the circumcision is to the Christian year somewhat as the poem is to the symbolic year of the poetic speaker's life. The joy at the birth of God into a needy, anticipating world is once more acknowledged, and the denouement of a penitential Lent and culminating Easter are lightly prefigured with a stronger sense of infidelity to "that great Cov'nant" ("Upon the Circumcision," 21) and with the circumcision as micro-Passion. The Passion has been domesticated, but at a critical cost in scale: the last three lines acknowledge that. Milton, like George Herbert, had so large a sense of the Passion that it took his entire poetic career to show him usable terms for it.

This speaker's uneasy stand in pseudocanzone involves other problems. Less established than epic Bard or Miltonic Deity, he merely asserts just law and exceeding love. And even if "that great Cov'nant which we still transgress" (line 21) has been "intirely satisfi'd" (line 22), what do we do the rest of the Christian year, or even tomorrow? The question has yet to be faced, and with it the cost of whatever "seals obedience" (line 25) in the speaker and the sweepingly included remainder of us. The speaker may know important things common to us all—our fallibility and death-wardness, say, our constitution as creatures of symbol, even—but does he know enough about what divides humanity?

"At a solemn Musick" suggests that he knows a great deal about divisions and, in the perennial metaphor with which he earlier enriched the nativity ode and *A Mask,* discord. Some celebratory poetry draws its energy from the opposition between noticing the subject and neglecting to notice. "At a solemn Musick" draws power from opposition to diverse adversaries, and the many adjectives point to these menacing oppositions: *undisturbed* ("At a solemn Musick," 6), *saintly* (line 9), *solemn* (line 9; versus *trivial,* for Milton), *victorious* (line 14), *devout* (line 15), *holy* (line 15), *undiscording* (line 17). The grammar also underscores life's contingency with a new resonance: "That we . . . May rightly answer . . . O may we" (lines 17–25). Indeed, the Fall is recapitulated as a quasi-originary event—not quite a Manichaean opposite to the new creation in Christ but rather an ongoing "harsh din," a failure to get in loving tune.

So "that Song" (line 25) has been posited as truly originary, the enactment of divine love, "consort" (line 27) of disparities. It is a noble conception: harmonious song, even dance ("thir motion sway'd"; line 22), fulfillment in aesthetic action for all the committed, together. This heavenly perspective, construed from the fallen world, traditionally articulates itself in paradox: the song both atemporal and temporal, and the "endles morn of light" (line 28). Dark negatives and adversities that resist explanation or domestication—even by paradox—have been sighted but have not been grappled with.

SHOCKS, WITHDRAWALS, RETURNS

The next seven poems circle closer to the subject of everything that seems to betoken evil, and they dally with doubtful surmises: "An Epitaph on the Marchioness of Winchester," "Song: On *May* Morning," "On Shakespear," "On the University Carrier," "Another on the same," "L'Allegro," and "Il Penseroso." Four are occasioned by deaths, and the other three engage death antiphonally. The marchioness has died of being what she is, a mother: "That to give the world encrease, / Short'n'd hast thy own lives lease" ("An Epitaph on the Marchioness of Winchester," 51–52). Even the baby has died. This poem's speaker can assimilate some peripheral facts, but not the death of the virtuous or innocent.

Assimilation of the peripheral produces the poignant opening of the poem, epitaphically cataloging the dead woman as almost "heiress of all the ages":[38] she has noble descent and alliance, as well as art, virtue, and breeding. But she is dead at twenty-three. So in a tactic elaborated in "Lycidas," the poem reorients us to a metaphor of the world—or to a

38. The phrase is Henry James's, in description of Millie Theale, in *The Wings of the Dove.*

sample life-world, in a shift from macrocosmic to microcosmic—as a mixed bouquet of entities and sequences: Hymen's garland with a "Cipress bud" (line 22). But the developing elegist cannot claim "you might have seen a Cipress bud," only that "ye might discern" it now, in retrospect. And this uncertainty provokes a formula that is almost a parody of the Manichaean, at once so domestic and so classically distanced as to suggest a psychological avoidance in fantasy: "whether by mischance or blame / *Atropos* for *Lucina* came" (lines 27–28).

Evidently, though, the formal yet troubled speaker of the poem resists the nightingale song of fancy to return where baby and mother are not "fruit and tree" (line 30) but where the life-given may give death. He consults common experience: "So have I seen som tender slip . . . Pluck't up by som unheedy swain" (lines 35–38). This approach might open toward the idea that "As flies to wanton boys, are we to the gods." Instead we find ourselves led out of the savaged garden into a comfortable convention: "Pearls of dew" appear on a flower as

> presaging tears
> Which the sad morn had let fall
> On her hast'ning funerall.
>   (Lines 43–45)

Still, the elegist does what he can. He prays for rest and certifies the contributions of ritual and art to order the mourning. But what meaning does the marchioness' life have in a world that would so interrupt it by death? The biblical analogue of Rachel, mother "after years of barrenness" to Joseph and then, fatally, to Benjamin, vexes the question. We seem to be told in the poem's lines to take that as the parallel, never mind other matters in the biblical context: broken bargains, stolen idols, slain Shechemites, and the like. Yet if Rachel's death is not vindicated by her place in salvific history, why mention it at all? But the anxious assurance that the wife in Genesis 35, "much like thee, / Through pangs fled to felicity" (lines 67–68) comes from the poet, not the Bible, and the solace that she is "no Marchioness, but now a Queen" (line 74) is mere assertion. A more appealing feature of this poem is the growing sense of "House" (line 54), of society organized, of maturation and lineage embedded in a destiny that may on occasion mysteriously allow a fatal vagary. The poem is an attempt to respond to her sacrificial gift to the world's "encrease" (line 51) by philadelphically giving her living story to the community.

Modern editions of *Poems* that break the order of 1645 obscure the degree of antiphonal resemblance between the "epitaph" and the "song." John T. Shawcross helpfully reminds us that the meter of the "salute" in lines 5–8 replicates that of the "epitaph" and of the later "L'Allegro" and "Il Penseroso." There's more: "Garland . . . fruit and tree . . . flowr . . . vernall showr . . . blossom . . . som Flowers, and som Bays" (lines 21–57) on the "sad morn" (line 45) of the death-stricken mother modulate to the "bright morning Star" ("Song," 1) of "Flowry *May,* who from *her* green lap throws / The yellow Cowslip, and the pale Primrose" (lines 3–4; our emphasis of pronoun). The metrically accented *Now* beginning this song and the phrase "wish thee long" with which it concludes surely emphasize a poignant transience. And the floral names anticipate the more famous catalog in "Lycidas." But this is not so much dalliance with a "false surmise" ("Lycidas," 153) as a kind of acknowledgment of limitation: to "welcom . . . and wish . . . long" ("Song," 10) what cannot be so is at least lively and generous, neither deathly nor meanspirited.

"On Shakespear" balances liveliness not against death or meanness but rather against ineffectuality: "to th' shame of slow-endeavouring art, / Thy easie numbers flow" ("On Shakespear," 9–10). The orders of nature and of art or vocation cohere for the playwright, the culture hero whose achievement transcends politics. But the poem invites a question about what order other doers and makers may stand in who can only wish for so noble a "Monument" (line 8).

It is a world order of long and mixed lineage. "My *Shakespear*" (line 1) seems to command the various generative forces. The playwright embodies classical being as "son of memory" (line 5) and author of "Delphick lines" (line 12) more vigorous than Latinate monuments.[39] He is akin to some Hebrew prophet, the witness of his name in the leaves of a sacred "Book" (line 11). He is no mere fading theme of medieval fame but rather her "great heir" (line 5). And the stones of the mostly Anglo-Saxon words in his lines monumentalize him in our Anglo-Saxon astonishment. Such quick, shorthand marshaling of society's resources—which becomes one of Milton's identifying moves—does not always proceed so univocally, as we shall see.

Milton's two poems "On the University Carrier" and "Another on the same" stand as finely buoyant, partly because placed as—so to speak—

39. Shawcross notes Horace's "exegii monumentum aere perennius," with reference to "Monument" in line 4.

satyr pieces to the solemn celebration of Shakespeare. However humble Hobson the campus character was, he resembled Shakespeare in doing the work that was his. If Hobson's work was not completed in the sense in which Shakespeare's was, who would impute a fault to orders of nature, culture, or language that made ease his chief disease—at age eighty-seven? "Rest that gives all men life, gave him his death, / And too much breathing put him out of breath" ("Another," 11–12). With death domesticated to a long-due "Chamberlin" ("On the University Carrier," 14) and the dying man himself conceived as chirping "For one Carrier put down to make six bearers" ("Another," 20), everything coheres in the most jolly-serious elegiac performance in English between Ben Jonson's "On S.P." and John Dryden's on Anne Killigrew. In these two poems formally about death, death's victory is swallowed up in the collegial wit of the ongoing community—in contrast to "Hobsons Epitaph," where the wit flags and the animation dies. In "On Shakespear," the suggestion is of a kind of nation, a permanent society of English readers and writers, and in the Hobson poems of a homelier community of students and letter writers. Yet there is the leavening of historicity in the contrast—which is perhaps not a dichotomy here—between inspiration and "slow-endeavouring art" ("On Shakespear," 9), and between witty point and Hobson's perennial activity. There is some cost in immediacy, in presence. Shakespeare's fluency reproaches "slow-endeavouring art," yet Shakespeare lived long and a young poet has long to live, does he not? What of more immediate options and their consequent lifeways? Hobson is other to collegians, almost an archetypal old man, "Obedient to the Moon . . . to the mutual flowing of the Seas" ("Another," 29–31).

It is in the context of such concerns that "L'Allegro" and "Il Penseroso" appear as texts and as life trials. We bracket for the moment the lively arguments whether the two options these poems present are in balance, joined, tilted, or cyclically related.[40] Whatever Milton himself may

40. Compare especially the point tangential to this made by Leslie Brisman in "'All Before Them Where to Choose': 'L'Allegro' and 'Il Penseroso,'" *Journal of English and Germanic Philology*, LXXI (1972), 226–40, esp. 228. Compare also Leonora Leet Brodwin, "Milton and the Renaissance Circe," *Milton Studies*, VI, (1974), 21–83, esp. 45–46. For paths more rhetorical and topographic than those emphasized here, see Harold Toliver, "Milton and Others Walking, Soaring, and Falling" in *Lyric Provinces in the English Renaissance* (Columbus, Ohio, 1985), Chap. 8. See also the emphasis on progress toward prophetic vision in Wittreich's *Visionary Poetics*, Chap. 20. In contrast, see Michael Wilding, "Milton's Early Radicalism," in *Dragon's Teeth: Literature in the English Revolution* (New

have felt at one youthful hour or another about the ways of personal life available to him, the finished "L'Allegro" and "Il Penseroso" should be understood as ironic—poignantly, wryly, or humorously so at differing moments. The irony starts in the titles: deliberate, Miltonic joking mystifications, which betoken by their foreignness both the distance from the author of what follows and its familiarity to him. Milton could be polite and witty and poetic in Italian. Had he wanted to be impolite, blunt, and prosaic, he might have given English titles, not as editors do in footnote translations of the Italian ("Happy man" and "Thoughtful man"), but more like "Sport" and "Muser," almost "Ninny" and "Pedant." We are willing to risk exaggeration in order to convey the subsiding—the almost night-sea voyage—into estrangement of these middle poems, thirteenth and fourteenth of twenty-seven.[41]

Milton's readers have been presented with birth—death coming with it—and lineages and fulfillment in a cosmic order, in "An Epitaph on the Marchioness of Winchester," "On Shakespear," and the poems about Hobson, which were likely, with "L'Allegro" and "Il Penseroso," the production of little more than a year. If those last two have the general form of a scholastic exercise, still, whence such verve, and why place them just here?

Everyone notices that both poems begin with paired descriptions of generation: "L'Allegro" with the "horrid shapes, and shreiks" ("L'Allegro," 4) that, unlike the pangs of Rachel and Jane Paulet, herald no flight "to felicity" ("An Epitaph on the Marchioness of Winchester," 68), and with, on the other hand, easy triplets, the Graces, perhaps by Bacchus out of "lovely *Venus* at a birth" (line 14) or else created by a pagan *hagia pneuma* in a kind of creeping inflation; "Il Penseroso" with the subhuman

---

York, 1987), Chap. 2; and Thomas M. Greene, "The Meeting Soul in Milton's Companion Poems," *English Literary Renaissance,* XIV (1984), 159–74. Greene writes, "He tries on each sensibility in turn" (p. 174). See also Casey Finch and Peter Bowen, "The Solitary Companionship of *L'Allegro* and *Il Penseroso,*" *Milton Studies,* XXVI (1990), 3–24.

41. Brodwin likewise notes estrangement, in "Milton and the Renaissance Circe," 44–45. Woodhouse and Bush note it, as well, in *Variorum Commentary,* Vol. II, Pt. 1, pp. 25–26. Woodhouse and Bush also adduce as sources Jonson's Mere-Foole and Sir Thomas Overbury's Melancholy Man, who "thinks business, but never does any . . . all contemplation, no action" (Vol. II, Pt. 1, p. 239). Tillyard shrewdly suggests that there is parody in the poems. See his *Studies in Milton,* 4–21. But neither Tillyard nor, to our knowledge, anyone else has pursued this insight.

"brood of folly without father bred" ("Il Penseroso," 2), in macabre contravention of human or sacred nature, and even more startlingly, with the fantasized incestuous generation of Melancholy out of Vesta by her father, "solitary *Saturn*" (line 24). Whether the reader is armed in the complete steel of Claude Lévi-Strauss or not, Milton's suggestion of the radical irregularity, inversion, and impoverishment of Melancholy's line is patent. Milton's speaker gives us the otherwise pointless word *solitary* and proffers the pedantic and alienating nonexplanation "In *Saturns* raign, / Such mixture was not held a stain" (lines 25–26). Surely if any explanation is needed, no explanation will help, and it is so much the more foolish for the pedantic Penseroso—call him—to think otherwise. He is caught like Saturn the father in self-focus tending toward self-pity, with no possibility of interchange or reciprocity. Somewhat like the egregious Adam, he is "fixt" as if asleep in "thoughts abstruse" (*Paradise Lost,* VIII, 3, 40).

Allegro's way of being in the world seems similarly impaired. Set aside, for now, the rousing conclusion of the couplet "Sport that wrincled Care derides, / And Laughter holding both his sides" ("L'Allegro," 31–32). Sport, hypostatized in boisterous personification, can deride Care and chase it out of mind: that is one of the reasons play is recreation. But sport, play, and game presuppose a delimiting, contrastive context; cares may be temporarily ignored, but Care abides. Is something like that implicit in making "sweet Liberty" a "Mountain Nymph" (line 36), distant and estranged from a speaker who strolls the plow-furrowed lowlands?

Allegro hopes that if he gives Mirth "honour due" (line 37), he will be admitted to her "crew" (line 38). His efforts in ritual homage are almost as thorough as the Book of Common Prayer's canticle of praise for the works of God, especially regarding what is visual and audible. There is also that specially Miltonic alternation of near detail and framing structure, as in "nibling flocks . . . Mountains . . . clouds . . . Daisies pide . . . Battlements . . . high in tufted Trees . . . tann'd Haycock in the Mead . . . Nut-brown Ale . . . bed [and] whispering Winds . . . Towred Cities" (lines 72–117).[42]

Yet something is wrong. Giving Mirth due honor in parsing the horizon of her world—"mine eye . . . Whilst the Lantskip round it measures"

---

42. Perhaps too problematical to belong in the main argument are the "Mountains on whose barren brest / The labouring clouds do often rest" ("L'Allegro," 73–74). That sounds oddly abstractive and unimplicated, if not gauche, given the context of blessed and fatal fertility in the edition of 1645. Compare Jonson's Cokes, in *Bartholomew Fair*.

(lines 69–70)—seems costly. True, Allegro walks "not unseen" (line 57), but that puts him in a detached, passive relationship. He "hath caught new pleasures" (line 69) with eye or ear or other senses only in a severely limited way, detached and noncommittal. What has he really been given or even received? Nor is it an answer to say that Allegro is merely fantasizing an anatomy of Mirth's world as a set of possibilities—hence the dreamily abrupt shifts like that from cottage to "Towred Cities." For Allegro evidently cannot imagine Mirth's world at the same time that he imagines himself in it, implicated and committed. Think of how different a congregation is when it sings as one a canticle of praise.[43]

The poem develops the consequences of an initial choice that, like the jealousy of Leontes and the disburdened exactions of Lear, must entail an exorbitant price. Beautiful women, for example, seem to subsist far from "Mirth and youth, and warm desire" ("Song," 6) and hover, if anywhere, in a scenically and existentially distant perhaps, as objects of an anonymous gaze, the "Cynosure of neighbouring eyes" ("L'Allegro," 80) remote from the speaker's own. Propinquity yields hardly more intimacy: the cottagers "creep" (line 115) to bed as if insects, and the speech of cities is "busie" (line 118)—not urbane, polite, civil, or even political, but a mere "humm of men" (line 118).

Service in Mirth's crew evidently becomes more hectic. The ceremony of cities involves "Ladies, whose bright eies / Rain influence" (line 121) and do not possess a merely presumed beauty (line 79). Those eyes may have the familiar office of stars, but they are near enough to judge prizes "of Wit, or Arms" (line 123). That should bode well for poets, witty that they are, but abruptly the nearness is distanced by the ambiguous status of dream and its dispersion among bemused poets (lines 129–30).[44]

43. Two centuries ago, Samuel Johnson observed in his "Life of Milton" that "both Mirth and Melancholy are solitary, silent inhabitants of the breast that neither receive nor transmit communication. . . . No mirth can indeed be found in his melancholy; but I am afraid that I always meet some melancholy in his mirth. They are two noble efforts of imagination." Brooks and Hardy have tried to resolve the seeming, but not actual, non sequitur of this final sentence. See "Essays in Analysis," esp. 131, 139. See also Christopher Grose, "The Lydian Arts of 'L'Allegro' and 'Il Penseroso,'" *Journal of English and Germanic Philology*, LXXXIII (1984), 183–99.

44. That what we are given is feeble and disjunctive, as dream vision, is scrupulously worked out by Herbert J. Phelan in "What Is the Persona Doing in 'L'Allegro' and 'Il Penseroso'?" *Milton Studies*, XXII (1986), 3–19. But the article does not attend to implications or the framing context. That dream is no vision.

Should the stage be furnished with a play by one of the most celebrated playwrights of the speaker's national drama, that will just be "learned" Jonson (line 132) or "*Shakespear* fancies child" (line 133) warbling. Ezra Pound could never have damned this as Milton's obtuseness had he considered the external context as including "On Shakespear," and the internal context the opening lines of "L'Allegro" and those which follow immediately the reference to Shakespeare: "And ever against eating Cares, / Lap me in soft *Lydian* Aires" (lines 135–36).[45] It seems the woodnotes must ever be accompanied, not with madder music and stronger wine but with the support and release of Lydian airs to "lap me in," and with voice to unchain the "hidden soul of harmony" (line 144). Melancholy, kicked out the door to begin the poem, has reappeared as regression in the heart's core. The poem's speaker may still dream of simple freedom from a Plutonic underworld, may only have learned enough caution to change the entreaty "And if I give thee honour due, / Mirth, admit me of thy crew" (lines 37–38) to the tougher conditional of "if thou canst give" (line 151; not "if I can take").

But the irony is enforced by the behavior of Allegro's creator, who abruptly projects a trial of the antithetical option. The very different partial or tentative or intermittent self of "Il Penseroso" can see the mote in his neighbor's eyes but not the beam in his own ("Il Penseroso," 8). He is made to call for Peace, Quiet, and "Spare Fast, that oft with gods doth diet" (line 46). He does not say "spare time, oft with gods to diet" in Spenserian temperance or even a conventional austerity. He personifies skinny abstinence, as if as Milton's joke on his speaker. What a later poet characterized as "eternal passion, eternal pain" in the song of Philomela Penseroso and "Cherub Contemplation" (line 54) reduce to "sweetest, saddest plight, / Smoothing the rugged brow of night" (line 57). This is not unlike Orsino on music, or Comus speaking of the Lady's song "smoothing the raven down / Of darknes till she smil'd" (*A Mask,* 251–52).

The instruction of quasi companions gives way to fancied circumstances ("Il Pensoroso," 56–97); then the speaker's fancy shifts to stage scenes apparently inspired by texts, the object of private study rather than the medium of playhouse entertainment. Still later, dawn arrives (lines 121–22), the earlier incidents having occurred in a night world. This

45. See Ezra Pound, *ABC of Reading* (New Haven, 1934), 91; and Ezra Pound, *The Literary Essays,* ed. T. S. Eliot (London, 1954), 72.

darkness reiterates the evolving estrangement from the opening matters of the poem, including Melancholy's own "looks commercing with the skies" (line 39)—commercing inconsequentially, it seems. Does Penseroso attenuate the personal immediacy and consequentiality of the Philomela legend for himself in observing the nightingale's song as "Most musicall, most melancholy!" (line 62) in shunning the "noise of folly" (line 61)? He does more than that; he separates himself entirely: "And missing thee, I walk unseen" (line 65). The odd darkness in which he walks lacks the omnipresence of acoustical or dance space, and it lacks also the differentiating qualities of visual and geographical or goal-oriented space. The protagonist is unseen, the moon is a confused or confusing marker even though near the zenith, the "far-off" curfew cry (line 74) is apparently an identifier of separation more than it is of connection, the place of the ocean's "roar" (line 76) is indefinitely "som" shore (line 75), the radiance of embers is almost as decharacterized as the celebrated "darkness visible" (*Paradise Lost,* I, 63): "Where glowing Embers through the room / Teach light to counterfeit a gloom" ("Il Penseroso," 79–80). The cricket on the hearth does not sing to this night fellow, though it is nearby like the bellman (line 83), whose "drousie," or failing, speech blesses "dores" (line 84) rather than lone thinkers.

The contingent mode of being here seems that of the most reclusive self Milton can imagine choosing to be. Penseroso does speak in his own voice. "Unseen" (line 65), he envisions himself passively inferable from his tower lamp (lines 85–86). As if shrinking from that faint human contact, though, he at once supposes himself not reciprocally inferring the other but instead aggrandizing himself in cosmic speculation. His removals from human association immediately measure themselves by their effect: whereas Allegro's way with drama and life automatizes it, Penseroso's withdrawal of self into abstraction reduces tragedy to costumed spectacle, so that even "Pelops line" (line 99) and the Trojan War become a passing parade. Similarly, the songs of Spenser or the most cluttered tale of Chaucer would parade through Penseroso's ear hopelessly denatured and shallow. We may attribute more substantial qualities to this speaker or his occasions, but for him, in his lethargic passivity, the very moon in "pale career" (line 121) is a kind of parade figure. The sun—uncomfortably importunate—must be avoided, in favor of a pageant projected on the screen of inner "eye-lids" (line 150). Heaven itself is the ultimate spectacle before the eye, not even in it, like beauty. Human chronology and history have evaporated in this contingent as-if time. There is neither love, to render time fulfilled, the emblem of eternity, nor hatred, to render time ever more onerous and repetitious, the mode of hell.

We have slighted certain lines embarrassing to the idea that there is a uniformity of outlook within each of these two poems. Milton, the rising poet of love, makes the embarrassment either Allegro's or Penseroso's. The power of poetry evidently resists reduction to mirth or to musing—or to schema. It tugs back toward the society that constructed the language and its life, toward love that resists death, toward committed action, engaged sympathy, failure, whatever else the potent figures of Orpheus and Eurydice embody. Their story situates by contrast both Allegro and Penseroso, as even fragments can remind us (our emphasis): "would have *won* the ear" ("L'Allegro," 148), "His *half*-regain'd Eurydice" (line 150); "Drew Iron *tears*" ("Il Penseroso," 107), "made Hell *grant* what Love did *seek*" (line 108). Down either Allegro's or Penseroso's path, Satan lies.

Of course, Melancholy cannot raise Musaeus nor secure a song from murdered Orpheus, any more than Mirth can anesthetize with Lydian airs—at least for Milton and his speakers. Evasions cannot prevail; they can only deny even a subsistence, as Milton has caused the Orphic references and other touches in both poems to suggest, and as he reiterates when he leaves Penseroso groping in subjunctives.[46]

Penseroso finally proposes for himself a sort of motion that would have the labor of journey but no *telos,* the repetition of dance but little of its expression and no joy: "never fail / To walk the studious Cloysters pale" (lines 155–56). He proposes a quasi-liturgical "Service high" (line 163) but imagines himself uninvolved in the "people's work" that *liturgy* comprises; instead he is estranged "into extasies" (line 165) and a heaven of spectacle, a sexless version of Comus' "round" (*A Mask,* 144).

For the remainder of the 1645 edition of *Poems,* the poet seems resolved not to sidestep the trials of life and commitment but rather to embrace them, either appraising them through mutual and straightforward speaking selves to a greater degree than before, or rendering them actively and interpersonally in the secular liturgy of entertainment or masque.

46. Those subjunctives are too often glossed over. But see Hill, "Poet-Priest," 56. Penseroso's final proposal may superficially look priestly-poetic enough to be Miltonic, but it is neither preacherly-active enough nor poetic-prophetic enough to represent the Milton whose studying was always for some kerygmatic purpose.

The speaker of Sonnet 1, "O Nightingale," acknowledges radical adversity: "Bird of Hate . . . hopeles doom" (Sonnet 1, lines 9–10). He is conscious of puzzles, in phrases like "hast sung too late . . . no reason why" (lines 11–12). He stops short of asking, What am I doing wrong? But by implication in Sonnet 7, "How soon hath Time," it will be the speaker's wrongdoing if he does not accept the grace to abide his time somehow fruitfully. Similarly, the Italian sonnets and "Canzone" present a speaker involved with love. An acquaintance with Italy and the state of love provoke him to a good-naturedly ironic self-awareness of change, of the "new flower of alien speech" (fior novo di strania favella; Sonnet 3, line 7) and of "unknown and alien language" (lingua ignota e strana; "Canzone," 3). He confesses to Diodati in Sonnet 4 that he has earlier scoffed yet now "entangles himself": (s'impiglia; Sonnet 4, line 4). He knowingly joins the conventional and perennial society of young lovers—which by generic and historic definition is a high-comic society.

The speaker in Sonnets 7, 8, 9, and 10—to say *speakers* seems unnecessary—shows a growing confidence in the power of the imaginative word as a mode of action and participation in the world. The "can requite thee" (Sonnet 8, line 5) and "can spread thy name" (line 7), are capable of becoming a directive to the self (as in Sonnet 9) or of defining the virtue of a father and daughter so as to give it a kind of presence for the hearers (as in Sonnet 10).[47] But a new split seems to be suggested by these successive sonnets, different from that between the committed life and uninvolved mirthfulness or contemplativeness. The world has come to be seen as fallen yet offering Christian redemption, a world in which it makes sense either to wait or to do, if waiting is not slack but oriented toward the hill of heavenly truth, and if to do is to do what one is, to wield words insofar as one is a poet. If the immediate public realm is more fallen than the private, it makes sense to seek privacy, or to seek an alternative, al-

---

47. For this condensed assimilation of the sonnets in the edition of 1645 to our thesis, we have found support in Nardo's extended and persuasive treatment of all Milton's sonnets as a coherent series in exploration of community. See her *Milton's Sonnets,* esp. Chaps. 2, 3, and pp. 60–66. For the importance of the Italian community of letters to the sonnets, see her "Milton and the Academic Sonnet," in *Milton in Italy: Contexts, Images, Contradictions,* ed. Mario A. DiCesare, Medieval and Renaissance Texts and Studies, XC (Binghamton, N.Y., 1991), 489–503. Leo Miller has argued persuasively that "Ladie, that in the prime" was prenuptial reassurance. See his "Milton's 'Lost' Sonnet to Mary Powell," *Milton Quarterly,* XXV (1991), 102–107.

ready existing public realm, or to reform the public realm—which might begin as reforming the private self, as the model and antecedent for reforming the great world. Such a schema of possibilities helps identify the troubled moves of the last English portions of *Poems*, in the edition of 1645. It also helps delineate the profundity of the crisis in "Lycidas."

Solitary privacy seems for Milton never to have been a life-supporting answer to the questions posed by the fallen world. His Messiah in *Paradise Regain'd* finds Satan and all the world in solitude. The Bard there, as in *Paradise Lost,* is a public character. The Messiah and the Bard minister in their respective ways to society. Blind Samson defines himself as a public character even "at the Mill with slaves" (*Samson Agonistes,* 41). That contrasts with Allegro and Penseroso, as with the followers of Comus, headed like various animals and forgetful of their native homes.

The great world is reciprocally necessary to authenticate the self, and parliaments are exactly the place to certify an "Old man eloquent" (Sonnet 10, line 8). Words are the essential medium for certain "noble Vertues" (line 12), as are "feastfull freinds" (Sonnet 9, line 12). These sonnets touch on elements in the classical, Hebraic, natural, and public English worlds which can sustain and be sustained by the poetic voice, elements that are the cause of virtue, in behalf of what the Book of Common Prayer has always called the "blessed company of all faithful people."

"Arcades" seems to have as its main claim to space in the volume its animated tableau of such a grace-given public reality: a noble matron and social hierarchy al fresco, night itself redeemed by "glad solemnity" ("Arcades," 39), the "daughters of *Necessity*" (line 69) lulled, an order constituted where rightly Alpheus "by secret sluse" (line 30) steals "under seas to meet his *Arethuse*" (line 31). More than *A Mask,* this may claim to be Milton's festive comedy.[48]

48. We allude to C. L. Barber's *Shakespeare's Festive Comedy* (Princeton, 1959), and to his disinclination to treat *A Mask* that way in "*A Mask Presented at Ludlow Castle:* The Mask as a Masque." *A Mask* seems as distinct generically as it does bibliographically from the other English works of the 1645 edition of *Poems*. We suggest that within the wide range of masque, it may be thought of as a counterritual. See Mara Selvini Palazzoli, *Self-Starvation: From Individual to Family Therapy in the Treatment of Anorexia Nervosa* (New York, 1978), esp. Chaps. 23–27; and Mara Selvini Palazzoli *et al., Paradox and Counter-Paradox: A New Model in the Therapy of the Family in Schizophrenic Transaction* (New York, 1978). *Arcades,* in contrast, has been explicated as a largely nonparadoxical *conversio,* pagan to Christian, by John Malcolm Wallace, in "Milton's *Arcades*," *Journal of English and Germanic Philology,* LVII (1959), 627–36.

"Lycidas" earns its just celebration not least as the climactic struggle of the edition of 1645. The universe is called in question because the prepublic self, the model or reflection of the unrealized speaker, can be absurdly aborted. Reforming a public world, or even seeking out an already achieved less fallen public world, may be a vertiginous project in a world that drowns a would-be poet-priest "ere his prime" ("Lycidas," 8). Yet he cannot avoid his long time of preparatory learning, for without it a priest will likely be an unheard, unread blind mouth. The insufficiently learned priest-poet's songs will be insubstantial, in contrast to both the presencing words of "Honourd *Margaret*" (Sonnet 10, line 14) and the words of this poet, who makes present "thy loss to shepherds ear" ("Lycidas," 49).

So this speaker, the last in the series, comes forward as an engaged young man in profound crisis over Lycidas' death. In a world contiguous with the other scenes of the volume—even if he does not at first know that—what is there for him to do? He can act fraternally in traditional rituals of loyal mourning. He can acknowledge the kinship of work and of death: the sable shroud will in time be the speaker's, as it might have been already. An intimacy with death is finally achieved. After a few more steps in this poem he will be able to confront—as the speaker can in Sonnet 18—the indignity of death. What he envisages then is no sable shroud but "bones . . . hurl'd" (line 155) in the "monstrous world" (line 158) he imaginatively visits and acknowledges.

That Lycidas and his mourner were creatures of history—of the same culture, apprenticeship, and mentorship—renders the loss more poignantly as loss of self, analogous to an epidemic of small deaths in nature (lines 45–49). So the speaker begins the major coping tactic of the poem, that tactic familiar from life of marshaling one source of reinforcement after another. The achieved poem presents the tactic as a testing of possible helps in a time of adversity.

Except for the last of the tested reinforcements, they are all destroyed, like troops committed piecemeal in a military debacle. Nymphs of Druidic association, even "the Muse her self that *Orpheus* bore" (line 58)—the aids from the deeps of the mind and the Orphic life-seeking powers of poetic vocation are savagely negated by the "hideous roar" (line 61) and "goary visage" (line 62). Allegro's balletic youths dancing in the checkered shade and hailed into the immediacy of "tangles of *Neaera's* hair" (line 69) are painful to contemplate because ambition for achievement has precluded participation in their frolic—the more painful because the "blind *Fury*" (line 75) may thwart achievement and eros alike.

That fame for earthly deeds is correctly recorded in heaven is an Apollonian thought that establishes a line of resistance to engulfment by desperation, but only so long as the world permits such deeds. The spirits who represent nature fail to achieve dominion over such realities as a "perfidious bark" (line 100) and "curses dark" (line 101). Similarly, Camus, the (notably male) representative of the Cantabrigian alma mater, can only lament. And the "Pilot of the *Galilean* lake" (line 109) can neither explain nor assuage the sinking that has occasioned the mourner's grief. He can identify abusers of the tradition he represents, the tradition of corporately dealing with mysteries, but his harshness only shrinks the streams without recovering Lycidas. Condemnatory judgment lacks life-fostering power; even when the judgment is just.

The struggling poet gains brief respite foreshadowing Robert Herrick's familiar strategy of fractionation into fine bits. He turns his thought to "bells, and flowrets of a thousand hues" (line 135). This strategic withdrawal "to interpose a little ease" (line 152) affords the strength to address the otherness of the "monstrous world" (line 158). The life world of "som melodious tear" (line 14) balances the death world of "watry bear" (line 12) in an important way. But the contrariety of fable and hurled bones "to our moist vows deni'd" (line 159) must be faced.

Remarkably, the effort to face it permits the train of association that leads to the last emotional, intellectual, geographical verge. It is the crisis from which help comes. Surely William Madsen is right: Saint Michael's voice answers.[49] The saint can affirm—whether within the speaker's entranced mind or from outside—the mysterious ways of heaven, and of transcendence. He does not provide a new name of God, not the Greek ecclesiastical name Christ. Rather, he gives the particularly appropriate quasi-Hebraic sort of description by power and thing done: "the dear might of him that walkt the waves" (line 173). By dramatic implication, nothing works but grace. Grace lets the poet's ears hear the enabling revelation of Michael. And just as this poet invited his readers into his

49. William Madsen, "The Voice of Michael in Lycidas," *Studies in English Literature,* III (1963), 1–9.

nativity song, here he invites them to leap with him in faith to an acceptance of the authenticity of Michael's vision, or at least of the authenticity of the poet's *agape*.

The dear might was alike precious and costly to both the Savior and those who would be saved. Such a duality is the mark of involvement. And the image of it enabled the poet to accept it, and accept Lycidas as an image of fidelity. Lycidas, in fidelity to his vocation, perseveres past the boundary between the known and the unknown, and by so doing becomes the "Genius of the shoar" (line 183). His fidelity and salvation attest to the boundedness of the sea; the monstrous world cannot utterly engulf being. Yet the concurrent existence of the monstrous world testifies to the mysterious power of his God. All of that gives the poet strength to accept realistically the world and to move "to fresh woods and pastures new" (line 193) even if they lie beyond the boundary of the known. A "great redemption" ("On the Morning of Christs Nativity," 4) from the desperately realized hopelessness of our deathly world has been brought, *both* "from above" (line 4) and from below, to a poet who in "Lycidas" has come far from the poignant innocence in which he applauded redemption in "On the Morning of Christs Nativity." This poet has joined the company of those who would repair the ruins of our first parents—who would, that is, attend to their duty as Milton defines it in "Of Education." He has qualified to attempt the instruction of his country, as he envisions in his preface to Book II of *The Reason of Church Government*. He has come to something he must know as Bard: that it is the very essence of history to impute to us responsibilities that are never entirely ours.[50]

When Milton came to look back with his inner—his only remaining—eye on his poetic beginnings, he made certain changes for an augmented edition of *Poems* in 1673. He could by then consider his beginnings by his endings and consider both in the light of the remarkable national history in between. His efforts of responsibility throughout could be in his thought, as well. *Paradise Lost, a Poem in Ten Books* had appeared in 1667, and *Paradise Regain'd, to which is added Samson Agonistes* in 1671.

The title page of 1645 carries the words "*Poems* of Mr. John Milton, Both English and Latin, Compos'd at Several Times . . . The Songs were set in Musick by Mr. Henry Lawes." In 1673, the songs of Lawes, "His

---

50. Maurice Merleau-Ponty, "The Yogi and the Proletarian," trans. Nancy Metzel and John Flodstrom, in *The Primacy of Perception*, ed. James M. Edie (Evanston, Ill., 1964), 223.

Maiesties Private Musick," have yielded to a greater emphasis on historicity and to essayistic discourse: "*Poems, &c.* upon Several Occasions, by Mr. John Milton . . . composed at several times. With a small Tractate of Education To Mr. Hartlib." It is difficult not to see the programmatic essay on education, with its concern for repairing—very much in history—what it refers to as the "ruins of our first parents," as a weighty footnote to *A Mask*.

The table of contents included a listing of printer's errata, of which the most interesting for our purposes is the indication that the elegy "On the Death of a Fair Infant Dying of a Cough" (inserted in 1645 immediately after the two psalms) should have been followed immediately by "At a Vacation Exercise" (which was actually printed late in the sequence of English poems). Thus, another poem about death appears in a sequence already marked with elegy. Its opening imagery of "Fairest flower no sooner blown but blasted . . . Bleak winters force" ("On the Death of a Fair Infant," 1–4) contrasts with the refrain from the paraphrase of Psalm 136: "For his mercies ay endure, / Ever faithfull, ever sure." The text notes that the two paraphrases were "done by the Author at fifteen years old," whereas the textual headnote to "On the Death of a Fair Infant" puts it "Anno aetatis 17"—an apparent typographical error for nineteen, as Shawcross observes.

Placing "At a Vacation Exercise" next after "On the Death of a Fair Infant" would appear to reflect the order of composition. Somewhat more provocatively, the poet wanted to set it just before his abortive "The Passion." Milton, who had ultimately indeed soared with no middle flight, was willing to position there a bookishly, boyishly sportive poem hailing native language and submitting in its early lines that "the deep transported mind may soar . . . and at Heav'ns dore / Look in" ("At a Vacation Exercise," 33–34).

The other changes for the edition of 1673 are all interpolations. Although it is simple to list them, their suggestiveness is not simple. The sonnets, which begin immediately after "Il Penseroso," are augmented by an eleventh, "A book was writt of late call'd *Tetrachordon,*" through nineteenth, "Mee thought I saw my late espoused saint." The additions continue with the translation of Horace's Fifth Ode, "What slender Youth"; the poem "On the New Forcers of Conscience"; and the misplaced "Vacation Exercise." "Arcades," "Lycidas," and *A Mask* follow, as in 1645. But then, before the Latin poems, there come Psalms 1–8, "done into

Verse, 1653," and Psalms 80–88, "done into [conventional] Metre," in "April 1648."

Clearly, what the new edition's sonnets add—including the "tailed," or augmented, "On the New Forcers"—is a profound reinforcement of cultural, social, vicissitudinary historicity.[51] The ill reception of *Tetrachordon* is set against enculturating figures like Apollo, Quintilian, and Sir John Cheke and thus associated with such as Pindar and "sad *Electra's* poet" (Sonnet 8, line 13). The appropriate reception by a public-spirited man of letters of a kindred effort is modeled not only by Dante toward Casella but also by Milton himself in Sonnet 13, entitled "To Mr. *H. Lawes, on his Aires*" in the edition of 1673. Lawes, whose name may have faded from the title page, reappears in this celebration of his "tunefull and well-measur'd song" (Sonnet 13, line 1).

At the same time, history seems to keep vicissitude from becoming chaotically bewildering. Rather, it articulates and situates it—indeed, puts it in its place—in a nonabsurd, non-Manichaean world. Old priest can define new presbyters. The sower of the biblical parable, Cadmus, and "*Babylonian* wo" (Sonnet 18, line 14) ominously locate and sentence the "bloody *Piemontese*" (line 7).

At the same time, the charities said in *Paradise Lost* to flow from wedded love are given habitation and name in these added sonnets: in Sonnet 14, "When Faith and Love," and Sonnet 23, "Mee thought I saw," and in the two on earned, recreative leisure—Sonnet 20, "*Lawrence* of vertuous Father," and Sonnet 19, "Cyriack, whose Grandsire on the Royal Bench." These touch hands with the earlier Sonnet 9, "Ladie that in the prime," and Sonnet 10, "Daughter to that good Earle." Here are testimony to the lineages of love and a gallery of orientations toward love's heavenly source.

Yet the last words of Sonnet 23 are "I wak'd, she fled, and day brought back my night." There are triumphant, or more exactly triumphantly

51. For sociopolitical contexts and intertextuality in these translations, see William B. Hunter, "Milton Translates the Psalms," *Philological Quarterly*, XL (1961), 485–94; Margaret Boddy, "Milton's Translation of Psalms 80–88," *Modern Philology*, LXIV (1966), 1–9; Collette, "Milton's Psalm Translations"; and Lee A. Jacobus, "Milton Metaphrast: Logic and Rhetoric in Psalm I," *Milton Studies*, XXIII (1987), 119–32. For Milton and the Psalter in general and particular, see Mary Ann Radzinowicz, *Milton's Epics and the Book of the Psalms* (Princeton, 1989). For further reflections on the 1645 and 1673 orders—mainly in their defense—see Wittreich, *Visionary Poetics*, 67–68, 89; and Ian Jack, "A Choice of Orders: The Arrangement of 'The Poetical Works,'" in *Textual Criticism and Literary Interpretation*, ed. Jerome J. McGann (Chicago, 1985), 127–43.

encouraging, endings to "Lycidas" and *A Mask,* but the psalms Milton appends to *A Mask* in 1673, along with the ending of the final sonnet of the volume, make for a sober and finally somber anthology. The poet subordinates his own order of work to the biblical order. The metrical experimentation of 1653, in Psalms 1–8, thus precedes Psalms 80–88, which are in the ballad meter of 1648.

Are there rewards to this beyond keeping the faith of biblical order? Perhaps there is an advantage in placing first the translations that apparently were made early in his blindness and his first widowhood. The first eight psalms bring to the foreground a God of wrathful justice who in a landscape of tumultuous Gentiles, dispersed "Like to a potters vessel" ("Psalm 2," 21), "Hast broke the teeth" ("Psalm 3," 23) of the ungodly. In this respect, the adaptations differ little from the translations in the Book of Common Prayer. But there are idiosyncratic touches, as in Milton's version of Psalm 1, which opens "Blest is the man who hath not walk'd astray" ("Psalm 1," 1). *Astray* provides a rhyme for *way* (the way of sinners) in the next line but also goes beyond the Book of Common Prayer's translation in an Augustinian and anti-Manichaean direction patent to readers looking back from *Paradise Lost* to this. And where the Book of Common Prayer has, "His leaf also shall not wither," Milton wrote, "his leaf shall not fall" (line 9). His son John had died in 1652. In Psalm 6, where the Book of Common Prayer has, "My beauty is gone for very trouble, and worn away," here there is, "mine Eie / Through grief consumes, is waxen old and dark" ("Psalm 6," 13–14). Psalm 8, with its great question "O what is man that thou . . . think'st upon him" is—may we say?—ever so slightly reoriented toward assertions of eternal providence by changing the Book of Prayer's repeated "excellent is thy Name" to "glorious is thy name" ("Psalm 8," 2, 24).

Psalms 80–88, rendered into ballad meter in 1648, reinforce the Hebraic recasting of the classical material so prominent in *A Mask,* somewhat as the transcendent vision enabling closure in "Lycidas" recasts the preceding classical, and monstrous, world. For these psalms, Milton adapts to the typographic mode the familiar rhetorical figure of modest disclaimer. "All but what is in a different Character, are the very words of the Text, translated from the Original," reads Milton's headnote. His expansions are highlighted (in fact, whether or not by intention) in italic type.

The first eight of the nine adaptations offer a few amplifications of the biblical and Augustinian figure of life as a journey, the figure we have emphasized as fundamental to Milton's early poetry and *A Mask* and to *Paradise Lost: "wayes of sin"* ("Psalm 80," 74), *"swerve"* ("Psalm 81," 16), *"led thee"* (line 28), *"never slide"* ("Psalm 86," 40). There are, closely related, elaborations on worldly vicissitude: *"time of need"* ("Psalm 80," 2), *"We cry and do not cease"* ("Psalm 83," 4), *"No quiet let find"* (line 50), *"chide no more"* ("Psalm 85," 16), *"sad decay"* ("Psalm 86," 4), *"where proud Kings / Did our forefathers yoke"* ("Psalm 87," 11–12). But of course the petitionary grammar and rhetoric confirm what Milton saw in Books XI and XII of *Paradise Lost:* that history need never be *merely* vicissitude. And he gives this hermeneutic recasting in the diction of the New Testament: *"give light"* ("Psalm 80," 7), *"and thy grace divine"* (line 29), *"thou the same . . . art one"* ("Psalm 83," 67–68), *"thou dost dwell so near!"* ("Psalm 84," 4), *"life in us renew"* ("Psalm 85," 28), "set free / *From deepest darkness foul"* ("Psalm 86," 47–48), "O turn to me *thy face at length"* (line 57), "*And* all my fountains *clear"* ("Psalm 87," 28).

Still, Milton concludes his sequence of "Psalms done into Metre" with the terrible eighty-eighth, in which the poetic of parallelism and iteration normal to the psalms appears in a faithful yet desolate utterance that Milton has made yet more intense. In the opening address to the God of salvation, the Book of Common Prayer's "I have cried" becomes "I cry . . . *weep,* / Before thee *prostrate lie"* ("Psalm 88," 2–4). *Slain,* in verse 4 in the Book of Common Prayer, becomes "slain *in bloody fight"* (line 19) in *"Deaths hideous house"* (line 24). The postulant cries from "lowest pit *profound . . . all forlorn"* (lines 25–26), which occur in a "place of darkness" in the Book of Common Prayer, come for Milton from a place where, palpably, "thickest darkness *hovers round"* (line 27). An ambiguity in the Hebrew, compressed in the Book of Common Prayer as "thou hast vexed me with all thy storms," expands here to "Thou break'st upon me all thy waves, / And all thy waves break me" (lines 31–32). Milton reiterates *waves* (line 68) where the Book of Common Prayer speaks of water, in verse 17. He adverts to *"gloomy* land" (line 51) and *"dark* oblivion" (line 52), and in a personally prefiguring simile substitutes "as in darkness are" (line 72) for the Book of Common Prayer's "out of sight." This, though, is symbolic darkness, not the optical darkness that would close in somewhat later. At the conclusion of Psalm 88, the prayer book's psalmist laments "lovers and friends . . . put away . . . hid." Milton's psalmist reduces the number and darkens the drama: "Lover and friend . . . remov'd / And sever'd . . . *fly me now*" (lines 69–71). The lines might have an unbearable pathos were it not for a subtle adjustment of volitional dynamism and temporality some lines earlier. Verse 13 of the Book of Common Prayer reads, "Unto thee have I cried, O Lord; and early shall my prayer come before thee." In Milton's version, there is something closer to the devout ideal of praying without cease, prayerful reiteration ever new:

> But I to thee O Lord do cry
> *E're yet my life be spent,*
> And *up to thee* my praier *doth hie*
> Each morn, and thee prevent.
>
> (Lines 53–56)

SEVEN

Confessions in the Desert, Motions in the Theater

We have argued that understanding Milton's end, of asserting and justifying by theodicean epic, entails a reunderstanding of his poetic beginnings. And the beginnings must also be reunderstood in the light of the end. This can be the case even for a reader who demurs at the terms we have used or at our emphases. Indeed, Milton's own understanding may have had ends informed by beginnings, and beginnings by ends, so far as the edition of *Poems* in 1673 is a *renewed* volume. Moreover, the provisional end of the beginnings in *Paradise Lost,* and the beginnings of the end in the early poetry, together invite a return to the middle of readers' engagement with Milton's final fully new volume. Reconsidering in this way *Paradise Regain'd,* "to which is added *Samson Agonistes,*" as the title page of 1671 reads, can complement *Paradise Lost* with a compatible consideration of postlapsarian aspects of knowing, naming, movement, and love engaged, abused, and occluded by power—all these being phenomena deeply incarnate in human, experiential time.

THE PARADIGM OF TRIAL AND CONFESSION OF THE WORD

In *Paradise Regain'd,*

> the Son of God . . .
> Musing and much revolving in his brest,
> How best the mighty work he might begin
> Of Saviour to mankind, and which way first
> Publish his God-like office now mature,
> One day forth walk'd alone, the Spirit leading;
> And his deep thoughts, the better to converse
> With solitude, till far from track of men,

> Thought following thought, and step by step led on,
> He enter'd now the bordering Desert wild
> *(Paradise Regain'd, 183–93)*

The Son is sinless but lives in the world after the fall in the garden of and from wedded love, and the civic fall in the power project of Babel of and from lesser charities. The Son leaves the known human world and crosses the boundary into the place negatively named as the Desert, the place of the not yet known. He does so faithfully as Lycidas, for Milton the "Genius of the shoar" ("Lycidas," 183), risking all to his calling. Milton's portrayal of the Son's commissioning at the baptism by the River Jordan is overtly dramatic but cryptic too. The Son's receptive movement step by step and thought by thought is from the first to his final stand on the pinnacle of the temple more graceful to the eye and more grace blessed than Satan's avid clamber through Chaos precisely because the Son is moved by love. The mark of that is the Son's aptness for carrying heaven with him even more surely than Satan carries hell.

The cryptic temptations, so many more than the biblical three—"obedience . . . Through all temptation . . . Tempter foil'd / In all his wiles" *(Paradise Regain'd, I, 4–6)*—have been suggestively called a "meditative combat" by Louis Martz, but have been supposed lacking in drama by many readers. The series of temptations might better be seen as intensely dramatic, but gracefully so, precisely in the avoidance of a quasi-Manichaean power struggle like that in Book VI of *Paradise Lost.* Even at the end, with Satan's fall, it is not the military farce of stumbling exits "ten paces huge" *(Paradise Lost, VI, 193)* but a dying swoop to midair crew in consult—a fall ultimately though not immediately parallel to those of Antaeus and Chimaera and initially like that of Mammon which is seemingly alleviated in the long trajectory of classical "Mulciber." Here heavenly love outdoes hellish hate (to adapt the divine promise of *Paradise Lost, III, 298)*: Satan's love, displaced and degraded to lust for power, receives "many a foil" *(Paradise Regain'd, IV, 569)* at the very wellspring of human worldly life, language. Language as narcissistic knowing, and the naming that is for power advantage, are consistently foiled by steadfast responses not of power but of obedient love.

A power dialectic of "windlesses and assays of bias"—the project of Polonius describes the rhetoric of Satan—is occluded, aborted, and finally obviated by confessions of true divinity. The speaker in "Lycidas" foils demoralization when the graced gift of Michael's voice supplies—or prompts (it comes to the same thing)—the apposite name of God for the crisis: "him that walkt the waves" ("Lycidas," 173). Paradigmatically expanded, the situation here is similar: the Son meets the spectral range of seductive misnamings with confession—utterance after utterance of the loved and truly apposite name of God.

Virtually every speech by Satan is a temptation to respond in kind to a tendentious naming, to become thereby misoriented or at least, like the Lady in *A Mask,* immobilized. Satan's first line is to tempt into misconception of the self in general and into self-pity in particular: "Sir, what ill chance hath brought thee to this place . . . ?" (*Paradise Regain'd,* I, 321). That this is misnaming is implied by the Son's prompt rectifying designation of God as Guide, with the accordant definition of himself as one who is guided. Even a meeting with Satan can thus work for good.

Satan alleges the need for bread to the person before him, baptized forty days since, so that "we wretched" (I, 345) in the desert may survive. The Son of God restates the need as the Word, and like Augustine in his doctrine of prevenient grace, confesses God to be the feeder—historically so of "Our Fathers here with Manna" (I, 351).

When "th' Arch Fiend, now undisguis'd" (I, 357), in a speech of nearly fifty lines names himself by term and tone as "unfortunate" (I, 358), pained, and pitiable, the temptation is to a sentimental sympathy. An acceptance of Satan's misnaming of his circumstances would entail a derangement and misorientation in the hierarchy of love, with the abuse of personal power involved in sentimentality. Hence it is that Milton's "Saviour sternly . . . reply'd" (I, 406) at far greater length than to Satan's earlier and biblical appeal to him to turn stones to bread. By tone and term, the Savior, choosing true guidance for his ministry, excoriates the "liar in four hundred mouths" (I, 428) and rejects all oracles as false and riddling in order to open the way for the "Oracle" (I, 460) who will "*henceforth* . . . dwell / In *pious* Hearts" (I, 462–63; our emphasis) in his identity as "Spirit of Truth" (I, 462). Right loving has fostered right naming, and right naming has fostered right loving; another long thought and step have been taken toward the pinnacle and cross.

Satan would attempt, as if by judo, to divert his opponent's force into a fall, in this case into a fall originating in pride in power or in abuse of power, either one betokening an excessive love of self. That is the two-sided temptation in the speculative slander and subtle trap of his claim that "Thy Father . . . Suffers the Hypocrite or Atheous Priest / To tread his Sacred Courts" (I, 486–88) and in his entreaty to the Son to "disdain not such access to me" (I, 492). "Our Saviour," moving toward his stand on the very point of the pinnacle, treads the exceedingly narrow line of word and attitude between, I dare you, and, Begone. To "bid not or forbid" (I, 495), and that "with unalter'd brow" (I, 493), is to give an outward visible and audible sign of inward and spiritual grace, free alike from pride or mistrust. The absence of mistrust is relevant, because in deferring to the need to seek "Permission from above," the Son is recognizing and rejecting Satan's Manichaean implications and is commending his spirit into divine hands. Such implications inhere in the secondary implicit suggestion that access might be denied out of mistrust of God, and in the disjunctively reifying language of "Hard . . . ways of truth [yet] tuneable as Silvan Pipe" (I, 478–80). The Bard, just as emphatically no Manichaean, closes Book I with Satan "Into thin Air diffus'd" (I, 499) by the Son's rejection of that suggestion.

The Bard reminds us in Book II of Andrew and Simon, and of Mary, who made lesser, partially contrastive hermeneutic journeys—day by day and thought by thought led on after the baptismal scene, led into demoralization in the first case and into anxiety in the second.

The Son, who earlier meditated on Mary's counsel to him and "again revolv'd / The Law and Prophets" (I, 259–60), must in the temptations of the "Table richly spred" (II, 340) somehow avoid denying that the firmament showeth God's handiwork, on the one hand, and valuing creatures idolatrously or the self's enjoyment narcissistically, on the other.[1] Thus, Satan, who misnames admiration of beauty *weakness* of mind, and love of woman as insufficiently manly, promises to "let pass / No [supposed] advantage" (II, 233–34) to assay the Son's *strength* and *constancy*.

The Bard invites the reader to appraise and, after due thought, approve the validity of those last two terms. The Son's very dream connects him with a usable past, the past in which the needs of Elijah and Daniel were differently but providentially supplied. Hence, when Satan cites a different past in tempting the Son toward a resentment over what might be named neglect, Jesus constantly affirms the adequacy thus far of providence to real need and, with that, the connection of gift and giver. The

1. See Dayton Haskin, "Milton's Portrait of Mary as Bearer of the Word," in *Milton and the Idea of Woman,* ed. Julia M. Walker (Urbana, Ill., 1988), 169–84.

cathedral-like scene, "High rooff" (II, 293) and a fit "haunt" (II, 296) for idolatrous fictions like "Wood-Gods and Wood-Nymphs" (II, 297) and "Knights of *Logres*" (II, 360), the table's "regal mode" (II, 340), with meats of the "noblest sort" (II, 341), the acolytelike "stripling youths" (II, 352) at a quasi-eucharistic "stately side-board" (II, 350), the masque-like vestals, the Bardic exclamation at the difference of everything from the "simple . . . crude Apple that *diverted Eve*" (II, 349; our emphasis of verb)—all the "Splendour" evidences a temptation to power as sensory indulgence, which is a form of self-worship. That would be a misled step, diverted and averse indeed.

Jesus rejects idolatrous excess by tone: "temperately" (II, 378). He rejects wrong naming by naming true connections: "of my own . . . I can command" (II, 381–82), "pompous Delicacies . . . no gifts but guiles" (II, 390–91). For Satan has condescendingly rejected Belial's advice to "set women in his eye" (II, 153), only to draw upon it in offering a more complex temptation to power as self-indulgence.

Since the Son, even though hungry, has constantly moved, exchange by exchange, through this temptation without succumbing, perhaps Satan can gain the advantage he seeks by tempting with power not for self-indulgence but as the leverage for however unselfish a project the acquirer of power might cherish, or for a project for its own sake—for glory. Thus, the temptation's modal dimension—namely, to substitute power for love—has a temporal dimension: to exploit impatience so as to short-circuit the hermeneutic, providential journey of receptivity to providence.

So when Jesus "patiently reply'd" (II, 432), he in effect confessed the essentiality and benign timelessness of God over any mere accident of occasion or instrumentality. Even poverty "May . . . perhaps" (II, 450–51) work for good for those who love the Lord. That sentiment, with its correlative point about kingly rule over "Passions, Desires, and Fears" (II, 467) is Pauline. The Son's subsequent naming of the "yet more Kingly" is as explicitly Augustinian and hermeneutic as anything in Milton's poetry:

> But to guide Nations in the way of truth
> By saving Doctrine, and from errour lead
> To know, and knowing worship God aright,
> Is yet more Kingly, this attracts the Soul
>
> (II, 473–76)

From noun to verb, from *way* to *lead,* by dynamic ministry dynamically received, as in participial *saving* and *knowing,* this movement toward an end half known at the beginning (from a beginning imperfectly understood until the end) will make a kingship—presumably akin to Protestant priesthood—of all believers on the way.

Satan's response throughout Book III to the checks in Book II upon his "fallacious drift" and "weak arguing" (III, 4) that had the intent of leading astray from the path toward salvation in the true God is to name categories that are either false or baneful. Obscurity of life, he names hiding (III, 21); patience in obscurity he names affectation (III, 22). He speaks as if motives and circumstances were necessarily at odds, and this in a rhetoric of what had once seemingly been Miltonic personal anxiety about "years ripe, and over-ripe" (III, 31).[2] He rhetorically disjoins the essence of glory from a reified glory the Son's "great Father" (III, 110) is alleged to *seek,* or *require* (III, 110, 113, 117), not be.

"Our Saviour" (III, 121), as the Bard feelingly names him here—in suggestive contrast to *Jesus* (II, 432) and the *Son of God* (III, 1)—our Savior foils what may be called an anxiety attack by speaking calmly (III, 43). Calmly he confesses the God who is prime in all, rendering any means—"wealth / For Empires sake . . . Empire . . . For glories sake" (III, 44–46)—absurdly subordinate and ineffectual unless directed back to the source of all. Moreover, the *time* of the hermeneutic journey is confessed to be, as much as the glory, "his / Who sent me" (III, 106–107) for witnessing "whence I am" (III, 107) without abbreviation, in *patience* and even suffering (III, 92, 98).

The Savior, who makes mention to Satan of Socrates, "For truths

2. The commonplace that the rising poet Milton could be troubled on this point is less to our purpose than that his final volume—that is, his final volume so greatly new—defines in the Savior an ideal response to such anxiety. See Laurie Zwicky, "Kairos in *Paradise Regain'd:* The Divine Plan," *English Literary History,* XXXI (1964), 241–77. Low ramifies Louis Martz's earlier argument for *Paradise Regain'd* as an apotheosis of Vergil's *Georgics.* See Low, "Milton and the Georgic Ideal," where the Savior of *Paradise Regain'd* is a georgic agent. He is Nestorian in Hugh MacCallum's *Milton and the Sons of God: The Divine Image in Milton's Epic Poetry* (Toronto, 1986). Stuart Curran perceives *Paradise Regain'd* as an act of literary criticism—which we take to be roughly analogous to the cultural criticism we see in *Paradise Regain'd* and, more emphatically, in *Samson Agonistes.* See Curran, *"Paradise Regain'd:* Implications of Epic," *Milton Studies,* XVII (1983), 209–24.

sake suffering death unjust" (III, 98), leads us to think of the crucifixion, as he did earlier in a speech in which he referred to "they know not what" (III, 52) to specify radically what "the people but a herd confus'd, / A miscellaneous rabble" (III, 49–50) admire and extol. The powerful theological and ethical point—that only the God who will die for love of those people is warranted to judge them—is perhaps no more important for literary criticism than the more general point about Milton and the crucifixion implicit here and throughout *Paradise Regain'd*. Among the constellation of seventeenth-century devotional poets, Milton scants the Passion, it is often said. And his own early poem on the subject "the Author finding to be above the yeers he had . . . and nothing satisfi'd with what was begun, left . . . unfinisht" ("The Passion," appended note), so that it scarcely stands to the contrary, any more than do brief allusions in "On the Morning of Christs Nativity" or *Paradise Lost*. But he does not quite take humble refuge in *adunatio*, like George Herbert's speaker in "The Thanksgiving": "I will do for that—Alas, my God, I know not what!" Rather, what conceivably need not transcend the feeling, loving capability of any Christian—who is counseled to be perfect, we may uneasily recall—is indirectly presented for imitation in the witty quotidian analogue of the Passion in Book III of *Paradise Regain'd*. Jesus, after an interval as if apart from human historical time, is isolated differently in a concentrated life world of physical distress—but of a familiar kind, hunger—and spiritual antagonism. In a succession of thoughts, steps, and rejoinders, he through the Bard enunciates to himself, to adversary, and to the Bard and his readers a complete position of sober, alert, patient, and obedient love. The stations of such a progress evidently imply for the Bard and his readers multiple descents of the Dove, that is, visitations of grace. This can be as important a reason for Milton's several recensions of the baptismal scene at the Jordan as that scene's supple adaptability to the beholder's eye.[3] The complete position of loving obe-

3. It is as if Milton expanded almost playfully on the hermeneutic circle with his differing accounts in *Paradise Lost* of the creation and fall of angels, and carried the tactic farther in *Paradise Regain'd,* where it appears in connection with the annunciation and the nativity, as well as the baptism. By implication, any understanding will reflect the reader's situation. A line of argument we wish to reinforce and extend concerns implications of the conjuncture of *Paradise Regain'd* and *Samson Agonistes*. See, notably, Balachandra Rajan's argument for thematic complementarity in "'To Which Is Added *Samson Agonistes*—,'" in *The Prison and the Pinnacle*, ed. Balachandra Rajan (Toronto, 1973), 82–110. See John

dience to God, in Milton's sternly orthodox view of a genuinely fallen and sinful world, entails an extremity where deliverance and resurrection must and will come by miracle.

Put from the other direction, the crucifixion is for Milton "Recover'd Paradise to all mankind" (*Paradise Regain'd,* I, 3) by virtue of the way Christly obedience foils the previously successful Tempter "in all his wiles" (I, 6). The poet's Christ may be assumed to take a confessional stand on the threatening height of the cross—"Father, into thy hands I commend my spirit"—and is bodily removed from it in a descent not immediately apparent as a triumph. Only subsequent events, understandingly believed and believingly understood, make it so. The Bard has exemplified the Christian duty to be present at the crucifixion—present not in mere physical propinquity, nor in quasi-angelic apprehension of the Deity, nor in engulfment in the human pain of mere sympathy. Being present at the crucifixion, being open to and understanding it as atonement and redemption, must work through allegory, that is to say, through extended metaphor. The poem on the Passion that Milton was able to complete is this poem. After imagining the transformative and triumphant heavenly moments in *Paradise Lost,* he approached the Passion— including the crucifixion, the resurrection, and the ascension—by considering the worldly steps that readied a divine yet human Jesus for the cross.

But first it was necessary to breast the temptation to a reductive arithmetic of temporality: "The happier raign the sooner it begins" (III, 179). Such arithmetic is transcended, without the impedance of adverbial qualification or of other than neutral tone, by the Savior's reply about the fulfillment of prophecies in "due time" (III, 182). (There is a little subsequent ironic questioning, and playtime is not reductively arithmetical either.)

What is biblically but sometimes too briefly called the temptation of the kingdoms, the mountaintop survey, begins with temptations offered to the Savior to configure or comport himself reductively, we think, as a simple opposite of Satan—in particular, to oppose Satanic haste with

---

T. Shawcross' argument for thematic and generic complementarity, in *"Paradise Regain'd"—Worthy T'Have Not Remain'd So Long Unsung* (Pittsburgh, 1988), esp. Chaps. 3, 7–8. Joseph Wittreich's rich argument for something like hermeneutic complementarity—not his terminology—appears in *Interpreting "Samson Agonistes"* (Princeton, 1986). For explication of a self-removing narrator, see Merrilee Cunningham, "The Epic Narrator in Milton's *Paradise Regain'd," Renaissance and Reformation,* XIII (1989), 215–32.

similar abruptness (III, 223–24) or in a spirit contrary to Satan's to lapse into a combination of vanity and false humility (III, 228–32). This is a more psychological version of the physical-theological quasi dilemma of the temple spire; there, too, the Savior answers "unmov'd" (III, 386) though with a wider lexicon of right naming, related to a place of becoming and unbecoming far below godly Being: "Vented . . . policy" (III, 391), "projects" ironically "deep" (III, 391), "prediction" oxymoronically alleged by Satan to "unpredict" (III, 394–95), "cumbersome / Luggage of war" (III, 400–401), Satanic "zeal" (III, 413) characterized by simile as murderous. Just as later, with the anti-Manichaean propriety characteristic of Milton's whole poetic career, Satan's "wiles" are thus "made void" (III, 442) and his speech "to shameful silence brought" (IV, 22).

But awareness of the process of fallen speech, and of all the human temporality of history, eases the conundrum of how sin can be nothing (*peccatum nihil* in the Scholastic formulation) despite being experienced as reality. Only what is not *quite* nothingness may in fallen language be named by images of insubstantiality, as in the Limbo of Vanity in Book II of *Paradise Lost,* and in the "froth or bubbles" (IV, 20) here. Moreover, in fallen time and to fallen consciousness, ever on the move, the assault of dilemmas and worse choices may always be renewed. Comus is still master of the wood, Satan "humming" (IV, 17) in compulsive dialectic with the occasion.

If the Savior is unwilling to degrade the sense of prediction or strength or precedent, if he instead names them recuperatively and acknowledges limits to happenstance in confessing their subordination to the Father's "due time and providence" (III, 440), Satan can perhaps seduce him into an idolatry of signs: "Lictors and rods the ensigns of thir power" (IV, 65), "Civility of Manners, Arts, and Arms" (IV, 83). The kingdoms of the world, presented, as in dream vision, "in a moment" (IV, 162; Luke 4:5), would be an ironic sign indeed if they were accepted as a gift from Satan "as . . . superior Lord" (IV, 167).

Both speeches in rejoinder by the Son of God, the first made "unmov'd" (IV, 109) at the "majestic *show*" (IV, 110; our emphasis), the second "with disdain" (IV, 170) for "Th' abominable terms" (IV, 173), redeem the Babel of perverted signs by a just appraisal and right naming. Luxury is but "call'd magnificence" (IV, 111), and the mummery of the "Embassies thou shew'st" (IV, 121) amounts only to "hollow compliments and lies" (IV, 124). The kingdoms of the world were not given by fate or even in fee simple but were given by God—in the anti-Manichaean sense, "Permitted rather" (IV, 183). Milton found in the inspired word of the Book of Daniel a better-defining image of the Savior's season and of his incumbency on "*David's* Throne" (IV, 471): the simile of Nebuchadnezzar's dream vision of a world tree, as Merritt Y. Hughes has noted.[4] Milton recognized that which is "written / The first of all Commandments" (IV, 176) as the absolutely valid and reliable signifier, the ground from which conclusive consequences and implications can be drawn. But Satan has demonstrated himself *void* of gratitude, fear, or shame (IV, 188–89) with regard to the kingdoms "permitted" him. Here is illustrated the Thomist axiom that the nothingness of sin is a nothingness of love in the sinner. Satan has been made an arch-sign of fallen definition.

Does that help with the *locus desperatus* in which the notorious rejection of "*Athens* the eye of *Greece*" (IV, 240) is so seemingly implicated in the rejection of Satanic names for classical Greece's "Arts / And Eloquence" (IV, 240–41)? Plainly there is the usual, Satanic diversionary attack, in this instance an obvious variant of the invitation to idolatry—not only in the panegyric diction and tone from Athenian "eye" to "*Aeolian* charms" (IV, 257) but in the extremist diction of *best* (IV, 262, 266), *resistless* (IV, 268), and *all the schools* (IV, 277). The attraction of classical models is eventually dismissed by the Savior with ironic concision as centered in "The top of Eloquence, Statists indeed, / And lovers of thir Country, as may seem" (IV, 354–55).

But as countless readers have noticed, and as many find to be a source of embarrassment, there appears an overplus of animus, almost overkill: "false, or little else but dreams . . . built on nothing firm" (IV, 291–92; *cf.* again the Limbo of Vanity and the Satanic "froth or bubbles," p. 210 above). The words *vain* (IV, 307), *boast* (IV, 306, 307), *shifts* (IV, 308), and *empty* (IV, 321) are let fly. We hear of "Gods ridiculous . . . Epithetes thick laid / As varnish on a Harlots cheek, the rest, / Thin sown" (IV, 342–45). Surely there is in the whole passage a kind of Miltonic ambivalence in the language composed by the Bard but placed in the mouth of "our Saviour." The positive aspect has perhaps been put best by Martz in his argument that even what is as beloved as classicism will be cast aside at need, as a sort of offering on the altar of the true God. William Kerri-

---

4. Merritt Y. Hughes, ed., *The Complete Poems and Major Prose of John Milton* (New York, 1957), 519.

gan epitomizes the negative concept: "The best teacher takes revenge on the impositions of the Renaissance Name-of-the-Father," that is, classical education.[5] Like Ben Jonson rhyming against rhyme, Milton inveighs against classicism in epic; he would put aside the "tedious talk" (IV, 307) of the Name-of-the-Father in favor of better spokesmen for the Father, "our Prophets" (IV, 356) by and with whom "better teaching" (IV, 357) is "plainest taught, and easiest learnt" (IV, 361). It is learned in the Miltonic (Uranic) Bard's mother tongue, notice, not except secondarily in patristic classical language taught by males.

Yet the interpretations of Martz and Kerrigan are informed by their knowledge of where the poem's journey is leading, and by their extrinsic knowledge about Milton. Some of the subtlety of the Tempter's major attack, and of the Savior's counter to it is thus obscured. Once again, the temptation by which Satan tries to ensnare is that of intellection and aesthesis as power rather than love. That is what the Savior opposes by insisting on an orientation that does "not mislead" (IV, 309) but is toward the true God rather than toward "nothing firm" (IV, 292), just an "empty cloud" (IV, 321), by insisting on having "God . . . prais'd aright" (348), and by insisting on distinguishing between "What makes a Nation happy, and keeps it so, / What ruins Kingdoms, and lays Cities flat" (IV, 362–63).

By the time Satan has become the "Fiend" (IV, 499), he has exhausted the thematic paradigm of "all temptation" (I, 5). As the Bard twice insists of Satan's "darts" (IV, 366) and of his every "device" (IV, 443), all "were spent." And he describes the subsequent actions of Satan as implicitly Molochian, explicitly the venting of "his rage, / And mad despight" (IV, 445–46), "now swoln with rage" (IV, 499). Insufficiently noticed is the thematic appositeness: the attempted assault, foiled on the front of discourse, is remounted on the front of dream vision, where an assault had some success in demoralizing Eve directly and Adam indirectly. Indeed, if one conceives the body of *Paradise Regain'd* from the Savior's first forty days in the desert onward as a daring Miltonic apotheosis of the literary tradition of dream vision, the final Satanic assault is in a dream within a dream and is on the most hidden levels of the psyche. Still, in *Paradise Regain'd,* the rejecter of love can, like Moloch in Pandaemonium and the artillerists of heaven, only propose more power.

5. Martz, *The Paradise Within,* 197–99; Kerrigan, *The Sacred Complex,* 116.

The drama of the abstracting of the Son from the desert to the pinnacle of the temple—like the cannonade in heaven—may be told in terms of weight, but those terms are taxonomically thin: "The Son of God I also am, or was / And if I was, I am; relation stands" (IV, 518–19). Yes, and no. Geoffrey Harpham argues that the temptation to regard the Word as altogether interpretable comprises a presumption to aggrandize one's own level of being. But method never quite encompasses truth. Satan has succumbed to that temptation, as did Adam and Eve, variously, in Books IX and X of *Paradise Lost*. Harpham is, however, if consistently structuralist, not altogether wise for our purposes in adverting to innocence as a static point, and he is so again when he remarks that "response—even Get thee behind me Satan—merely confirms conversation and so constitutes a yielding to temptation." He is more hermeneutic and Miltonic in paraphrasing Prov. 17:3: "As fire proves iron, so temptation proves the just man."[6]

Satan is forever a son of God, yet the relation both "stands" and degrades. The Son can by a magic-muscular marvel suggestive of technological power be moved to the seeming necessity of either mistrusting or presuming upon God. For the Son then to stand long enough to do neither but rather utter the lovingly, unpresumptuously ambiguous command "Tempt not the Lord"—as referring to himself or the Father as it needs to be—is precisely enough to repulse the rebel who, in earthly as in heavenly war, by strength would measure all.

THE PARADIGM OF POWER AND OCCLUDED LOVE

We have considered the assertions and justifications of *Paradise Lost* as deepened and elaborated both prospectively and retrospectively by the fall (which is no Fall) of the Word into history, in *Paradise Regain'd*. There, "all temptation" (I, 5) appears as multiple trials of the Word by misrepresentative words, trials and lies coherent and consistent in their occlusion of love by power. Loving obedience empowers in the Savior the witty

6. Geoffrey Harpham, *The Ascetic Imperative* (Chicago, 1991), 48–55. We see the whole poem as metaphor and synecdoche of the believer meditatively—and incompletely—taking in the Passion. We agree that redemption is implicit, even explicit, but do not see the temptations as connecting with the Passion as figural humiliation. But see Charles Huttar, "The Passion of Christ in *Paradise Regain'd*," *English Language Notes*, XIX .(1982), 23–60. See also, especially for the critique of previous structural analyses, Jeffrey B. Morris, "Disorientation and Disruption in *Paradise Regain'd*," *Milton Studies*, XXVI (1990), 219–38.

intelligence and active patience—a paradox for those preoccupied with power—eventuating in the triumph obvious to all readers. The Bard's ability to constitute imaginatively the account of temptation transcended, expanded so paradigmatically from the biblical account, implies a general human capacity by grace to imitate the Savior in steps toward the redemption that is uniquely the Savior's to accomplish, and uniquely the believer and understander's to accept.

With *Samson Agonistes,* we would redress the apparent critical balance of our day by emphasizing the differences over the similarities between this poem and Milton's other works, notwithstanding the solitary blind protagonist. *Samson Agonistes* extends *Paradise Lost* by exploring the unloving world of power after the Fall and absent the Redeemer. That is obviously a world of body power—muscle, sex, fatigue, abused power, and abused bodies—and less obviously a world of such power represented as a secondary sign of political power. It is the world of Babel that Milton was not too blind to see increasingly dominant in the projects of his age.

The waiting bodies of the Son, Mary, and the disciples (a middle case, imperfectly patient), and the hungering but patiently enduring body of the Savior in *Paradise Regain'd,* contrast with the abused bodies of *Samson Agonistes,* most obviously of Samson and his past and present victims. In contrast to Shakespeare's Duke Vincentio, who preferred not to "stage" himself to his people's eyes—but did, in a monk's costume—Samson is recognizably the stage prop of objectifying gazers: he unwillingly figures in whatever moralistic or political tableau vivant his choral compatriots or a Philistian overlord may attend to for their interpretations—interpretations that have unloving power as their object. Manoa will stage himself as an obsequious suppliant, playing manipulatively to Philistian greed and grandiosity. Ultimately, his wish is to make Samson's monument a mise-en-scène for pageant or masque. Dalila, costumed ambiguously as a ship of sexuality and a ship of state besieged by public officers, plays out with an extemporizing Samson some preconceived scenarios designed to bring him and his significance and sexual power within her power.[7] Harapha, Milton's least biblical expansion of his story, wants to

---

7. John Guillory, in a brilliant but perverse article, is quite right to note that Dalila's quest for Samson's "capital secret" is for "knowledge that is also power." But he tends to reduce the play to a conflict between husband and wife, and to reduce that to the "contra-

stage—that is, fix—a supposititious show of his muscle power, and recoils in fearful impotence from Samson's blunt, sardonic proposal of a radically unfixed and indecorous encounter. The very Chorus self-consciously stages itself and presumes, however unconvincingly, to stage-direct: "so various, / or might I say contrarious" (*Samson Agonistes*, 668–69). There are also its other segues into rhyme, and its concluding speech, most blatant among others, of how we should interpret the action and indeed how we should feel about what has happened.[8] The powers of Philistia, unsatisfied to use up their vanquished foe, seek to confect a civic pageant, a masque of Dagon's power. And so they do, with the producers becoming participants, though in no conventional concluding dance. Milton makes the unpromising generic material something of a generic supersession of Christopher Marlowe's Jew and of the courtly masque of Ben Jonson and Inigo Jones.

These prominent features, which will likely strike any reader reflecting on *Samson Agonistes* after reading *Paradise Lost* and *Paradise Regain'd* and which in any case begin to situate the dramatic poem with respect to them, invite hermeneutic elaboration in two directions. One, enforced by Milton's preface, goes to the mode of being, generic and institutional, of his tragic poem. The other direction, partially coinciding with the first, reaches to the dynamics within the work of love (including grace), to knowing and naming, and to movement.

---

diction between work and home." See Guillory, "Dalila's House: *Samson Agonistes* and the Sexual Division of Labor," in *Rewriting the Renaissance: The Discourses of Sexual Difference in Early Modern Europe,* ed. Margaret W. Ferguson, Maureen Quilligan, and Nancy J. Vickers (Chicago, 1986), 106–22, pp. 110, 118, 121 quoted. But for the neglected "her at Timna," as for much else, see Philip J. Gallagher, *Milton, the Bible, and Misogyny,* ed. Eugene R. Cunnar and Gail L. Mortimer (Columbia, Mo., 1990), esp. Chap. 3. Especially on theatricalism, see Mary Ann Radzinowicz, "The Distinctive Tragedy of *Samson Agonistes,*" *Milton Studies,* XVII (1983), 249–80. On aspects of player, mocker, masker, and fool, see Paul R. Sellin, "Milton's Epithet *Agonistes,*" *Studies in English Literature,* IV (1964), 137–62; and Anna Nardo, "'Sung and Proverb'd for a Fool': Samson as Fool and Trickster," *Mosaic,* XXII (1989), 1–16. See also Steadman, *Milton and the Paradoxes of Renaissance Heroism,* Chap. 9.

8. Clearly the Chorus' misogyny is part of its pathetic self-aggrandizement. We are intrigued by a suggestion by our student Rosa Garza that the misogyny should also be understood as classical Greek, which is to say questionable for Milton. Greek or Hebraic, it is another instance of "thus they relate, / Erring" (*Paradise Lost,* I, 746–47).

Milton's "Of That Sort of Dramatic Poem Which Is Call'd Tragedy"—surely the weightiest preface to an English play before George Bernard Shaw—emphatically places the playwright in history. Inevitably, it is a powerfully selective history—his past so far as it is usable for his transaction with us—as he invokes Saint Paul, along with the Euripides, David Pareus, Martial, "Antients and *Italians*," and Aeschylus and Sophocles of his understanding. He invokes them with regard to both action and imitation or representation. Yet we read, surprisingly enough, that his poem "never was intended" for the stage—only to be reassured, "It suffices if the whole Drama be found not produc't beyond the fift Act."

Whenever the play was first drafted and however it was revised for publication, *Samson Agonistes* is Milton's definitive descent from mountaintop vision and inconstantly (or constantly) loving obedience to God, into the Babel of tongues in the mill, street, and arena—a welter for him certainly unredeemed and at best uncertainly regenerate. By an act of creative power affectionately if somberly exerted on the biblical narrative, he constructed a drama of power which he might hope to stand against the "evil communications" that "corrupt good manners."

Philistia, and Samson's career there, constitutes a compelling metaphor of what Milton increasingly after the late 1630s understood as the burgeoning and doomed Baroque world of power.[9] The "fable" rings changes on the fact and the theme of power, and drama is the genre for representing interpersonal power dynamics with the least mediation—and in that

9. This metatheme of the shift from a world of salvific journey and greed or ungraced dynamism to a world of secularized power—and anticipations of that shift—can constitute a companion study to this one, as we hope to show soon. Neither within Milton nor at large is it satisfactory to adduce a movement from metaphor to metonymy or to irony, from allegory to typology, or the like, for many reasons ontological and epistemological: for example, the credibility of the Chain of Being, and such rhetorical construals as make "*allegories* . . . a long and perpetuall Metaphore" and "all these [modalities of irony] souldiers to the figure allegoria . . . under the banner of dissimulation" (George Puttenham [or should it be "George Puttenham"?], *The Art of English Poesie* [1589], Bk. III, Chap. 18). For various thematic and conceptual perspectives suggestive in their disagreements with this and with one another, see Gregory F. Goekjian, "Suicide and Revenge: *Samson Agonistes* and the Law of the Father," *Milton Studies*, XXVI (1990), 253–70; Daniel T. Lochman, "'Seeking Just Occasion': Law, Reason, and Justice at Samson's Peripety," *Milton Studies*, XXVI (1990), 271–88; and Burton J. Weber, "The Worldly End of Samson," *Milton Studies*, XXVI (1990), 289–309.

sense most powerfully. Yet producing a drama not only introduces the mediation of players—Hamlet's concern—but, as Milton well knew, implicates the producer in the power structures of commerce, even those of Restoration London. Hence, the intentionality of this offering to his society—textually attached to *Paradise Regain'd* and at least in that sense subsequent to *Paradise Lost*—is toward uncoercive productions in the private mind, productions that might be mounted as so many acts of devotion or at least of civic affection or concern.

What sort of action unfolds in these theater productions of the mind? It is not sufficient to think of *Samson Agonistes* as merely the fifth act if that implies the absence of any drama but the resolution of drama. Of course, there was antecedent action back to the Fall; of course, there will be subsequent action, all of it inconclusive if not indeed inconsequential, until the incarnational and apocalyptic steps of redemption, since that is what history meant to Milton. Of course, too, there is the agonistic struggle of Samson with the five visitants—counting the Chorus and "Publick Officer"—and with himself. But it is critical to construe the dialogues as naming contests lest the action be obscured or seen as disjunctive, and to recognize the internal relationships of power and love.

After the caretaking "guiding hand" (line 1) that helps Samson to "choice of Sun or shade" (line 3), nearly every move is for an advantage in power, and virtually every verbal exchange contests the power of naming and thereby of configuring how the signified is articulated in the range of available human orientations. Samson insists, against Manoa or the Chorus, that his situation manifests not divine abandonment but divine justice. He insists on "Traytress" (line 725) as the name Dalila has exchanged for *Wife,* insists that "lust" (line 837) rather than "Love constrain'd" her (line 836), insists that her touch will mean her end rather than his seduction (lines 952–54), insists that the right name for what she has wrought is not "Love-quarrels" but "wedlock-trechery" (line 1009).

Dalila makes a show—or a feint?—of arguing "womans frailty" (line 783), saying that she was "commanded, threat'n'd, urg'd, / Adjur'd" (lines 852–53) by "powerful arguments" (line 862). But she has by then already confessed that she designed to hold Samson "firmest" (line 796) and get into her "power / Thy key of strength and safety" (lines 798–99) as "Mine and Loves prisoner" (line 808). And she finally acknowledges that she desires to be "nam'd among the famousest / Of Women, sung at solemn festivals" (lines 982–83)—not unlike Harapha, who wants the "highest name" (line 1101).[10]

Naïve and presumptuous faith in the power of human naming is proleptically disqualified in Harapha's case by Samson's invitation not to see or hear "but taste" (line 1091) in prelinguistic, subdecorous violence that abolishes the distinction between inside and outside.[11] That was more explicitly and egregiously brought out earlier in the Chorus' notorious lines that "Just are the ways of God, / And justifiable to Men" (lines 293–94), for what could this affirmation be but an act of intellectual fiat, if not hubris, in the absence of Urania of *Paradise Lost* and the Savior of *Paradise Regain'd?* The Chorus' suspiciously jingling remark immediately thereupon, that there is no "School / But the heart of the Fool" (line 298), confirms the point: however many opponents Milton may explicitly or implicitly have damned with the name of fool in his polemical prose, the late poetry's preoccupation with love includes a correlative awareness of the New Testament's injunction that to affix that name to someone is damnable—the beguiling juxtaposition of "Embryo's and Idiots, Eremits and Friers" (*Paradise Lost,* III, 474) notwithstanding.

Samson's agony with himself yields, again and again, confessions of failures or of misdirections not of love but of power: "a foolish Pilot have shipwrack't / My Vessel" (*Samson Agonistes,* 198–99), "Gave up my fort of silence" (line 236), "The secret wrested" (line 384), "Tongue-batteries" (line 404), "Weakly at least" (line 499). He anticipates rest: "My race of glory run, and race of shame" (line 597). Here Milton makes him anticipate and evaluate a wealth of anthropological and psychoanalytic material about the contrast between guilt and shame, and about the relationship of shame to relative impotence or to loss of control to someone else.[12]

10. Obviously we agree with Radzinowicz, Woods, and others who see Milton attributing moral responsibility to Dalila and acknowledging cultural pressures on her, rather than attributing fault to gender (thereby absolving her). See Radzinowicz, *Toward "Samson Agonistes": The Growth of Milton's Mind* (Princeton, 1978), 40; and Woods, "How Free Are Milton's Women?" in *Milton and the Idea of Woman,* ed. Walker, 15–31.

11. See Kilgour, *From Communion to Cannibalism,* esp. Chap. 3. Our disagreements are merely local.

12. Here as elsewhere the insights of well-conducted psychoanalytic criticism, illuminating as they can be, are only marginally relevant to our purpose, and insofar as they tend to the power move of preemptive closure, they are at odds with the Miltonic argument we attempt to construe. But see Kerrigan, *The Sacred Complex,* 125–29; Herman Rapaport, *Milton and the Postmodern* (Lincoln, Nebr., 1983), 131–64; and Jim Swan,

When in a broken parallel to the unfallen naming of *Paradise Lost* or the Savior's confessions of divine preeminence in *Paradise Regain'd,* Samson is ready to confess God, his confessions are sharply limited. He confesses a God of power far more than a God of creativity and love, and prays accordingly, "No long petition, speedy death" (line 650). The "God of *Abraham*" (line 465) who "will arise and his great name assert" (line 467) is a God of power, and so, predominantly, is the God confessed in Samson's verbal combat with Harapha to be the just sender of his afflictions yet "Whose ear is ever open; and his eye / Gracious to re-admit the suppliant" (lines 1172−73).

The nearest approach to an attitude of loving trust in a mysteriously creative God, of patient openness, comes in his ominous acknowledgment after Harapha's rebuff:

> But come what will . . .
> Yet so it may fall out, because thir end
> Is hate, not help to me, it may with mine
> Draw thir own ruin
>
> (Lines 1262−67)

He confesses a God who may mysteriously and unexpectably enable decisive violence. That is a tragically limited confession. Its secular counterpart, and Samson's dark vision into the mysterious human nexus and conjuncture or disjunction of love and power, appears as a confession of earthly hearts weakly disposed: "to love Bondage more then Liberty / Bondage with ease then strenuous liberty" (lines 270−71), "feeble hearts, propense anough before / To waver, or fall off and joyn with Idols" (lines 455−56).

Nothing here helps answer the question, Liberty for what? Or rather, there is the minimum requisite for tragic seriousness: the godhead potentially present to suppliants, and a human world graced by, in some sense, love. But when Samson reproaches Dalila, as if decisively, "Love seeks to

---

"Difference and Silence: John Milton and the Question of Gender," in *The (M)other Tongue: Essays in Feminist Psychoanalytic Interpretation,* ed. Shirley N. Garner, Claire Kahane, and Madelon Sprengnether (Ithaca, N.Y., 1985), 151−69. For a convincing application of Proverbs 7, a suggestive problematizing of the status of proverbiality, and the argument that Milton adduces divine wisdom as the only counter to foolishness and harlotry "of both male and female," see Laura Lunger Knoppers, "'Sung and Proverb'd for a Fool': *Samson Agonistes* and Solomon's Harlot," *Milton Studies,* XXVI (1990), 239−51.

have Love" (line 837), the reflective reader of *Paradise Lost* and *Paradise Regain'd* must recognize a tragic misnaming. Loving is there defined in the Augustinian fashion as not a bargain, not an investment, not a deal, but rather a gift. One loves the other either for God's sake or for one's own, and in the latter case, love is more or less a misnomer. Narcissism and rancor in action are powermongering and power abuse. Power worship, institutionalized to serve corporately and reflexively now the more narcissistic, now the more rancorous, may in a celebrated formulation of Walter Benjamin compare with fascism aestheticizing political violence or communism politicizing art. [13]

So what becomes of love in Gaza? Any stagers of *Samson Agonistes* in the theater of the mind may well reflect on what place can be the norm for love in Milton's urbanized landscape of subjugators and subjugated. Should we settle on a metaphor, saying that love is there red-shifted or modulated into power? The Shakespearean imagery of disease comes to mind, and the Chorus and Samson speak of stings (lines 20, 623). Samson in a moment of aborted teleology—of a collapsed hermeneutic loop, like a fallen angel's—even names gangrene (line 621). But such a voice is not that of Urania, and there is also the Miltonic and Bardic imagery of music and of hierarchy, which is ironic on occasions of bad eminence. In an enveloping context of the salvific journey toward God, red shifts and centrifugal flights are not grossly inapposite metaphors, despite the anachronism. Yet none of these is as dominant or explicit in *Samson Agonistes* as the framing fact of representation: the fact that love is dramatized—in the sense of being brought into contention—and tragedized. Manoa, Dalila, and Samson are figures in the contention.

But what of divine love in its mode as grace? How certainly is Samson God's champion? Granted that Milton's God is partly hidden, "Dark with excessive bright" (*Paradise Lost,* III, 380), and that the authentic image of his power and "wisdom, and effectual might" (III, 170), his Son, is not available to Samson or his compatriots, how confidently are we invited by the play to *suppose* that its protagonist is God's champion, an agent or at least recipient of grace? Not confidently, perhaps not at all. [14]

---

13. Walter Benjamin, *Illuminations* (New York, 1975), 242.

14. The dominant line of discourse of the past critical generation has concluded that Samson is finally regenerate. See Albert C. Labriola, "Divine Urgency as a Motive for

Samson married her "at Timna" (*Samson Agonistes*, 219), led allegedly by God. But even if he was "motion'd . . . of God" (line 222), he troped into a lawyerlike argument from precedent in taking Dalila. As to the "rouzing motions" (line 1382) that move him to accompany the Publick Officer to where the Philistines would "make a game," a motion, of Samson's "calamities" (line 1331), can we be sure that those impulses and (imagined?) scenarios are from God? Or are the rousing motions more closely related to earlier triumphs of power about which we have been

Conduct in *Samson Agonistes*," *Philological Quarterly*, L (1971), 99–107; Lynn Veach Sadler, "Regeneration and Typology: *Samson Agonistes* and Its Relation to *De Doctrina Christiana*, *Paradise Lost*, and *Paradise Regained*," *Studies in English Literature*, XII (1972), 141–56; Anthony Low, *The Blaze of Noon: A Reading of "Samson Agonistes"* (New York, 1974); Christopher Grose, "'His Uncontrollable Intent': Discovery as Action in *Samson Agonistes*," *Milton Studies*, VII (1975), 49–76; Joan S. Bennett, "Liberty Under the Law: The Chorus and the Meaning of *Samson Agonistes*," *Milton Studies*, XII (1978), 141–63; John Mulryan, "The Heroic Tradition of Milton's *Samson Agonistes*," *Milton Studies*, XVIII (1983), 214–34; Kathleen M. Swaim, "The Doubling of the Chorus in *Samson Agonistes*," *Milton Studies*, XX (1984), 225–45; Nicholas José, "*Samson Agonistes*: The Play Turned Upside Down," in *Ideas of the Restoration in English Literature, 1660–1671* (Cambridge, Mass., 1984), Chap. 8; Darryl Tippens, "The Kenotic Experience of *Samson Agonistes*," *Milton Studies*, XXII (1986), 173–94; William Kerrigan, "The Irrational Coherence of *Samson Agonistes*," *Milton Studies*, XXII (1986), 217–32; Daniel T. Lochman, "'If There Be Aught of Presage': Milton's Samson as Riddler and Prophet," *Milton Studies*, XXII (1986), 195–216; and Leonard Mustazza, "The Verbal Plot of *Samson Agonistes*," *Milton Studies*, XXIII (1987), 241–58. But there is an adversarial position not to be erased, an undernoticed view of a less than regenerate Samson. See John T. Shawcross, "Irony as Tragic Effect: *Samson Agonistes*, and the Tragedy of Hope," in *Calm of Mind: Tercentenary Essays on "Paradise Regain'd" and "Samson Agonistes" in Honor of John S. Diekhoff*, ed. Joseph A. Wittreich (Cleveland, 1971), 298–306; Helen Damico, "Duality in Dramatic Vision: A Structural Analysis of *Samson Agonistes*," *Milton Studies*, XII (1978), 91–116; Wendy Furman, "*Samson Agonistes* as Christian Tragedy: A Corrective View," *Philological Quarterly*, LX (1981), 169–81; and John T. Shawcross, "Milton and Covenant: The Christian View of Old Testament Theology," in *Milton and Scriptural Tradition: The Bible into Poetry*, ed. James H. Sims and Leland Ryken (Columbia, Mo., 1984), 160–91. Finally, there has been emerging something like a hermeneutic Samson reconsidered, though not, it seems to us, in our sense. See Northrop Frye, "Agon and Logos: Revolution and Revelation," in *The Prison and the Pinnacle*, ed. Balachandra Rajan, 135–63; Radzinowicz, "The Distinctive Tragedy of *Samson Agonistes*"; Radzinowicz, *Toward "Samson Agonistes*," 149–77; John C. Ulreich, "'Beyond the Fifth Act': *Samson Agonistes* as Prophecy," *Milton Studies*, XVII (1983), 281–318; Ernest B. Gilman, *Iconoclasm and Poetry in the English Reformation*, Chap. 6; and Wittreich, *Interpreting "Samson Agonistes.*"

reminded, all of them memorable to Manoa, the Philistines, and the Chorus, but all ephemeral except insofar as remembrance moves to reciprocal violence or to the motions of masque? What God does the play suggest which Samson could know how to imitate if he were truly divinely moved? It is the God of the exodus, of war and deliverance from captivity. The God who is to send the Savior in "unexampl'd love" (*Paradise Lost*, III, 410), to live exemplarily and die forgiving his assailants, is unknown to Samson from salvific history and is also evidently unknown to him by grace.

"*Samson* hath quit himself / Like *Samson*, and heroicly hath finish'd / A life Heroic," Manoa declares (*Samson Agonistes*, 1709–11), and he goes on to decry Samson's "nuptial choice, / From whence captivity and loss of eyes" (lines 1743–44). But we have seen Manoa's confused immersion in materiality and, as here, material causes. His sense of the world squares well enough with the Philistian conception of powers avenged or greedy. But he has quite missupposed that the God who allows Samson's strength to grow back with his hair will regrow Samson's eyes, at least in this world. And he uses what by 1671 had come to be one of the most loaded words in the Miltonic corpus: *heroic*. Samson, historic, is not of the "fabl'd Knights" (*Paradise Lost*, IX, 30), nor is his havoc "tedious" (IX, 30), as the messenger's stunning report witnesses. But the apparently apocalyptic violence is, we know, inconclusive vicissitude in a larger schema.

And the conflict between reality at the more particular level and reality at the more general level is part of the essence of tragedy for Milton, with the tragic mode of being always available as a kind of choice. Samson has quit and acquitted himself like Samson indeed, no less and no more. The tragically chosen world is perfused with the presence of a darkly mysterious divinity—"O dark, dark, dark" (*Samson Agonistes*, 80)—and one dies violently of being what one is, dies less violently only by forgoing what one is. Samson "Bore witness gloriously" (line 1752) both to his divinely sanctioned strength and to the inability of strength to measure all or of war to do much. Perhaps we live mostly in New Gaza, but Milton implies that we need not be eyeless.

CONCLUSION

"Knowledge is as food" (*Paradise Lost*, VII, 126), Raphael has explained to Adam and Eve. Analogies are not congruities, even in unfallen paradise. But one implication borne out from that point forward in the poetry, and in Milton's earlier poetry, is that human life requires regular reinforcement by knowledge even more than by material food, the intake of which may be abated for forty days during certain steps into knowledge. The surfeit of knowledge that Raphael gives warnings about in Book VIII of *Paradise Lost* we construe as a delusionary sense of exhaustive plenitude, of a system's having all the answers. That sense might well prove nauseating to Milton and others even if not immediately to the ingesters of the surfeit that "oppresses" and that may ultimately enslave them.

Late in Adam and Eve's instruction and their accommodation to the fallen world, it is recognized that God is open to vouchsafing the knowledge needful to their new life. For Milton, anti-Manichaean and no proto-Luddite, it could not be otherwise. Neither technological knowledge nor any other would ever heave its head but by the help or sufferance of God. Any evaluation put on knowledge and any use made of it constitute a step onward or aside or retrograde in the salvific journey.

The opposite of the knowledge that surfeits is for Milton, accordingly, not ignorance. Education rightly understood can "repair the ruins of our first parents," as he held in "Of Education." Rather, the opposite of the knowledge that surfeits is divine love and creativity, which education can assert and justify in human terms but never define or circumscribe. Nor can human steps be compelled along the path toward what by definition exceeds definition, however emphatically education may indicate the steps or the path. This is a corollary of divine love that provokes a spectrum of responses, from outrage to exhilaration, whether the idea is accepted or merely entertained. Control in the sense one intends by saying, "He's an overcontrolling person," always implies closure. A playscript is in an obvious way a closed system, although the play of suggestiveness it excites may circle indefinitely in steps of hermeneutic reflection. The absence of closure in a system is likely to be unsettling to an orientation toward or a preoccupation with power. On the other hand, openness in a system, especially toward surprising developments and the play of loving creativity both delights, and paradoxically, meets the expectations of, the lover. Anyone can be a lover receptive to the uncontrolled; Milton's pervasive faith and hope on this point contrasts with Augustine's occasional gloom and tempers his own practical supposition that in the world of impending history most will opt for power and the illusion of power rather than love. The worldly knowledge and phantasms of power that may oppress with surfeit need not do so—though they might someone who failed to see that deterministic inclusiveness or closure is not inevitable on psychological or economic or socioanthropological or bioethological or any other grounds. For Milton, neither height nor depth nor any other creature "shall," in the language of the Book of Common Prayer's burial service, "keep us from the love of God."

So assertion and justification must be understood to continue in receptive consciousnesses. Arrangement entails rearrangement, reading rereading, scholarly dialogue rejoinder. Hans Georg Gadamer has eloquently argued that "a nonobjectifying consciousness always accompanies the *process* of understanding, understanding is not suitably conceived at all as consciousness of something."[15] Both, Milton seems to demur; both, we agree.

15. Gadamer, *Essays in Philosophical Hermeneutics,* 123. Our emphasis.

BIBLIOGRAPHY

Adams, Robert Martin. *Ikon: John Milton and the Modern Critics*. Ithaca, N.Y., 1955.

————. "A Little Look at Chaos." In *Illustrious Evidence: Approaches to English Literature of the Early Seventeenth Century*, edited by Earl Miner, 71–89. Berkeley and Los Angeles, 1975.

Adelman, Janet. "Creation and the Place of the Poet in *Paradise Lost*." In *The Author in His Work*, edited by Louis L. Martz and Aubrey Williams, 51–69. New Haven, 1978.

Aeschylus. *Agamemnon*. Translated by Robert Fagles. London, 1977.

Allen, Don Cameron. "Milton's *Comus* as a Failure in Artistic Compromise." *English Literary History*, XVI (1949), 104–19.

Allen, M. J. B. *The Platonism of Marsilio Ficino: A Study of His Phaedrus Commentary, Its Sources and Genesis*. Berkeley and Los Angeles, 1984.

Amorose, Thomas. "Milton the Apocalyptic Historian: Competing Genres in *Paradise Lost*, Books XI–XII." *Milton Studies*, XVII (1983), 141–62.

Anderson, Douglas. "Unfallen Marriage and the Fallen Imagination in *Paradise Lost*." *Studies in English Literature, 1500–1900*, XXVI (1986), 125–44.

Anselm of Canterbury. *De casu diaboli*. Translated and edited by Jasper Hopkins and Herbert Richardson. In *Truth, Freedom, and Evil: Three Philosophical Dialogues by Anselm of Canterbury*. New York, 1967.

————. *Proslogion*. Edited by F. Schmitt. Stuttgart, 1961.

Anselm of Canterbury: Why God Became Man and the Virgin Conception and Original Sin. Translated and edited by Joseph M. Colleran. Albany, N.Y., 1969.

Arden, Heather M. *The Romance of the Rose*. Boston, 1987.

Arthos, John. *On "A Mask Presented at Ludlow-Castle."* Ann Arbor, Mich., 1954.

Asclepius. In *Hermetica*, edited by Walter Scott. Vol. I of 4 vols. London, 1924–36.

Augustine. *The City of God*. Translated by Marcus Dods; edited by Thomas Merton. New York, 1950.

————. *The Confessions of Saint Augustine*. Translated by Rex Warner. New York, 1963.

————. *De doctrina christiana*. In *Patrologiae Cursus Completus . . . Series Latina*, edited by J. P. Migne. Vol. XXXIV of 221 vols. Paris, 1844–1903.

————. *De Genesi ad litteram, imperfectus liber.* In *Patrologiae . . . Latina,* edited by Migne. Vol. XXXIV.

————. *De qualitate animae.* In *Patrologiae . . . Latina,* edited by Migne. Vol. XXXIV.

————. *De trinitate.* In *Patrologiae . . . Latina,* edited by Migne. Vol. XLII.

————. *Enarrationes in Psalmos,* XXXVIII, 7, CXXI, 8. In *Patrologiae . . . Latina,* edited by Migne. Vol. XXXVII.

————. *Enchiridion . . . de fide, spe et caritate,* C, 26. In *Patrologiae . . . Latina,* edited by Migne. Vol. XXXV.

————. *In Joannis evangelium.* In *Patrologiae . . . Latina,* edited by Migne. Vol. XXXV.

————. "On the Grace of Christ." Translated by Peter Holmes. In *St. Augustin: Anti-Pelagian Writings,* edited by Philip Schaff, 217–36. Select Library of Nicene and Post-Nicene Writings, V. New York, 1887.

————. *Sermones ad populum.* In *Patrologiae . . . Latina,* edited by Migne. Vol. XXXVIII.

Badel, Pierre Yves. *Le Roman de la rose au XIVe siècle: Etude de la reception de l'oeuvre.* Geneva, 1980.

Barber, C. L. "*A Mask Presented at Ludlow Castle:* The Mask as a Masque." In *The Lyric and Dramatic Milton,* edited by J. H. Summers, 35–63. New York, 1965.

————. *Shakespeare's Festive Comedy.* Princeton, 1959.

Barkan, Leonard. *The Gods Made Flesh: Metamorphosis and the Pursuit of Paganism.* New Haven, 1986.

Barker, Arthur. "The Pattern of Milton's 'Nativity Ode.'" *University of Toronto Quarterly,* X (1940–41), 167–81.

Batany, Jean. *Approches du "Roman de la rose."* Paris, 1973.

Benedict, Saint. "Regula." In *Patrologiae Cursus Completus . . . Series Latina,* edited by J. P. Migne. Vol. LXVI of 221 vols. Paris, 1844–1903.

————. *The Rule of Saint Benedict.* Translated by Anthony Meisel and M. L. del Mastro. Garden City, N.Y., 1975.

Benjamin, Walter. *Illuminations.* New York, 1975.

Bennett, Joan S. "'Go'": Milton's Antinomianism and the Separation Scene in *Paradise Lost,* Book 9." *PMLA,* XCVIII (1983), 388–404.

————. "Liberty Under the Law: The Chorus and the Meaning of *Samson Agonistes.*" *Milton Studies,* XII (1978), 141–63.

————. *Reviving Liberty: Radical Christian Humanism in Milton's Great Poems.* Cambridge, Mass., 1989.

Berry, Boyd M. *Process of Speech: Puritan Religious Writing and "Paradise Lost."* Baltimore, 1976.

Blessington, Francis. "'That Undisturbed Song of Pure Concent': *Paradise Lost* and the Epic-Hymn." In *Renaissance Genres: Essays on Theory, History, and Interpretations,* edited by Barbara K. Lewalski, 468–95. Cambridge, Mass., 1986.

Bloom, Harold. *A Map of Misreading.* New York, 1975.

———. *Ruin the Sacred Truths: Poetry and Belief from the Bible to the Present.* Cambridge, Mass., 1989.

Boddy, Margaret. "Milton's Translation of Psalms 80–88." *Modern Philology,* LXIV (1966), 1–9.

Booty, John E., ed. *The Book of Common Prayer, 1559: The Elizabethan Prayer Book.* Charlottesville, Va., 1976.

Bouchard, Donald. *Milton: A Structural Reading.* London, 1974.

Bowers, R. H. "The Accent on Youth in 'Comus.'" In *SAMLA Studies in Milton,* edited by J. Max Patrick. Gainesville, Fla., 1953.

Breasted, Barbara. "Comus and the Castlehaven Scandal." *Milton Studies,* III (1971), 201–24.

Bretzius, Stephen. *Shakespeare in Theory.* Forthcoming.

Brisman, Leslie. "'All Before Them Where to Choose': 'L'Allegro' and 'Il Penseroso.'" *Journal of English and Germanic Philology,* LXXI (1972), 226–40.

Broadbent, J. B. *Some Graver Subject: An Essay on "Paradise Lost."* London, 1960.

Brockbank, Philip. "'Within the Visible Diurnal Sphere': The Moving World of *Paradise Lost.*" In *Approaches to "Paradise Lost,"* edited by C. A. Patrides, 199–221. Toronto, 1968.

Brodwin, Leonora Leet. "The Dissolution of Satan in *Paradise Lost:* A Study of Milton's Heretical Eschatology." *Milton Studies,* VIII (1975), 165–207.

———. "Milton and the Renaissance Circe." *Milton Studies,* VI (1974), 21–83.

Brooks, Cleanth. "Milton and Critical Re-Estimates." *PMLA,* LXVI (1951), 1045–54.

Brooks, Cleanth, and John E. Hardy. "Essays in Analysis." Bound with *Poems of Mr. John Milton: The 1645 Edition.* New York, 1951.

Brown, Cedric C. *John Milton's Aristocratic Entertainments.* New York, 1985.

Browning, Judith E. "Sin, Eve, and Circe: *Paradise Lost* and the Ovidian Circe Tradition." *Milton Studies,* XXVI (1990), 135–58.

Bryan, Robert A. "Adam's Tragic Vision in *Paradise Lost.*" *Studies in Philology,* LXII (1965), 197–214.

Budick, Sanford. *The Dividing Muse: Images of Sacred Disjunction in Milton's Poetry.* New Haven, 1985.

———. "Milton and the Scene of Interpretation: From Typology Toward Midrash." In *Midrash and Literature,* edited by Geoffrey Hartman and Sanford Budick, 195–212. New Haven, 1986.

Burden, Denis. *The Logical Epic: A Study of the Argument of "Paradise Lost."* Cambridge, Mass., 1967.

Bush, Douglas. *Mythology and the Renaissance Tradition in English Poetry.* 2nd ed. New York, 1963.

Calhoun, Thomas O. "On John Milton's *A Mask at Ludlow.*" *Milton Studies,* VI (1974), 165–79.

Campbell, Joseph. *The Hero with a Thousand Faces.* Princeton, 1949.

Canfield, J. Douglas. *Word as Bond.* Philadelphia, 1989.

Carrithers, Gale H., Jr. *Donne at Sermons: A Christian Existential World.* Albany, N.Y., 1972.

Cervantes Saavedra, Miguel de. *Don Quixote.* Translated by J. M. Cohen. London, 1950.

Chew, Samuel C. *The Pilgrimage of Life.* New Haven, 1962.

Cicero, Marcus Tullius. *De re publica.* Edited by K. Ziegler. Tübingen, 1969.

Cinquemani, A. M. "Henry Reynolds' 'Mythomystes' and the Continuity of Ancient Modes of Allegoresis in Seventeenth-Century England." *PMLA,* LXXV (1970), 1041–49.

Cirillo, Albert R. "Noon-Midnight and the Temporal Structure of *Paradise Lost.*" *English Literary History,* XXIX (1962), 372–95. Reprinted in *Critical Essays on Milton from "ELH"* (Baltimore, 1971).

Clanchy, M. T. *From Memory to Written Record, England, 1066–1307.* Cambridge, Mass., 1979.

Clark, James Andrew. "Milton Naturans, Milton Naturatus: The Debate over Nature in *A Mask. . . .*" *Milton Studies,* XX (1984), 3–27.

Clark, Mili. "The Mechanics of Creation: Non-Contradiction and Natural Necessity in *Paradise Lost.*" *English Literary Renaissance,* VII (1977), 207–42.

Cohn, Norman. *The Pursuit of the Millennium.* New York, 1961.

Colie, Rosalie. "Time and Eternity: Paradox and Structure in *Paradise Lost.*" In *Paradoxia Epidemica: The Renaissance Tradition of Paradox.* Princeton, 1966.

Colish, Marcia L. *The Mirror of Language: A Study in the Medieval Theory of Knowledge.* New Haven, 1968.

Collette, Carolyn P. "Milton's Psalm Translations: Petition and Praise." *English Literary Renaissance,* II (1972), 243–59.

Connerton, Paul. "Gadamer's Hermeneutics." *Comparative Criticism,* V (1983), 107–28.

Cook, Albert. *The Dark Voyage and the Golden Mean.* Cambridge, Mass., 1952.

Cook, Eleanor. "Melos Versus Logos; or, Why Doesn't God Sing? Some Thoughts on Milton's Wisdom." In *Re-Membering Milton: Essays on the Texts and Traditions,* edited by Mary Nyquist and Margaret Ferguson, 197–210. New York, 1987.

Cope, Jackson. *The Metaphoric Structure of "Paradise Lost."* Baltimore, 1962.

———. *The Theater and the Dream: From Metaphor to Form in Renaissance Drama.* Baltimore, 1973.

Cox, John D. "Poetry and History in Milton's Country Masque." *English Literary History,* XLIV (1977), 622–40.

Creaser, John. "'The Present Aid of This Occasion': The Setting of *Comus.*" In *The Court Masque,* edited by David Lindley, 111–34. Manchester, Eng., 1984.

Cressy, David. *Literacy and the Social Order: Reading and Writing in Tudor and Stuart England.* New York, 1980.

Crewe, Jonathan. *Trials of Authorship: Anterior Forms and Poetic Reconstruction from Wyatt to Shakespeare.* Berkeley and Los Angeles, 1980.

Cunningham, Merrilee. "The Epic Narrator in Milton's *Paradise Regain'd.*" *Renaissance and Reformation,* XIII (1989), 215–32.

Curran, Stuart. "*Paradise Regain'd:* Implications of Epic." *Milton Studies,* XVII (1983), 209–24.

Curry, Walter Clyde. *Milton's Ontology, Cosmogony, and Physics.* Lexington, Ky., 1957.

Damico, Helen. "Duality in Dramatic Vision: A Structural Analysis of *Samson Agonistes.*" *Milton Studies,* XII (1978), 91–116.

Danielson, Dennis. "Milton's Arminianism and *Paradise Lost.*" *Milton Studies,* XII (1979), 47–75.

———. *Milton's Good God: A Study in Literary Theodicy.* New York, 1982.

———. "Through the Telescope of Typology: What Adam Should Have Done." *Milton Quarterly,* XXIII (1989), 121–27.

Davies, Stevie. *The Feminine Reclaimed: The Idea of Woman in Spenser, Shakespeare, and Milton.* Lexington, Ky., 1986.

———. *Milton.* New York, 1991.

Davies, Walter R. "The Languages of Accommodation and the Styles of *Paradise Lost.*" *Milton Studies,* XVIII (1983), 103–27.

Davos, Joseph R. *A Concordance to the Roman de la Rose of Guillaume de Lorris.* Chapel Hill, N.C., 1975.

Demaray, John G. *Milton and the Masque Tradition: The Early Poems, "Arcades," and "Comus."* Cambridge, Mass., 1968.

———. *Milton's Theatrical Epic: The Invention and Design of "Paradise Lost."* Cambridge, Mass., 1980.

Derrida, Jacques. *Dissemination.* Translated by Barbara Johnson. Chicago, 1981.

———. "Living On: Border Lines." In *Deconstruction and Criticism,* edited by Harold Bloom *et al.,* 75–176. New York, 1979.

———. *Margins of Philosophy.* Translated by Alan Bass. Chicago, 1982.

———. *Of Grammatology.* Translated by Gayatri Spivak. Baltimore, 1976.

———. *Writing and Difference.* Translated by Alan Bass. Chicago, 1978.

Dix, Gregory. *The Shape of the Liturgy.* London, 1945.

Doherty, M. J. "Salvation History, Poetic Form, and the Logic of Time in Milton's Nativity Ode." *Milton Studies,* XXV (1989), 21–42.

Donne, John. *The Sermons.* Edited by George Potter and Evelyn Simpson. 10 vols. Berkeley and London, 1951–59.

DuRocher, Richard J. *Milton and Ovid.* Ithaca, N.Y., 1985.

Eisenstein, Elizabeth. *The Printing Press as an Agent of Change: Communications and the Cultural Transformations in Early Modern Europe.* 2 vols. New York, 1979.

——. *The Printing Revolution in Early Modern Europe.* New York, 1983.

Empson, William. *The Structure of Complex Words.* London, 1951.

Entzminger, Robert L. *Divine Word: Milton and the Redemption of Language.* Pittsburgh, 1985.

——. "Epistemology and the Tutelary Word in *Paradise Lost.*" *Milton Studies,* X (1977), 93–109.

——. "Michael's Options and Milton's Poetry: *Paradise Lost* XI and XII." *English Literary Renaissance,* VIII (1978), 197–211.

Erickson, Peter. *Rewriting Shakespeare, Rewriting Ourselves.* Berkeley and Los Angeles, 1991.

Euripides. *The Bacchae.* Translated by William Arrowsmith. In *The Complete Greek Tragedies.* Volume IV of 4 vols. Chicago, 1955–59.

Everett, Barbara. "The End of Big Names: Milton's Epic Catalogues." In *English Renaissance Studies Presented to Dame Helen Gardner in Honour of Her Seventieth Birthday,* edited by John Carey, 254–70. New York, 1980.

Falck, Colin. *Myth, Truth, and Literature: Towards a True Post-Modernism.* New York, 1989.

Fallon, Stephen M. *Milton Among the Philosophers: Poetry and Materialism in Seventeenth-Century England.* Baltimore, 1991.

——. "Milton's Sin and Death: The Ontology of Allegory in *Paradise Lost.*" *English Literary Renaissance,* XVII (1987), 329–50.

Faustus of Rhegium. *Epistola ad Lucidum.* In *Patrologiae Cursus Completus . . . Series Latina,* edited by J. P. Migne. Vol. LIII of 221 vols. Paris, 1844–1903.

Ferry, Anne. *Milton's Epic Voice: The Narrator in "Paradise Lost."* Cambridge, Mass., 1963; rpr. Chicago, 1983.

Ficino, Marsilio. *Commentary on Plato's Symposium.* Translated by Sears Jayne. 2nd ed. Dallas, 1985.

——. *Theologica platonica de immortalite animorum: XVIII libaris comprehensa.* New York, 1975.

Finch, Casey, and Peter Bowen. "The Solitary Companionship of *L'Allegro* and *Il Penseroso.*" *Milton Studies,* XXVI (1990), 3–24.

Fineman, Joel. *Shakespeare's Perjured Eye: The Invention of Poetic Subjectivity in the Sonnets.* Berkeley and Los Angeles, 1985.

————. *The Subjectivity Effect in Western Literary Tradition: Essays Toward the Release of Shakespeare's Will.* Cambridge, Mass., 1991.

Fiore, Peter. *Milton and Augustine: Patterns of Augustinian Thought in "Paradise Lost."* University Park, Pa., 1981.

Fisch, Harold. *Jerusalem and Albion.* New York, 1968.

Fish, Stanley. "Authors-Readers: Jonson's Community of the Same." In *Representing the English Renaissance,* edited by Stephen Greenblatt, 231–63. Berkeley and Los Angeles, 1988. Reprinted from *Representations,* No. 7 (1984).

Fixler, Michael. "All-Interpreting Love: God's Name in Scripture and in *Paradise Lost.*" In *Milton and Scriptural Tradition: The Bible into Poetry,* edited by James H. Sims and Leland Ryken, 117–41. Columbia, Mo., 1984.

Fleming, John V. *Reason and the Lover.* Princeton, 1984.

————. *The Roman de la Rose: A Study in Allegory and Iconography.* Princeton, 1969.

Fletcher, Angus. *The Transcendental Masque: An Essay on Milton's "Comus."* Ithaca, N.Y., 1971.

Flinker, Noam. "Courting Urania: The Narrator of *Paradise Lost* Invokes His Muse." In *Milton and the Idea of Woman,* edited by Julia M. Walker, 86–99. Urbana, Ill, 1988.

Foucault, Michel. *The Order of Things: An Archaeology of the Human Sciences.* New York, 1970. Translation of *Les Mots et les Choses* (Paris, 1966).

Freedman, Barbara. *Staging the Gaze: Postmodernism, Psychoanalysis, and Shakespearean Comedy.* Ithaca, N.Y., 1991.

Freeman, James A. *Milton and the Martial Muse: "Paradise Lost" and European Traditions of War.* Princeton, 1980.

Friedman, Donald M. "*Comus* and the Truth of the Ear." In *The Muses Commonweale: Poetry and Politics in the Seventeenth Century,* edited by Claude Summers and Ted-Larry Pebworth, 119–34. Columbia, Mo., 1988.

Froula, Christine. "When Eve Reads Milton: Undoing the Canonical Economy." *Critical Inquiry,* X (1983), 321–47.

Frye, Northrop. "Agon and Logos: Revolution and Revelation." In *The Prison and the Pinnacle,* edited by Balachandra Rajan, 135–63. Toronto, 1973.

————. "The Four Forms of Fiction." In *Anatomy of Criticism.* Princeton, 1957.

Fulgentius, Fabius Planciades. *De aetatibus mundi et hominis.* In *Fabii Planciadis Fulgentii Virgilianae Continentiae Opera,* edited by R. Helm, 2nd ed., 127–79. Stuttgart, 1970.

————. *Expositio virgilianae continentiae secundum philosophos moralis.* In *Fabii Planciadis Fulgentii Virgilianae Continentiae Opera,* edited by Helm, 2nd ed., 81–107.

Fulgentius the Mythographer. Translated by Leslie George Whitbread. Columbus, Ohio, 1971.

Furman, Wendy. "*Samson Agonistes* as Christian Tragedy: A Corrective View." *Philological Quarterly,* LX (1981), 169–81.

Gadamer, Hans Georg. *Essays in Philosophical Hermeneutics.* Translated and edited by David E. Linge. Berkeley and Los Angeles, 1976.

———. *Truth and Method.* New York, 1975.

Galileo [Galileo Galilei]. "Letter to Grand Duchess Christina." In *Discoveries and Opinions of Galileo,* translated by Stillman Drake. Garden City, N.Y., 1957.

Gallagher, Philip J. *Milton, the Bible, and Misogyny.* Edited by Eugene R. Cunnar and Gail L. Mortimer. Columbia, Mo., 1990.

———. "Real or Allegoric: The Ontology of Sin and Death in *Paradise Lost.*" *English Literary Renaissance,* VI (1976), 317–35.

Germanus, Saint. *De liturgica gallicana.* In *Patrologiae Cursus Completus . . . Series Latina,* edited by J. P. Migne. Vol. LXXII of 221 vols. Paris, 1844–1903.

Gilman, Ernest B. *Iconoclasm and Poetry in the English Reformation: Down Went Dagon.* Chicago, 1986.

Goekjian, Gregory F. "Deference and Silence: Milton's Nativity Ode." *Milton Studies,* XXII (1985), 119–35.

———. "Suicide and Revenge: *Samson Agonistes* and the Law of the Father." *Milton Studies,* XXVI (1990), 253–70.

Gossman, Ann. "The Ring Pattern: Image, Structure, and Theme in *Paradise Lost.*" *Studies in Philology,* LXVIII (1971), 326–39.

Greene, Thomas M. "The Meeting Soul in Milton's Companion Poems." *English Literary Renaissance,* XIV (1984), 159–74.

Gregerson, Linda. "The Limbs of Truth: Milton's Use of Simile in *Paradise Lost.*" *Milton Studies,* XIV (1980), 135–52.

Gregory, E. R. "Three Muses and a Poet: A Perspective on Milton's Epic Thought." *Milton Studies,* X (1977), 35–64.

Gregory the Great. *In librum primum regum,* IV, 7. In *Patrologiae Cursus Completus . . . Series Latina,* edited by J. P. Migne. Vol. LXXIX of 221 vols. Paris, 1844–1903.

Grose, Christopher. "'His Uncontrollable Intent': Discovery as Action in *Samson Agonistes,*" *Milton Studies,* VII (1975), 49–76.

———. "The Lydian Arts of 'L'Allegro' and 'Il Penseroso.'" *Journal of English and Germanic Philology,* LXXXIII (1984), 183–99.

———. *Milton and the Sense of Tradition.* New Haven, 1988.

———. *Milton's Epic Process: "Paradise Lost" and Its Miltonic Background.* New Haven, 1973.

Grossman, Marshall. *Authors to Themselves: Milton and the Revelation of History.* New York, 1987.

———. "Milton's Dialectical Visions." *Modern Philology,* LXXXII (1984), 23–39.

—. "Servile/Sterile/Style: Milton and the Question of Woman." In *Milton and the Idea of Woman*, edited by Julia M. Walker, 146–68. Urbana, Ill., 1988.

Guibbory, Achsah. "John Milton: Providential Progress or Cyclical Decay." In *The Map of Time: Seventeenth-Century English Literature and Ideas of Pattern in History*. Urbana, Ill., 1986.

Guillory, John. "Dalila's House: *Samson Agonistes* and the Sexual Division of Labor." In *Rewriting the Renaissance: The Discourses of Sexual Difference in Early Modern Europe*, edited by Margaret W. Ferguson, Maureen Quilligan, and Nancy J. Vickers, 106–22. Chicago, 1986.

—. *Poetic Authority: Spenser, Milton, and Literary History*. New York, 1983. "Ithuriel's Spear: History and the Language of Accommodation" (Chap. 6) reprinted in *Critical Interpretations,* ed. Harold Bloom (New York, 1987), 65–90.

—. "Reading Gender into *Paradise Lost*." In *Soliciting Interpretation: Literary Theory and Seventeenth-Century English Poetry,* edited by Elizabeth D. Harvey and Katharine Eisaman Maus, 68–88. Chicago, 1990.

Hagstrum, Jean. *Sex and Sensibility: Ideal and Erotic Love from Milton to Mozart.* Chicago, 1980.

Hale, John K. "Milton Playing with Ovid." *Milton Studies,* XXV (1989), 3–19.

—. "Milton's Self-Presentation in *Poems . . . 1645.*" *Milton Quarterly,* XXV (1991), 37–48.

Halewood, William H. *The Poetry of Grace: Reformation Themes and Structures in English Seventeenth-Century Poetry.* New Haven, 1970.

Halley, Janet E. "Female Autonomy in Milton's Sexual Politics." In *Milton and the Idea of Woman,* edited by Julia M. Walker, 230–53. Urbana, Ill., 1988.

Halpern, Richard. "Puritanism and Maenadism in *A Masque*." In *Rewriting the Renaissance: The Discourses of Sexual Difference in Early Modern Europe,* edited by Margaret W. Ferguson, Maureen Quilligan, and Nancy J. Vickers, 88–105. Chicago, 1986.

Hamilton, Gary D. "Milton's Defensive God: A Reappraisal." *Studies in Philology,* LXIX (1972), 87–100.

Hamlet, Desmond. *One Greater Man: Justice and Damnation in "Paradise Lost."* Lewisburg, Pa., 1976.

Hardison, O. B., Jr. "*In Medias Res* in *Paradise Lost*." *Milton Studies,* XVII (1983), 27–41.

Harpham, Geoffrey. *The Ascetic Imperative.* Chicago, 1991.

Harris, Roy. *Reading Saussure: A Critical Commentary on the "Cours de linguistique général."* London, 1987.

Hartman, Geoffrey. "Adam on the Grass with Balsamum." In *Beyond Formalism: Literary Essays, 1958–1970,* 124–50. New Haven, 1970.

————. *Criticism in the Wilderness: The Study of Literature Today*. New Haven, 1980.

Haskin, Dayton. "Milton's Portrait of Mary as Bearer of the Word." In *Milton and the Idea of Woman*, edited by Julia M. Walker, 169–84. Urbana, Ill., 1988.

Helgerson, Richard. *Self-Crowned Laureates: Spenser, Jonson, Milton, and the Literary System*. Berkeley and Los Angeles, 1983.

Heninger, S. K. "Sidney and Milton: The Poet as Maker." In *Milton and the Line of Vision*, edited by Joseph A. Wittreich, 57–95. Madison, Wis., 1975.

Hieatt, A. Kent. *Chaucer, Spenser, and Milton: Mythopoeic Continuities and Transformations*. Montreal, 1975.

Hill, John Spencer. "Poet-Priest: Vocational Tension in Milton's Early Development." *Milton Studies*, VIII (1976), 41–69.

Hollander, John. *The Figure of Echo: A Mode of Allusion in Milton and After*. Berkeley and Los Angeles, 1981.

Honorius of Autun. *De imagine mundi*. In *Patrologiae Cursus Completus . . . Series Latina*, edited by J. P. Migne. Vol. CLXXII of 221 vols. Paris, 1844–1903.

Hughes, Merritt Y., ed. *The Complete Poems and Major Prose of John Milton*. New York, 1957.

Hult, David. *Self-Fulfilling Prophecies: Readership and Authority in the First Roman de la Rose*. New York, 1986.

Hunter, William B. "John Milton: Autobiographer." *Milton Quarterly*, VII (1974), 100–104.

————. "Milton Translates the Psalms." *Philological Quarterly*, XL (1961), 485–94.

Huttar, Charles. "The Passion of Christ in *Paradise Regain'd*." *English Language Notes*, XIX (1982), 236–60.

Ignatius of Loyola. *The Spiritual Exercises of Saint Ignatius*. Edited by David L. Fleming, S.J. St. Louis, 1978.

Jack, Ian. "A Choice of Orders: The Arrangement of 'The Poetical Works.'" In *Textual Criticism and Literary Interpretation*, edited by Jerome J. McGann, 127–43. Chicago, 1985.

Jacobus, Lee A. "Milton Metaphrast: Logic and Rhetoric in Psalm I." *Milton Studies*, XXIII (1987), 119–32.

————. *Sudden Apprehension: Aspects of Knowledge in "Paradise Lost."* The Hague, 1976.

Jakobson, Roman. "Two Aspects of Language and Two Types of Aphasic Disturbances." In *Fundamentals of Language*, edited by Roman Jakobson and Morris Halle, 69–96. The Hague, 1956.

Jayne, Sears. "The Subject of Milton's Ludlow *Mask*." *PMLA*, LXXIV (1959), 533–43.

Jose, Nicholas. *"Samson Agonistes:* The Play Turned Upside Down." In *Ideas of the Restoration in English Literature, 1660–1671.* Cambridge, Mass., 1984.

Katzenellenbogen, A. *The Sculptural Programs of Chartres Cathedral: Christ, Mary, Ecclesia.* Baltimore, 1959.

Kelly, Kathleen. "Narcissus in *Paradise Lost* and *Upon Appleton House:* Disenchanting the Renaissance Lyric." In *Traditions and Innovations: Essays on British Literature of the Middle Ages and the Renaissance,* edited by David G. Allen and Robert A. White, 200–13. Newark, Del., 1990.

Kerrigan, William. "The Irrational Coherence of *Samson Agonistes.*" *Milton Studies,* XXII (1986), 217–32.

———. *Prophetic Milton.* Charlottesville, Va., 1974.

———. *The Sacred Complex: On the Psychogenesis of "Paradise Lost."* Cambridge, Mass., 1983.

Kerrigan, William, and Gordon Braden. *The Idea of the Renaissance.* Baltimore, 1989.

Kilgour, Maggie. *From Communion to Cannibalism: An Anatomy of Metaphors of Incorporation.* Princeton, 1990.

King, Archdale A. *Liturgies of the Roman Church.* Milwaukee, 1957.

Knoespel, Kenneth. "The Limits of Allegory: Textual Expansion of Narcissus in *Paradise Lost.*" *Milton Studies,* XXII (1986), 79–99.

Knoppers, Laura Lunger. "'Sung and Proverb'd for a Fool': *Samson Agonistes* and Solomon's Harlot." *Milton Studies,* XXVI (1990), 239–51.

Knowles, Julie Nall. "'The Course of Time': A Calvinist *Paradise Lost.*" *Milton Studies,* XVIII (1983), 173–93.

Kojève, Alexandre. *From the Closed Mind to the Infinite Universe.* Baltimore, 1965.

Kristeller, Paul Oskar. *The Philosophy of Marsilio Ficino.* New York, 1943.

———. *Studies in Renaissance Thought and Letters.* Rome, 1956.

Kristeva, Julia. *Desire in Language: A Semiotic Approach to Literature and Art.* Translated by Thomas Gora, Alice Jardine, and Leon S. Roudiez. New York, 1980.

———. *In the Beginning Was Love.* New York, 1987.

———. "The Speaking Subject." In *On Signs,* edited by Marshall Blonsky, 210–20. Baltimore, 1985.

———. *Tales of Love.* New York, 1987.

Labriola, Albert C. "Divine Urgency as a Motive for Conduct in *Samson Agonistes.*" *Philological Quarterly,* L (1971), 99–107.

———. "The Medieval View of Christian History in *Paradise Lost.*" In *Milton and the Middle Ages,* edited by John Mulryan, 115–32. Lewisburg, Pa., 1982.

Laistner, M. L. W. *Christianity and Pagan Culture in the Later Roman Empire.* Ithaca, N.Y., 1951.

————. *The Intellectual Heritage of the Early Middle Ages.* Ithaca, N.Y., 1987.

Law, Jules David. "Eruption and Containment: The Satanic Predicament in *Paradise Lost.*" *Milton Studies,* XVI (1982), 35–60.

Lawry, Jon S. *The Shadow of Heaven: Matter and Stance in Milton's Poetry.* Ithaca, N.Y., 1978.

Lehmann, Paul. "The Anti-Pelagian Writings." In *A Companion to the Study of Saint Augustine,* edited by Roy Battenhouse, 203–35. New York, 1955.

Leonard, John. *Naming in Paradise: Milton and the Language of Adam and Eve.* New York, 1990.

Lewalski, Barbara K. *"Paradise Lost" and the Rhetoric of Literary Forms.* Princeton, 1985.

————. "Structure and the Symbolism of Vision in Michael's Prophecy, *Paradise Lost* XI–XII." *Philological Quarterly,* XLII (1963), 25–35.

Lewis, C. S. *A Preface to "Paradise Lost."* London, 1942.

Lieb, Michael. *The Dialectic of Creation: Patterns of Birth and Regeneration in "Paradise Lost."* Amherst, Mass., 1970.

————. *Poetics of the Holy: A Reading of "Paradise Lost."* Chapel Hill, N.C., 1981.

Lochman, Daniel T. "'If There Be Aught of Presage': Milton's Samson as Riddler and Prophet." *Milton Studies,* XXII (1986), 195–216.

————. "'Seeking Just Occasion': Law, Reason, and Justice at Samson's Peripety." *Milton Studies,* XXVI (1990), 271–88.

Loewenstein, David. "Introduction: 'Labouring the Word.'" In *Politics, Poetics, and Hermeneutics in Milton's Prose,* edited by David Loewenstein and James Grantham Turner, 1–7. New York, 1990.

Loewenstein, Joseph. "The Script in the Marketplace." In *Representing the English Renaissance,* edited by Stephen Greenblatt, 265–78. Berkeley and Los Angeles, 1988. Reprinted from *Representations,* No. 12 (1985).

Lord, George de F. "Milton's Dialogue with Omniscience in *Paradise Lost.*" In *The Author in His Work: Essays on a Problem in Criticism,* edited by Louis L. Martz and Aubrey Williams, 31–50. New Haven, 1978.

Lorris, Guillaume de, and Jean de Meun. *Le Roman de la rose.* Translated by André Larly. 2nd ed. 4 vols. Paris, 1973–75.

————. *The Romance of the Rose by Guillaume de Lorris and Jean de Meun.* Translated and edited by Charles Dahlberg. Princeton, 1971.

Lovejoy, Arthur O. *The Great Chain of Being: A Study in the History of Ideas.* Cambridge, Mass., 1936.

————. "Milton and the Paradox of the Fortunate Fall." *English Literary History,* IV (1937), 161–79. Reprinted in *Essays in the History of Ideas,* by Arthur O. Lovejoy (Baltimore, 1948), 277–95.

Low, Anthony. *The Blaze of Noon: A Reading of "Samson Agonistes."* New York, 1974.

————. "Milton and the Georgic Ideal." In *The Georgic Revolution*, 296–352. Princeton, 1985.

Luria, Maxwell. *A Reader's Guide to the "Roman de la rose."* Hamden, Conn., 1982.

Lynch, Kathryn L. *The High Medieval Dream Vision: Poetry, Philosophy, and Literary Form.* Stanford, Calif., 1988.

MacCaffrey, Isabel. *"Paradise Lost" as "Myth."* Cambridge, Mass., 1959.

MacCallum, Hugh. *Milton and the Sons of God: The Divine Image in Milton's Epic Poetry.* Toronto, 1986.

McCanles, Michael. *"Paradise Lost* and the Dialectic of Providence." In *Dialectical Criticism and Renaissance Literature.* Berkeley and Los Angeles, 1975.

McColley, Diane. "Eve's Dream." *Milton Studies,* XII (1978), 25–45. Reprinted in *Milton's Eve,* by Diane McColley (Urbana, Ill., 1983).

McGuire, Maryann Cale. *Milton's Puritan Masque.* Athens, Ga., 1983.

MacLaren, I. S. "Milton's Nativity Ode: The Function of Poetry and Structures of Responsibility in 1629." *Milton Studies,* XV (1981), 181–200.

McMahon, Robert. *Augustine's Prayerful Ascent: An Essay on the Literary Form of the Confessions.* Athens, Ga., 1989.

————. "Eve's Reflection, and Ovid." Typescript, n.d.

Macrobius, Ambrosius Theodosius. *Commentarii in Somnium Scipionis.* Edited by Jacob Willis. Tübingen, 1953.

Macrobius, Commentary on the Dream of Scipio. Translated and edited by William Harris Stahl. New York, 1952.

Madsen, William. "The Idea of Nature in Milton's Poetry." In *Three Studies in the Renaissance.* New Haven, 1958.

————. *From Shadowy Types to Truth: Studies in Milton's Symbolism.* New Haven, 1968.

————. "The Voice of Michael in Lycidas." *Studies in English Literature,* III (1963), 1–9.

Mâle, Emile. *The Gothic Image: Religious Art in France of the Thirteenth Century.* 1913; rpr. New York, 1958.

Mansi, J. D. *Sacrorum Conciliorum Amplissima Collectio.* 31 vols. Florence and Venice, 1759–98.

Marcel, Gabriel. *Creative Fidelity.* Translated by Robert Rosthal. New York, 1964.

Marcus, Leah S. "Justice for Margery Evans: A 'Local' Reading of *Comus.*" In *Milton and the Idea of Woman,* edited by Julia M. Walker, 66–85. Urbana, Ill., 1988.

————. "Milton's Anti-Laudian Masque." In *The Politics of Mirth: Jonson, Herrick, Milton, Marvell, and the Defense of Old Holiday Pastimes,* 169–212. Chicago, 1986.

Maresca, Thomas E. *Three English Epics: Studies of "Troilus and Creseyde," "The Faerie Queene," and "Paradise Lost."* Lincoln, Nebr., 1979.

Martin, Jeanne S. "Transformations in Genre in Milton's *Comus.*" *Genre,* X (1977), 195–213.

Martindale, Charles. "Paradise Metamorphosed: Ovid in Milton." *Comparative Literature,* XXXVII (1985), 301–303.

Martz, Louis L. *The Paradise Within: Studies in Vaughan, Traherne, and Milton.* New Haven, 1961.

———. *Poet of Exile: A Study of Milton's Poetry.* New Haven, 1980.

———. *The Poetry of Meditation: A Study in English Literature.* New Haven, 1954.

———. "The Rising Poet." In *The Lyric and Dramatic Milton,* edited by Joseph Summers, 3–33. New York, 1965.

Merleau-Ponty, Maurice. "The Yogi and the Proletarian." Translated by Nancy Metzel and John Flodstrom. In *The Primacy of Perception,* edited by James M. Edie. Evanston, Ill., 1964.

Merrill, Thomas F. "Miltonic God-Talk: The Creation in *Paradise Lost.*" *Language and Style,* XVI (1983), 296–312.

Michelfelder, Diana P., and Richard E. Palmer, eds. *Dialogue and Deconstruction: The Gadamer-Derrida Encounter.* Albany, N.Y., 1989.

Miller, Leo. "Milton's 'Lost' Sonnet to Mary Powell." *Milton Quarterly,* XXV (1991), 102–107.

Milton, John. *The Complete Poetry of John Milton.* Edited by John T. Shawcross. Rev. ed. Garden City, N.Y., 1971.

———. *De Doctrina Christiana.* In *Complete Prose Works of John Milton,* edited by Don M. Wolfe *et al.* Vol. VI of 8 vols. New Haven, 1953–82.

———. *John Milton's Complete Poetic Works.* Edited by Harris Francis Fletcher. 4 vols. Urbana, Ill., 1943.

———. *Poems of Mr. John Milton: The 1645 Edition.* New York, 1951.

———. *Variorum Commentary on the Poems of John Milton.* Edited by A. S. P. Woodhouse and Douglas Bush. Additional vols. projected. New York, 1970–.

Miner, Earl. "*Felix Culpa* in the Redemptive Order of *Paradise Lost.*" *Philological Quarterly,* XLVII (1968), 43–54.

Mollenkott, Virginia R. "Some Implications of Milton's Androgynous Muse." *Bucknell Review,* XXIV (1978), 27–36.

Morris, Jeffrey B. "Disorientation and Disruption in *Paradise Regain'd.*" *Milton Studies,* XXVI (1990), 219–38.

Moseley, C. W. R. D. *The Poetic Birth: Milton's Poems of 1645.* Menston, Eng., 1991.

Mulder, John R. "The Lyric Dimension of *Paradise Lost.*" *Milton Studies,* XXIII (1987), 145–63.

Mullaney, Stephen. *The Place of the Stage: License, Play, and Power in Renaissance England.* Chicago, 1988.

Mulryan, John. "The Heroic Tradition of Milton's *Samson Agonistes.*" *Milton Studies,* XVIII (1983), 214–34.

Mumford, Lewis. *The Myth of the Machine.* 2 vols. New York, 1967–70.

Mundhenk, Rosemary. "Dark Scandal and the Sun-Clad Power of Chastity: The Historical Milieu of Milton's *Comus.*" *Studies in English Literature,* XV (1975), 141–52.

Murrin, Michael. *The Allegorical Epic: Essays in Its Rise and Decline.* Chicago, 1980.

Mustazza, Leonard. "The Verbal Plot of *Samson Agonistes.*" *Milton Studies,* XXIII (1987), 241–58.

Nardo, Anna. "Academic Interludes in *Paradise Lost.*" *Milton Studies,* XXVII (1991), 209–41.

———. "Milton and the Academic Sonnet." In *Milton in Italy: Contexts, Images, Contradictions,* edited by Mario A. DiCesare, 489–503. Binghamton, N.Y., 1991.

———. *Milton's Sonnets and the Ideal Community.* Lincoln, Nebr., 1979.

———. " 'Sung and Proverb'd for a Fool': Samson as Fool and Trickster." *Mosaic,* XXII (1989), 1–16.

Newman, John Kevin. *The Classical Epic Tradition.* Madison, Wis., 1986.

Nimis, Stephen A. *Narrative Semiotics in the Epic Tradition: The Simile.* Bloomington, Ind., 1987.

Nitchie, George W. "Milton and His Muses." *English Literary History,* XLIV (1977), 75–84.

Norbrook, David. *Poetry and Politics in the English Renaissance.* London, 1984.

Norford, Don Parry. "The Sacred Head: Milton's Solar Mysticism." *Milton Studies,* IX (1976), 37–75.

Nyquist, Mary. "Gynesis, Genesis, Exegesis, and Milton's Eve." In *Cannibals, Witches, and Divorce: Estranging the Renaissance,* edited by Marjorie Garber, 147–208. Baltimore, 1987.

———. "Reading the Fall: Discourse and Drama in *Paradise Lost.*" *English Literary Renaissance,* XIV (1984), 199–229.

———. "Textual Overlapping and Dalilah's Harlot Lap." In *Literary Theory / Renaissance Texts,* edited by Patricia Parker and David Quint, 341–72. Baltimore, 1986.

Obertino, James. "Milton's Use of Aquinas in *Comus.*" *Milton Studies,* XXII (1986), 21–43.

Ong, Walter J., S.J. *Fighting for Life: Contest, Sexuality, and Consciousness.* Ithaca, N.Y., 1981.

———. *Interfaces of the Word: Studies in the Evolution of Consciousness and Culture.* Ithaca, N.Y., 1977.

———. "Milton's Logical Epic and Evolving Consciousness." *Proceedings of the American Philosophical Society,* CXX (1976), 295–305.

———. *Orality and Literacy: The Technologizing of the Word.* New York, 1982.

———. *The Presence of the Word: Some Prolegomena for Cultural and Religious History.* New York, 1970.

———. *Ramus, Method, and the Decay of Dialogue: From the Art of Discourse to the Art of Reason.* Cambridge, Mass., 1958.

———. *Rhetoric, Romance, and Technology: Studies in the Interaction of Expression and Culture.* Ithaca, N.Y., 1971.

———. "Voice as Summons to Belief." In *Literature and Belief,* edited by M. H. Abrams, 80–105. New York, 1965.

Oram, William A. "The Invocation of Sabrina." *Studies in English Literature,* XXIV (1984), 121–39.

Ortega y Gasset, José. *Ideo del theatro.* Madrid, 1958.

———. *Meditations on Quixote.* New York, 1961.

Ovid. *The Metamorphoses.* Translated by Horace Gregory. New York, 1958.

Pagels, Elaine. *Adam, Eve, and the Serpent.* New York, 1989.

Palazzoli, Mara Selvini. *Self-Starvation: From Individual to Family Therapy in the Treatment of Anorexia Nervosa.* New York, 1978.

Palazzoli, Mara Selvini, *et al. Paradox and Counter-Paradox: A New Model in the Therapy of the Family in Schizophrenic Transaction.* New York, 1978.

Panofsky, Erwin. *Abbot Suger on the Abbey Church of Saint Denis and Its Art Treasures.* Princeton, 1946.

———. *Studies in Iconography.* New York, 1939.

Pare, G. *Le Roman de la rose et la Scolastique courtoise.* Paris, 1941.

Parker, Patricia A. *Inescapable Romance: Studies in the Poetics of a Mode.* Princeton, 1979.

Parker, William Riley. *Milton: A Biography.* 2 vols. New York, 1968.

Patrick, J. Max. "A Reconsideration of the Fall of Eve." *Etudes anglaises,* XXVIII (1975), 15–21.

Patrides, C. A. "'Something like Prophetic Strain': Apocalyptic Configurations in Milton." *English Language Notes,* XIX (1982), 193–207.

Patterson, Annabel. "'Forc'd Fingers': Milton's Early Poems and Ideological Constraint." In *The Muses Common-Weale: Poetry and Politics in the Seventeenth Century,* edited by Claude Summers and Ted-Larry Pebworth, 9–22. Columbia, Mo., 1988.

Pavlock, Barbara. *Eros, Imitation, and the Epic Tradition.* Ithaca, N.Y., 1990.

Peczenik, F. "Fit Help: The Egalitarian Marriage in *Paradise Lost.*" *Mosaic,* XVII (1984), 29–48.

Phelan, Herbert J. "What Is the Persona Doing in 'L'Allegro' and 'Il Penseroso'?" *Milton Studies*, XXII (1986), 3–19.

Pico della Mirandola, Giovanni. *Oration on the Dignity of Man.* Translated by Elizabeth L. Forbes. In *The Renaissance Philosophy of Man,* edited by Ernst Cassirer, Paul Oskar Kristeller, and John Herman Randall, Jr. Chicago, 1948.

Pinka, Patricia G. "Timely Timelessness in Two Nativity Poems." In *Bright Shootes of Everlastingnesse: The Seventeenth-Century Religious Lyric,* edited by Claude Summers and Ted-Larry Pebworth, 162–72. Columbia, Mo., 1987.

Pound, Ezra. *ABC of Reading.* New Haven, 1934.

———. *Literary Essays.* Edited by T. S. Eliot. London, 1954.

Quilligan, Maureen. "The Gender of Milton's Muse and the Problem of the Fit Reader." In *John Milton's "Paradise Lost": Modern Critical Interpretations,* edited by Harold Bloom, 125–31. New York, 1987.

———. *Milton's Spenser: The Politics of Reading.* Ithaca, N.Y., 1983.

Quinones, Ricardo. *The Renaissance Discovery of Time.* Cambridge, Mass., 1972.

Quint, David. *Origin and Originality in Renaissance Literature: Versions of the Source.* New Haven, 1983.

Radzinowicz, Mary Ann. "The Distinctive Tragedy of *Samson Agonistes.*" *Milton Studies,* XVII (1983), 249–80.

———. "Man as a 'Probationer of Immortality': *Paradise Lost* XI–XII." In *Approaches to "Paradise Lost,"* edited by C. A. Patrides, 31–51. Toronto, 1968.

———. *Milton's Epics and the Book of the Psalms.* Princeton, 1989.

———. "The Politics of *Paradise Lost.*" In *Politics of Discourse: The Literature and History of Seventeenth-Century England,* edited by Kevin Sharpe and Steven N. Zwicker, 204–29. Berkeley and Los Angeles, 1987.

———. "Psalms and the Representation of Death in *Paradise Lost.*" *Milton Studies,* XXIII (1987), 133–44.

———. *Toward "Samson Agonistes": The Growth of Milton's Mind.* Princeton, 1978.

Rajan, Balachandra. *The Lofty Rhyme.* Coral Gables, Fla., 1970.

———. "*Paradise Lost:* The Uncertain Epic." *Milton Studies,* XVII (1983), 105–19. Reprinted in *The Form of the Unfinished: English Poetics from Spenser to Pound,* by Balachandra Rajan (Princeton, 1985).

———. "'To Which Is Added *Samson Agonistes*—.'" In *The Prison and the Pinnacle,* edited by Balachandra Rajan, 82–110. Toronto, 1973.

Rapaport, Herman. *Milton and the Postmodern.* Lincoln, Nebr., 1983.

Rewak, William J., S.J. "Book III of *Paradise Lost:* Milton's Satisfaction of Redemption." *Milton Quarterly,* XI (1977), 97–102.

Revard, Stella P. "Eve and the Doctrine of Responsibility in *Paradise Lost.*" *PMLA,* LXXXVIII (1973), 69–78.

———. "Vergil's *Georgics* and *Paradise Lost:* Nature and Human Nature in a Landscape." In *Vergil at 2000: Commemorative Essays on the Poet and His Influence,* edited by John D. Bernard, 259–80. New York, 1986.

———. *The War in Heaven: "Paradise Lost" and the Tradition of Satan's Rebellion.* Ithaca, N.Y., 1980.

Ricoeur, Paul. *The Conflict of Interpretations.* Evanston, Ill., 1974.

———. *The Symbolism of Evil.* New York, 1967.

———. *Time and Narrative.* Translated by K. McLaughlin and D. Pellauer. 3 vols. Chicago, 1984.

Riggs, William G. *The Christian Poet in "Paradise Lost."* Berkeley and Los Angeles, 1972.

Roberts, S. E. "A Phenomenological Approach to Milton from Typology to Existentialism." Ph.D. dissertation, State University of New York at Buffalo, 1970.

Rollin, Roger B. "Milton's 'I's': The Narrator and the Reader in *Paradise Lost.*" In *Renaissance and Modern Essays in Honor of Edwin M. Moseley,* edited by Murray J. Levith, 35–55. Saratoga Springs, N.Y., 1976.

Rooney, Ellen. *Seductive Reasonings: Pluralism as the Problematic of Contemporary Literary Theory.* Ithaca, N.Y., 1989.

Rosen, Stanley. *Hermeneutics as Politics.* New York, 1987.

Rosenblatt, Jason P. "Adam's Pisgah Vision: *Paradise Lost,* Books XI and XII." *English Literary History,* XXXIX (1972), 66–86.

Rossi, Paolo. *The Dark Abyss of Time.* Chicago, 1984.

Ruegg, Maria. "Metaphor and Metonymy: The Logic of Structuralist Rhetoric." *Glyph,* VI (1979), 141–57.

Rumrich, John Peter. *Matter of Glory: A New Preface to "Paradise Lost."* Pittsburgh, 1987.

———. "Metamorphosis in *Paradise Lost.*" *Viator,* XX (1989), 311–26.

Ryken, Leland. *The Apocalyptic Vision in "Paradise Lost."* Ithaca, N.Y., 1970.

———. "*Paradise Lost* and Its Biblical Epic Models." In *Milton and Scriptural Tradition: The Bible into Poetry,* edited by James H. Sims and Leland Ryken, 43–81. Columbia, Mo., 1984.

Sadler, Lynn Veach. "Regeneration and Typology: *Samson Agonistes* and Its Relation to *De Doctrina Christiana, Paradise Lost,* and *Paradise Regain'd.*" *Studies in English Literature,* XII (1972), 141–56.

Said, Edward W. *Beginnings: Intention and Method.* New York, 1975.

———. "Narrative: Quest for Origins and Discovery of the Mausoleum." *Salmagundi,* IX (1970), 63–72.

———. "Notes on the Characterization of a Literary Text." In *Velocities of Change,* edited by Richard Macksey, 32–57. Baltimore, 1974. Reprinted in *Beginnings,* by Said.

————. "Reflections on Recent American 'Left' Literary Criticism." *Boundary 2*, VIII (1979–80), 11–30.

————. *The World, the Text, and the Critic.* Cambridge, Mass., 1983.

Samuel, Irene. "The Dialogue in Heaven: A Reconsideration of *Paradise Lost* III, 1–471." *PMLA*, LXXII (1957), 609–11.

Sasek, Lawrence A. "The Drama of Paradise Lost, Books XI and XII." In *Milton: Modern Essays in Criticism,* edited by Arthur Barker, 342–56. London, 1968.

Schindler, Walter. *Voice and Crisis: Invocation in Milton's Poetry.* Hamden, Conn., 1984.

Schwartz, Regina. *Remembering and Repeating: Biblical Creation in "Paradise Lost."* New York, 1988.

Schwarz-Bart, André. *Le Dernier des justes.* Paris, 1959.

Scoufos, Alice-Lyle. "The Mysteries in Milton's *Masque.*" *Milton Studies*, VI (1974), 113–42.

Sellin, Paul R. "Milton's Epithet *Agonistes.*" *Studies in English Literature*, IV (1964), 137–62.

Sessions, William A. "Abandonment and the English Religious Lyric of the Seventeenth Century." In *Bright Shootes of Everlastingnesse: The Seventeenth-Century Religious Lyric,* edited by Claude J. Summers and Ted-Larry Pebworth, 1–19. Columbia, Mo., 1987.

Shawcross, John T. "Irony as Tragic Effect: *Samson Agonistes* and the Tragedy of Hope." In *Calm of Mind: Tercentenary Essays on "Paradise Regain'd" and "Samson Agonistes" in Honor of John S. Diekhoff,* edited by Joseph A. Wittreich, 298–306. Cleveland, 1971.

————. "Milton and Covenant: The Christian View of Old Testament Theology." In *Milton and Scriptural Tradition: The Bible into Poetry,* edited by James H. Sims and Leland Ryken, 160–91. Columbia, Mo., 1984.

————. "Milton's Shorter Poems." In *Intentionality and the New Traditionalism: Some Liminal Means to Literary Revisionism.* University Park, Pa., 1991.

————. *"Paradise Regain'd"—Worthy T'Have Not Remain'd So Long Unsung.* Pittsburgh, 1988.

————. "Stasis, and John Milton and the Myths of Time." *Cithara*, XVIII (1978), 3–17.

————. *With Mortal Voice: The Creation of "Paradise Lost."* Lexington, Ky., 1982.

Shoaf, R. A. *Milton, Poet of Duality: A Study of Semiosis in the Poetry and the Prose.* New Haven, 1985.

Shuger, Debora K. "The Temptation of Eve." In *Traditions and Innovations: Essays on British Literature of the Middle Ages and the Renaissance,* edited by David G. Allen and Robert A. White, 187–99. Newark, Del., 1990.

Shullenberger, William. "Wrestling with the Angel: *Paradise Lost* and Feminist Criticism." *Milton Quarterly*, XX (1986), 69–85.

Sichi, Edward, Jr. "Milton and the Roman de la Rose: Adam and Eve at the Fountain of Narcissus." In *Milton and the Middle Ages,* edited by John Mulryan, 153–82. Lewisburg, Pa., 1982.

Siemon, James R. *Shakespearean Iconoclasm.* Berkeley and Los Angeles, 1985.

Simson, Otto von. *The Gothic Cathedral: Origins of Gothic Architecture and the Medieval Concept of Order.* New York, 1956.

Sloane, Thomas O. *Donne, Milton, and the End of Humanist Rhetoric.* Berkeley and Los Angeles, 1985.

Smith, George William, Jr. "Milton's Method of Mistakes in the Nativity Ode." *Studies in English Literature,* XVIII (1978), 107–23.

Snider, Alvin. "The Self-Mirroring Mind in Milton and Traherne." *University of Toronto Quarterly,* LV (1986), 313–27.

Steadman, John. *The Hill and the Labyrinth: Discourse and Certitude in Milton and His Near-Contemporaries.* Berkeley and Los Angeles, 1984.

————. *Milton and the Paradoxes of Renaissance Heroism.* Baton Rouge, 1987.

————. "Milton's *Haemony:* Etymology and Allegory." *PMLA,* LXXVII (1962), 200–207.

Stock, Brian. *The Implications of Literacy: Written Language and the Models of Interpretation in the Eleventh and Twelfth Centuries.* Princeton, 1983.

Stollman, Samuel S. "Satan, Sin, and Death: A Mosaic Trio in *Paradise Lost.*" *Milton Studies,* XXII (1986), 101–20.

Swaim, Kathleen M. "Allegorical Poetry in Milton's Ludlow Mask." *Milton Studies,* XVI (1982), 167–99.

————. *Before and After the Fall: Contrasting Modes in "Paradise Lost."* Amherst, Mass., 1986.

————. "The Doubling of the Chorus in *Samson Agonistes.*" *Milton Studies,* XX (1984), 225–45.

————. "The Mimesis of Accommodation in Book 3 of *Paradise Lost.*" *Philological Quarterly,* LXIII (1984), 461–75. Reprinted in *Before and After the Fall,* by Swaim.

Swan, Jim. "Difference and Silence: John Milton and the Question of Gender." In *The (M)other Tongue: Essays in Feminist Psychoanalytic Interpretation,* edited by Shirley N. Garner, Claire Kahane, and Medelon Sprengnether, 151–69. Ithaca, N.Y., 1985.

Tayler, E. W. *Milton's Poetry: Its Development in Time.* Pittsburgh, 1979.

————, ed. *Literary Criticism of Seventeenth Century England.* New York, 1967.

Taylor, Dick. "Milton and the Paradox of the Fortunate Fall Once More." *Tulane Studies in English,* IX (1959), 35–51.

Tertullian [Quintus Septimius Florentius Tertullianus]. *De carne Christi.* In *Patrologiae Cursus Completus . . . Series Latina,* edited by J. P. Migne. Vol. II of 221 vols. Paris, 1844–1903.

Thorne-Thomsen, Sara. "'Hail Wedded Love': Milton's Lyric Epithalamium." *Milton Studies,* XXIV (1988), 155–85.

Tillich, Paul. *The Courage to Be.* New Haven, 1952.

———. *Theology of Culture.* Edited by Robert C. Kimball. New York, 1959.

Tillyard, E. M. W. *Studies in Milton.* New York, 1951.

Tippens, Darryl. "The Kenotic Experience of *Samson Agonistes.*" *Milton Studies,* XXII (1986), 173–94.

Toliver, Harold. "Milton and Others Walking, Soaring, and Falling." In *Lyric Provinces in the English Renaissance.* Columbus, Ohio, 1985.

Treipe, Mindele. "*Comus* as 'Progress.'" *Milton Quarterly,* XX (1986), 1–12.

Turner, James G. *One Flesh: Paradisal Marriage and Sexual Relations in the Age of Milton.* New York, 1987.

Ulreich, John C. "'Beyond the Fifth Act': *Samson Agonistes* as Prophecy." *Milton Studies,* XVII (1983), 281–318.

———. "Milton and the Fortunate Fall." *Journal of the History of Ideas,* XXXII (1971), 351–66.

———. "Milton on the Eucharist: Some Second Thoughts About Sacramentalism." In *Milton and the Middle Ages,* edited by John Mulryan, 32–56. Lewisburg, Pa., 1982.

Waddington, Raymond B. "Milton Among the Carolines." In *The Age of Milton: Backgrounds to Seventeenth-Century Literature,* edited by C. A. Patrides and R. B. Waddington, 338–64. Manchester, Eng., 1980.

Walker, William. "Typology and *Paradise Lost,* Book XI and XII." *Milton Studies,* XXV (1989), 245–64.

Wallace, John Malcolm. "Milton's *Arcades.*" *Journal of English and Germanic Philology,* LVII (1959), 627–36.

Warfield, B. B. *Studies in Tertullian and Augustine.* New York, 1930.

Watkins, W. B. C. *An Anatomy of Milton's Verse.* Baton Rouge, 1955.

Watson, Thomas Ramey. "God's Geometry: Motion in the English Poetry of George Herbert." *George Herbert Journal,* IX (1985), 17–25.

Webber, Joan M. "The Politics of Poetry: Feminism and *Paradise Lost.*" *Milton Studies,* XIV (1980), 3–24.

Weber, Burton J. "The Worldly End of Samson." *Milton Studies,* XXVI (1990), 253–309.

Weinsheimer, Joel. *Gadamer's Hermeneutics: A Reading of Truth and Method.* New Haven, 1985.

———. *Philosophical Hermeneutics and Literary Theory.* New Haven, 1991.

Wells, Susan. *The Dialectics of Representation.* Baltimore, 1985.

Werman, Golda. "Repentance in *Paradise Lost.*" *Milton Studies,* XXII (1986), 121–39.

West, Rebecca. *The Meaning of Treason,* Epilogue. New York, 1945.

White, Hayden. *Tropics of Discourse*. Baltimore, 1978.

Wilcher, Robert. "Milton's Masque: Occasion, Form, and Meaning." *Critical Quarterly*, XX (1978), 3–20.

Wilding, Michael. "Milton's Early Radicalism." In *Dragon's Teeth: Literature in the English Revolution*. New York, 1987.

Wilkes, G. A. "'Full of Doubt I Stand': The Final Implications of *Paradise Lost*." In *English Renaissance Studies Presented to Dame Helen Gardner in Honour of Her Seventieth Birthday*, edited by John Carey, 271–78. New York, 1980.

Wilkinson, David. "The Escape from Pollution: A Comment on *Comus*." *Essays in Criticism*, X (1960), 32–43.

Williams, Arnold. *The Common Expositor: An Account of the Commentaries on Genesis, 1527–1633*. Chapel Hill, N.C., 1948.

Williamson, George. "The Education of Adam." *Modern Philology*, LXI (1963), 96–109.

Winegarden, Karl Lewis. "No Hasty Conclusions: Milton's Anti-Nicean Pneumatology." *Milton Quarterly*, XI (1977), 102.

Wittreich, Joseph. *Feminist Milton*. Ithaca, N.Y., 1987.

———. *Interpreting "Samson Agonistes."* Princeton, 1986.

———. "'John, John, I Blush for Thee!': Mapping Gender Discourses in *Paradise Lost*." In *Out of Bounds: Male Writers and Gender(ed) Criticism*, edited by Laura Claridge and Elizabeth Langland, 22–54. Amherst, Mass., 1990.

———. *Visionary Poetics: Milton's Tradition and His Legacy*. San Marino, Calif., 1979.

Wood, Elizabeth Jane. "'Improved by Tract of Time': Metaphysics and Measurement in *Paradise Lost*." *Milton Studies*, XV (1981), 43–58.

Woodhouse, A. S. P. "*Comus* Once More." *University of Toronto Quarterly*, XIX (1950), 218–23.

———. "Notes on Milton's Views on the Creation: The Initial Phases." *Philological Quarterly*, XXVIII (1949), 211–36.

Woods, Suzanne. "How Free Are Milton's Women?" In *Milton and the Idea of Woman*, edited by Julia M. Walker, 15–31. Urbana, Ill., 1988.

Zimmerman, Joyce Ann. *Liturgy as Language of Faith: A Liturgical Methodology in the Mode of Paul Ricoeur's Textual Hermeneutics*. New York, 1988.

Zimmerman, Shari A. "Milton's *Paradise Lost*: Eve's Struggle for Identity." *American Imago*, XXXVIII (1981), 247–67.

Zwicky, Laurie. "Kairos in *Paradise Regain'd*: The Divine Plan." *English Literary History*, XXXI (1964), 241–77.

INDEX